WINNING

RESEARCH

SKILLS

FOURTH EDITION

WINNING RESEARCH SKILLS

FOURTH EDITION

Nancy P. Johnson
Director of the Law Library and Professor of Law
Georgia State University

Robert C. Berring
Director of the Law Library and Professor of Law
University of California, Berkeley

Thomas A. Woxland
Legal Information Officer for the
Labour Law Information Branch,
International Labour Office
Formerly Director of the Law Library and Professor of Law
Northern Illinois University

WEST GROUP

Bancroft-Whitney • Clark Boardman Callaghan
Lawyers Cooperative Publishing • Westlaw® • West Publishing

Production Coordinator: Pat Britt
Copy Editing: Sheila Goeken, Ann Laughlin, Wil McClaren, Roberta Roban, Jay Shuck

About the Authors

Nancy Johnson has been the director of the Law Library at Georgia State University since 1986. Previously, she served as a reference librarian at Georgia State, the University of Illinois Law Library, and the University of Chicago Law Library. She teaches courses in legal research. She is the co-author of *Legal Research Exercises* and the author of *Sources of Compiled Legislative Histories*. Johnson received her B.A. from Marycrest College, M.L.S. from the University of Illinois, and J.D. from Georgia State.

Bob Berring has been the director of the Boalt Hall Law Library since 1982. Previously, he held positions at the University of Washington Law Library, the Harvard Law Library, the University of Texas Law Library, and the University of Illinois Law Library. He teaches courses in legal research. Berring is a past president of the American Association of Law Libraries. Berring has a B.A. from Harvard and an M.L.S. and a J.D. from the University of California at Berkeley.

Tom Woxland has been legal information officer for the Labour Law Information Branch of the International Labour Office since 1996. Previously, he served for seven years as director of the law library at Northern Illinois University College of Law, where he taught legal research courses. Prior to that he was assistant director for public services at the University of Minnesota Law Library. He has published several articles on research topics and on the history of legal publishing. He is also the co-author of instructional software used nationally for computer-assisted legal research training. Woxland has a B.A. from St. Olaf College and an M.A.L.S. and a J.D. from the University of Minnesota.

Acknowledgments

The authors wish to thank their staff at the Georgia State University Law Library, the Boalt Hall Law Library, and the Northern Illinois University Law Library. Nancy Johnson specifically thanks Rhonda Rosenberg, who helped with the initial phases of the book. A project of this kind is, in a genuine sense, a joint effort; we are grateful to all of the individuals at West Group who worked on this book, especially Bill Lindberg for his support of this project. Several others at West Group helped with various stages of preparation and completion of this work: Craig Runde, Ann Possis, Sharon Kavanagh, and Kara Johnson on the first edition; Pamela Brandt, Deborah Lanners, Kathleen Lepp, and Stacy Lenzen on the second edition; Joanne Smestad Claussen, Mark Cygnet, Anne Kelley, Melinda Peck, and Roberta Roban on the third edition; and Jay Shuck, Wil McClaren, Ann Crowe Heimerman, Monique Buursema, Ann Laughlin, Roberta Roban, and Sheila Goeken on the fourth edition. Finally, we thank each other for still being friends.

Contents

Introduction

Legal research is largely a matter of sex, drugs, and rock 'n' roll. Well, not really, but at least we have caught your attention. The point is, legal research is not the dull, plodding enterprise that it is often made out to be. Unfortunately, many law schools still do not have the resources to teach research well. Some students assume that the research training that is crammed into the first few weeks at those schools represents the full picture of legal research. Nothing could be further from the truth. The structure of how one finds the law is really the center of the legal education enterprise.

This is a book for first-year law students. If you are one, you have probably already heard, more than once, that one of the main goals of the first year is to teach you how to think like a lawyer. Most of your first-year courses will be concerned with teaching you methods of analyzing the law and facts in a particular situation. It is this type of thinking that is most important. Although the same core courses—Contracts, Torts, and Property—have been taught for over one hundred years, learning the content of these courses is of secondary importance to being able to analyze it. In most of these first-year courses, you are being taught to think, question, and analyze. The specific rules of law that you discuss are just part of the process, not the point. This is why you will know very little real law at the end of your first year. It is only in the legal research enterprise, and the legal writing experience, that you are actually taught how to do things. That's why we are here.

A number of books are devoted to the enterprise of legal research. They include large textbooks that explore everything in minute detail and friendly paperbacks that provide a broad overview of the research process and its bibliography. This book falls into neither of these categories. It is an attempt to introduce you to basic research materials and methods, and especially to the products of the nation's leading and most comprehensive legal publisher, West Group. In particular, we will devote much attention to Westlaw, the computer-assisted legal research (CALR) service from West Group. We are not going to make any attempt to argue that Westlaw (or West books for that matter) is a substitute for all of the other materials, nor would we pretend that using West Group products is the only way to do intelligent research. But we do see them as very important parts of the complete research picture. As such, they need to be placed in that context. That is the aim of this book.

West books have been an essential part of every lawyer's library for more than a century. But during the last twenty years, the computer revolution has reached law libraries. A major purpose of this book is to show you how computer-assisted legal research relates to the materials in a traditional law library. One reason we have presented the information in this way is to make clear that the online databases are more than just auxiliary case-finding mechanisms. Lots of people think this, but trust us, they are wrong. Both Westlaw and Lexis, the two major services, are, in themselves, law libraries filled with information.

A generational change is going on in the way people think about legal information. Many lawyers who graduated from law school more than ten or fifteen years ago will always think of law as something printed on a page. They may use computers, but in their minds, they will not be reading law until they see something on the page of a book or in a loose-leaf service. We believe that your generation of law students is riding the crest of what may become a flood tide of change. Information in online services is indeed information. A service like Westlaw contains primary sources, secondary sources, and links between them. With a modem, you can sit at your home personal computer and access much of the world of legal information.

In a way, this book is a hybrid product. It provides a little background on legal information in general and introduces you to relevant ways of using Westlaw as well as traditional print sources. It is a one-legged enterprise, however, and does not stand alone. It should be used with other tools and as a part of other courses, where it should be a legitimate help for you. Westlaw offers enormous advantages to users. You should be able to make the most of those advantages. You should also understand the context in which Westlaw operates. No one should graduate from law school without understanding what a case reporter is, both in its traditional printed format and in its online manifestation. Nor should you leave law school without understanding how statutory materials are organized and why using them online might be different or better—or worse. You should know why administrative rules and regulations are important and how you can find them online. And you should be aware of the role secondary sources and indexes play in the real world of legal research.

Of course, a book of this size must necessarily omit a great deal, and, believe it or not, we don't always agree on every point. Our goal, however, is to provide you with a guide. We recognize that we can only present the tip of the iceberg of legal research materials, and we'll try not to take ourselves too seriously as we present the information. If we were to leave you with only one injunction, it would be to look beyond the four corners of the research enterprise and understand how the tools work, how the pieces fit together, and how the body of research materials functions as a whole. This understanding may be the most important piece of the puzzle.

A Little History

Let's begin with a short history of legal research and go back to the earliest days of the American republic. Finding the law was pretty simple for the small group of American lawyers who practiced two hundred years ago. It is only a slight overstatement to say that all you needed to practice law in 1800 was the American edition of Blackstone's *Commentaries on the Laws of England*—the great, multivolume, comprehensive law text of the eighteenth century. With Blackstone, an inkwell, and a desk, you were a lawyer.

By the end of the nineteenth century, both the law and legal research were getting more complicated. In 1810, there were only eighteen volumes of American court reports; a lawyer of the time could literally read all the cases. But by 1885, a comprehensive law library had 3,500 volumes of reports, and not even with Evelyn Wood's assistance could you have read all the cases.

Speed reading courses might not have helped, but law book publishers did. Responding to lawyers' needs, large legal publishing companies developed during the last quarter of the nineteenth century to compile, and provide access to, the explosive growth in legal sources. Many of the commercial legal publishers, whose books you will use for the rest of your career, began their work during this period. Among the best known are West Publishing Company and Lawyers Cooperative Publishing (both now part of West Group) and the Frank Shepard Company (now Shepard's Company).

Between 1875 and 1900, these publishers introduced many of the now-familiar types of law books, including regional reporters and comprehensive digests from West, citators from Shepard's, and annotated reporters from Lawyers Cooperative. Along with a few other publishers, they also introduced most of the common features of today's legal publications. For example, during this time, publishers developed the basic types of modern supplementation techniques: pocket parts, advance sheets, and—slightly later—loose-leaf services.

In answer, then, to the anguished complaints of lawyers about the outpouring of law from the courts and legislatures, the legal publishers said, in effect: "Don't worry. We will publish all of it. And, not only will we publish it, but we will read and organize it for you as well. We will give you indexes and annotations and summaries and digests."

During the second half of the twentieth century, the lawyers' old lament was heard again. Now there were even more courts deciding even more cases. To make matters worse, to the steady stream of statutes coming out of the legislatures was added a river of regulations flowing from administrative agencies. Three million appellate cases were published. Federal statutes and regulations filled hundreds of thousands of pages. Fifty states multiplied this torrent by fifty times. The storage capacities of many law libraries were strained. Book budgets were burdened. New and competing publications confused lawyers, not to mention law librarians.

The publishers responded again. This time their answer was high technology. One of the first solutions was to use microfiche for mass storage. A filing cabinet of fiche could replace a whole library of books. This technology, however, never really took hold. It is hard to use and offers little in the way of added features. The less you see of it, the better.

The computer brought about the biggest change. Computer-assisted legal research systems, principally the Westlaw service of West Group and the Lexis service of Reed Elsevier, Inc., were developed in the 1970s and improved in the 1980s. These services contain millions of legal documents, including cases, statutes, regulations, and legal periodical articles, almost all of which can be fully displayed. Together, these documents contain tens of millions of words, each of which (with the exception of a few very common words) is searchable. The ability to search the *full text* of documents has made virtually every word in the databases a possible search term and a possible indexing term. In the legal publishing revolution of the nineteenth century, professional editors and indexers read and summarized cases for attorneys. The computer revolution of the twentieth century has added a different type of indexing tool for attorneys to use. The speed and capacity of a service such as Westlaw provide us all with a new level of access to the law's many sources.

The original versions of both Westlaw and Lexis were built using a search system called *Boolean logic*. This method of finding information is based on the theories of George Boole, a nineteenth-century mathematician. Boolean logic involves choosing key words or "terms" and specifying the relationship the terms have to each other by means of "connectors." Choosing the correct terms and understanding how to use connectors efficiently is no simple task. One ends up typing sentences like this:

government military /p warn*** /p soldier sailor "service member" serviceman military /p radiation

Twenty years ago, Boolean searching was front-page news and much effort was expended in trying to teach people how to use it. It was, and is, a very useful method for some, but its intricacies have kept many people from learning how to do it well.

In 1992, West introduced a new system called WIN (Westlaw is Natural) that can be used as an alternative to Boolean searching. WIN allows the researcher to type searches in normal language (or, at least, in language as normal as legal research ever gets). Instead of the above search, for example, one could simply type

what is the government's obligation to warn military personnel of the dangers of past exposure to radiation

Using sophisticated techniques, the WIN system figures out what you want and gives you answers. Despite what you may think, the WIN system is not based on mystical spells or communicating with UFOs; it's simply the next step in making computers work for you. But for jaded legal researchers, it's pretty amazing. Since you are just beginning this legal research journey, WIN will seem no different from other tools; but trust us, it's really a breakthrough.

Naturally, we will discuss both Boolean (called *Terms and Connectors* in Westlaw) and WIN searching in this book and in the appendix. We wouldn't want you to miss any of the fun.

The modern law library is a collection of old and new publishing technologies, books and computers, working together. Neither Westlaw nor Lexis is a panacea for all of your research needs. For some types of research, the old ways are still the best. For example, searching for broad concepts, such as *negligence* or *proximate causation*, is most effectively begun with treatises or digests. For other types of research, the speed, ease, and accuracy of computerized legal research should make Westlaw your starting point.

A Few Helpful Hints

Before we begin looking more specifically at the tools and techniques of legal research, we offer some general hints to remember about legal publications, both paper and electronic: (1) When the same material is published by both a government printer and commercial publisher, the latter is almost invariably more useful. The reason is no surprise. Private publishers, informed by the profit motive, add features designed to make their publications more user-friendly. (2) Different commercial publishers have different publishing philosophies—knowing the philosophy helps you understand the scope and content of their publications. (3) You will often find the same legal materials published in both a chronological arrangement and a subject-based arrangement. (4) Finally, the forms of publication for the law of the various states are very similar to the forms of publication for federal law; if you understand the system on the national level, you will understand it on a local level. Let us expand briefly on each of these points.

(1) Governments—both state and federal—often print the text of the primary sources of their law. They publish the statutes enacted by their legislatures, the decisions handed down by their appellate courts, and the regulations promulgated by their administrative agencies. All of these materials, of course, are in the public domain. Commercial publishers, like West Group, publish the same statutes, decisions, and regulations that the government printers publish. These *unofficial* publications are usually more helpful than the *official* government publications for two reasons.

First, the commercial publications are usually more up-to-date than the government publications. Laws change; new decisions appear. Government printers frequently are several years behind in their publications. In contrast, the commercial publishers publish new cases or statutes in "advance sheet" form within only a few weeks or months of their occurrence.

Second, the commercial publishers frequently add other useful information to their publications. For example, the officially published *United States Code* contains only the text of the federal statutes, but the commercially published *United States Code Annotated* also includes summaries of judicial cases that have construed or explained those statutes as well as references to other helpful interpretive sources.

(2) Perhaps it seems strange to think of legal publishers as having philosophies. But it's true. For example, while both Westlaw and Lexis have databases containing court opinions, West Group adds its traditional editorial enhancements—headnotes, key numbers, and other features that we will soon tell you about—to the text of court opinions in its computerized documents. It also applies the same editorial scrutiny to the online form that it does to the printed form, ensuring accuracy in matters of citations, spelling, and the like. Lexis, on the other hand, provides the language of the court alone, without the "added value" of any editor's or indexer's work. In addition, largely because Westlaw was created by a traditional book publisher and Lexis was not, West Group has emphasized the interconnectedness of books and databases, while Lexis sees the online service as central to the research process.

(3) Our third hint concerns chronological arrangement versus subject arrangement. Most primary sources, whether judicial, legislative, or administrative, are initially published in a chronologically arranged series. As more cases, statutes, or regulations appear, another volume or pamphlet is published. If these chronological materials were the only ones available, research would be impossible. How, in three million cases, would you be able to find cases on a certain topic? Publishers have recompiled this material by subject. Case digests are subject arrangements of points of law in cases. Statutory and administrative codes are topical arrangements of session laws and administrative registers.

(4) Finally, the forms of legal publication are common throughout different jurisdictions. Federal laws are published chronologically as session laws and recompiled as a statutory code. Federal regulations appear in a register and then in an administrative code. Federal cases are published in reporters and indexed in digests. The same is true, more or less, for each of the fifty state jurisdictions. Therefore, once you've learned the research tools for one jurisdiction, you've learned them for all.

Where to Go for More Help

This book is not going to answer all of your legal research questions. No one book could, and certainly not one as short as this. There are several very good and very comprehensive books. Examples are *Finding the Law, How to Find the Law,* and *Fundamentals of Legal Research.* All of them will be in your law school library and probably also in your law school's bookstore. Every truly compulsive legal researcher will constantly consult these books. Take a look at them. That research maniac who sits next to you in Torts already has.

Furthermore, the main focus of this book is *legal* research. This is the kind of research you will be doing as a first-year law student. But when you become a lawyer, you will quickly discover you will be doing a lot of *nonlegal* research as well. Depending on your practice, you may need news, business, medical, or some other kind of information to help you represent a client more effectively.

There is a whole world of information that is not contained in the books of a law library. A lot of that nonlegal information is now available on computer databases. Some of the largest providers of this kind of information are Dow Jones & Company, Inc., and the Dialog Corporation. For you, both as a law student and a lawyer, Westlaw provides access to Dow Jones Interactive and Dialog on Westlaw databases. We will tell you more about them in Chapter 7.

If you want to know more about the wide range of West's books and services, look at *Guide to West Group Legal Resources.* You have probably already received a complimentary copy. It is handy, helpful, and thin enough to keep in your briefcase.

If you have specific questions about Westlaw, your best bet is the print publication *Discovering Westlaw.* It is both informative and well written (unlike many computer manuals, which appear to have been written by people who scored 800 on the SAT math section and 350 on the SAT verbal). *Discovering Westlaw* is not only readable and informative, it has a good index. You can find answers in it.

If you have questions that *Discovering Westlaw* doesn't answer or a really tough question about searching your issue, call 1-800-850-WEST (1-800-850-9378). If you have a complex technical question—something like "How can I automatically disable and reactivate my laptop fax software when I use WestMate for Windows to access Westlaw through a PCMCIA modem with a nonstandard IRQ?"—you may be referred to the technical specialists (West Group's "computer jocks"). Don't be afraid to call. The call is free, and these people are paid to answer your questions. Go ahead and make their day.

What Follows

We have tried to keep this book short. You have a lot to read during your first year, and while we think that a book on legal research should be at the top of the list, we have known enough law students to realize that it won't be. So we will be as brief as possible.

Chapter 1 will introduce you to the basics of case reporting—how cases are published in hard-copy reporters as well as how they are organized in the Westlaw service. Chapter 2 explains how to find cases, and Chapter 3 how to update cases. Later chapters examine statutory and administrative sources and secondary nonlegal sources. Finally, Chapter 8 reviews the entire research process. Sprinkled liberally along the way are illustrations from both the hard-copy materials and the online databases. Even the most careful reader should need only a few hours to reach the end.

One last note: Throughout this book are suggestions on how Westlaw can be used in various research contexts. If you know nothing about the mechanics of full-text searching, you may want to look at the appendix on Westlaw searching before you begin reading Chapter 1.

Case Law

Since the ability to find and read cases is fundamental to legal study as well as to legal practice, we will begin with a description of how cases are organized. You will be introduced to the kind of information that is included in the hard-copy case reporters. You will also learn how cases are organized on Westlaw. The "stuff" of the cases—that is, the words of the judge or justice authoring the opinion—is the same in the hard copy and on Westlaw, but there are differences in the way the cases are grouped together in the reporters and in Westlaw databases.

From reading this chapter, you should acquire certain basic skills. You should be able to locate the correct case in a reporter from a legal citation. You should also be able to find parallel citations, a mandatory part of the proper citation form. And you should be able to recognize and understand the various elements of a case in a reporter volume and on Westlaw.

We will begin by explaining what a court reporter is, how cases are issued and published, and how cases are arranged within the different levels of the court system.

Court Reporters

Reporters are the books that contain the text of judicial opinions. These are real cases, not the edited versions that you find in your casebooks. In fact, you can often learn a great deal about a case in your casebook by reading the unexpurgated version in the reporter. Try it. You will notice that the title of the reporter in a citation is abbreviated. All of the reporters have standard abbreviations. For example, F. Supp.2d and F.3d are abbreviations for the *Federal Supplement, Second Series* and the *Federal Reporter, Third Series*, respectively. You will memorize these pretty quickly whether you want to or not. You can easily decipher the abbreviation by checking the last pages of *Black's Law Dictionary* or *The Bluebook: A Uniform System of Citation*, simply known as the *"Bluebook."* A typical F.3d citation, such as 155 F.3d 521 (5th Cir. 1998), includes the following components:

155	F.3d	521	(5th Cir. 1998)	
↓	↓	↓	↓	↓
Volume	Reporter	Page	Court	Year

One of the trickiest things about finding the right reporter is making sure you have the correct series. Many of the reporters are published in two or possibly three series. For example, the first series of the *Federal Reporter* goes up to volume 300, and the second series starts over at volume 1 and stops at volume 999. Lots of old series stopped at 300, but no one seems to follow that practice now.

It may come as a surprise to you that the great majority of judicial opinions are not published at all. Most state trial-level cases are not reported. A very high percentage of federal district court opinions are not reported either. In fact, not even all appellate cases are reported. The trend has been to publish considerably fewer opinions on a percentage basis. But since the absolute number of cases being decided continues to skyrocket, plenty are still published. Many are not reported, though, because the courts deem them to be redundant of previous decisions; others are not reported because they are determined to have no precedential value. Different states have different rules as to what should be published; even different federal courts of appeals have separate rules. It is not as straightforward as it appears.

The court rules of each jurisdiction indicate when publication of an opinion is appropriate. An appellate judge consults with the judges who participated in the opinion on whether it is desirable or necessary to publish the opinion. Occasionally, an editor will recommend that a case not be published, or that an accompanying order not be published.

Many cases that are not selected for publication in print do go into the Westlaw service, however. Both published and unpublished opinions appear on both Westlaw and Lexis.

There is great debate in legal circles as to whether these unpublished opinions, which may only appear online, may serve as precedent; that is, whether they can be cited as law. The argument goes as follows: since all persons, even those represented by attorneys, do not always have access to the computerized services, they could not possibly follow these unpublished rulings. The upshot of the argument is that, in most jurisdictions, unpublished opinions cannot be used as precedent or may be used only under certain guidelines requiring ample notice to the court and the opposing counsel. Even if unpublished opinions may not be useful as precedent, they may be very helpful in determining judicial thinking in similar cases. Think strategically—if you are going before Judge Smith in a products liability case, it may be valuable to know what Judge Smith has done in products liability cases in the past even if you do not use them as precedent. In practice, cases have many uses.

The cases that are reported by West Group are organized by court, jurisdiction, or geographic proximity. The arrangement of cases is determined by West attorney-editors. For example, in a regional reporter the cases from a single state are published together. The arrangement of cases may also be based on a hierarchy of courts within a state. There are also internal rules at West Group that govern the arrangement.

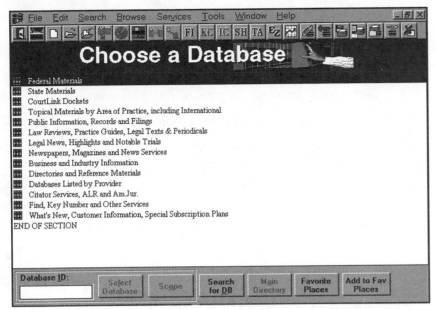

Figure 1.1
Online Directory of
Westlaw Databases

On Westlaw, cases are organized into databases. For example, Westlaw has federal databases, state databases, and specialized practice-area databases (Figure 1.1). Electronic information storage allows for much more flexibility in the arrangement of materials than the hard-copy reporters do. A database of electronically stored information can be reorganized repeatedly.

Opinions do not appear immediately in bound volumes. Instead, they appear first as official slip opinions issued by the court itself (Figure 1.2). Opinions of the U.S. Supreme Court first appear in slim pamphlets published by the U.S. Government Printing Office. Most law libraries do not collect slip opinions from courts other than the U.S. Supreme Court.

Slip opinions and unreported cases generally do not contain editorial enhancements. When West Group receives slip opinions, it adds them to Westlaw immediately. Therefore, the fastest way for you to read a new opinion is online. In fact, U.S. Supreme Court opinions are on Westlaw in the U.S. Supreme Court Cases database (SCT)* within thirty minutes of filing. Slip opinions from the other courts are online within different time periods, depending on the court.

The case is then scrutinized by the West manuscript staff, who check more than one million citations per year. They also add parallel citations to cases. The statute citations in the case are also checked, and many are corrected. All of the other editorial enhancements, which will be explained in this chapter, are added at this time.

---

*In this manual, the database identifier, that is, the abbreviation you use to access the database on Westlaw, is given in parentheses following the database name.

Figure 1.2
A Slip Opinion

CERTIFIED FOR PUBLICATION

IN THE COURT OF APPEAL OF THE STATE OF CALIFORNIA

SECOND APPELLATE DISTRICT

DIVISION FOUR

RECEIVED
OCT 0 5 1995
WEST

IN RE THE ESTATE OF ALICE JOSLYN, DECEASED.

MARCELLUS L. JOSLYN et al.,

Contestants and Appellants,

v.

HELEN MELAYNE DAVIS,

Claimant and Respondent.

B089496

(Super. Ct. No. SMP 4190)

COURT OF APPEAL - SECO...
FILED
OCT -4 1995
JOSEPH A. LANE   Clerk

APPEAL from a judgment of the Superior Court of Los Angeles County, Irving Shimer, Judge. Affirmed.

Mayer, Brown & Platt, Lee N. Abrams and Jacqueline R. Brady for Contestants and Appellants.

Rutan & Tucker, Theodore I. Wallace, Jr., and Matthew K. Ross for Claimant and Respondent.

Next, the opinions are gathered into softbound advance sheets (Figure 1.3). Advance sheets allow you to read the decision in the reporter format without having to wait until enough opinions are accumulated to make an entire bound volume. Most advance sheets from West Group are published on a weekly schedule. As you have learned in your classes, the rule of stare decisis demands access to the latest cases; law publishing has kept pace with this need for current cases either in print or online.

At the final stage, the bound case reporter volumes are published (Figure 1.4). The bound volumes contain a large number of decisions arranged in the same sequence as they appeared in the advance sheets. The citation will be identical in the advance sheet and in the bound volume, so you do not have to recheck your citation once the opinion appears in the bound volume.

There is a distinction in case reporting between official and unofficial reporters. When a statute or a court order directs the publication of court reports, they are called *official reports*. The official reports are no more accurate than the unofficial reports; in fact, the unofficial reports come into existence because they can be published more quickly than the official reports. Additionally, West editors may contact the court if clarification or corrections are needed, or if it appears that text has been omitted. Many times the corrections are initiated by the court itself. The key to a report being official is the political power of the state legislature or state court to declare it to be so.

U.S. Supreme Court and Lower Federal Court Decisions

You will study the jurisdiction of the federal courts during your first year of law school. At the top of the federal judicial pyramid is the Supreme Court of the United States. Almost all of its business consists of reviewing the judgments of lower courts. These may be the judgments of state courts of last resort that deal with questions of federal law, or they may be the decisions of lower federal courts. If a federal question arises in state litigation, that question must be pursued on appeal up through the state court system—to the state courts of last resort—before the case is eligible for review by the U.S. Supreme Court. The lower federal courts are the federal circuit courts of appeals and the federal district courts. Generally, the Supreme Court hears only cases that have already been appealed through a state's appellate courts or to one of the thirteen federal circuit courts of appeals.

The Supreme Court could not possibly hear all of the cases that come before it. It disposes of most appeals summarily by denying petitions for a *writ of certiorari*. This is a device used by the Court in choosing the cases it wishes to hear.

The decisions of the U.S. Supreme Court appear in published form in one official reporter and two unofficial reporters. The *United States Reports* (U.S.)* is the official reporter for the Supreme Court. It is published by the U.S. Government Printing Office. As with many official publications, the advance sheets and bound volumes of the *United States Reports* appear very slowly. Almost two years pass between the announcement of a decision and its appearance in the advance sheet, and yet another year passes before it is included in a bound volume. The decisions of the U.S. Supreme Court also

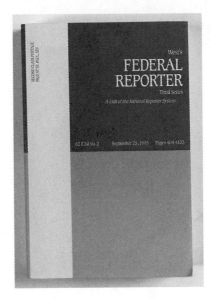

Figure 1.3
An Advance Sheet

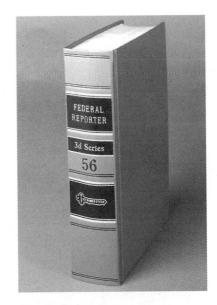

Figure 1.4
A Bound Case Reporter

*In this manual, the *Bluebook* abbreviation for a publication is given in parentheses following the publication name.

appear in the *Supreme Court Reporter* (S.Ct.) published by West Group and in the *United States Supreme Court Reports, Lawyers' Edition* (L.Ed. and L.Ed.2d) published by Lexis Law Publishing. The U.S. Supreme Court Cases databases (SCT and SCT-OLD) on Westlaw contain the Supreme Court decisions from the inception of the Court (1790). Although the *Bluebook* requires only the official citation to the *United States Reports,* most citations include all three sources:

Hustler Magazine v. Falwell, 485 U.S. 46, 108 S.Ct. 876, 99 L. Ed.2d 41 (1988)

Many law firm libraries and some court libraries have only one of the bound sets available, so parallel citations can be a big help.

Another source for U.S. Supreme Court decisions is *United States Law Week* (U.S.L.W.) published on a weekly basis by The Bureau of National Affairs, Inc. It is issued in two volumes: one contains all of the Supreme Court decisions as well as other actions taken by the Court; the other has abstracts of what the publisher considers to be important lower federal and state court opinions. Other than the online services, *U.S. Law Week* is the first place to find the full text of recent Supreme Court decisions.

Below the Supreme Court in the federal system are thirteen federal courts of appeals and numerous federal district courts (Figure 1.5). The jurisdiction of the federal courts of appeals, or circuit courts, is really very simple. It consists of appeals from decisions by district courts, together with appeals from decisions by federal administrative agencies, such as the Federal Communications Commission. The decisions of the federal courts of appeals since 1880 are published in West Group's *Federal Reporter* (F., F.2d and F.3d). West Group has also published a collection of earlier cases in a set called *Federal Cases.* Decisions of the courts of appeals, from the beginning of the court, are in the U.S. Court of Appeals Cases databases (CTA and CTA-OLD) on Westlaw. You can also search in individual courts of appeals databases, for example, the U.S. Court of Appeals for the Eighth Circuit Cases database (CTA8).

The jurisdiction of the district courts is the most complex part of federal jurisdiction. A case will be tried in a district court if it "arises under" federal law for purposes of federal trial court jurisdiction. In addition to these "arises under" cases, federal courts also have jurisdiction over civil cases involving parties from different states; these are known as *diversity cases.*

The criminal jurisdiction of the district courts includes all prosecutions for federal crimes. The decisions of the federal district courts since 1924 are published in West Group's *Federal Supplement* (F.Supp. and F.Supp.2d).

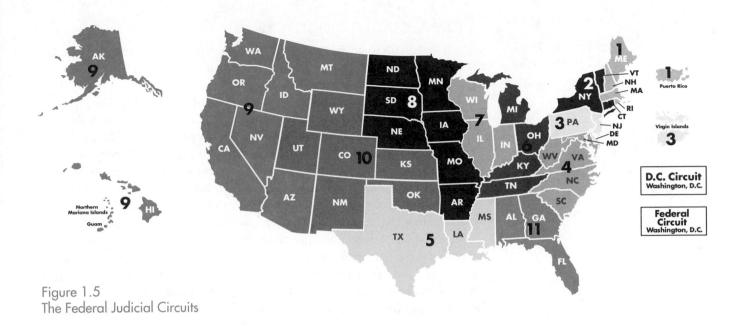

Figure 1.5
The Federal Judicial Circuits

Decisions of district courts can be found in the U.S. District Courts Cases databases (DCT and DCT-OLD) on Westlaw. The district courts are the federal trial courts and only a small percentage of their cases are reported in West Group's reporters; the DCT database on Westlaw includes both cases that appear in the reporters and those that are unreported.

West Group's *Federal Rules Decisions* (F.R.D.), first published in 1940, is a specialized reporter that contains selected opinions of the U.S. district courts on matters related to the Federal Rules of Civil Procedure and Criminal Procedure. In addition to these decisions, *Federal Rules Decisions* includes articles dealing with federal rules. These articles from the reporter are on Westlaw in the Federal Rules Decisions (Articles from the West Reporter) database (FEDRDTP); the cases themselves appear in the DCT database.

Decisions of Special Courts

A few special federal courts, such as the Tax Court, publish their own decisions. West Group publishes the *Bankruptcy Reporter*, which includes cases from the federal bankruptcy courts plus district court bankruptcy cases not reported in the *Federal Supplement*. It also publishes reporters compiling federal and state decisions in subject areas, such as the *Education Law Reporter*. The decisions from these reporters also appear on Westlaw.

State Court Decisions

It is difficult to generalize about the structure of state courts since each state has a different structure. Suffice it to say that each state has either a triple-layered or a two-tiered hierarchy of courts.

About half the states still publish their own official reports. Many states have ceased publishing their official reports, and attorneys rely on West Group's National Reporter System for reporting cases. In some states, the legislature or the courts have designated West Group's reporters as the official repository of state opinions. In other places, this has been done by default. It is surprising how informal much of this process is. Many states have discontinued their official reports because of long publication delays and untimely publication of new opinions. Even when states publish their own reports, attorneys often use West Group's reporters because of the many editorial enhancements—synopses, headnotes, topic and key number indexing—and because the headnotes link the researcher with the West Key Number System, which we will discuss in the next chapter.

West Group's National Reporter System is a set of reporters that divides the fifty states and the District of Columbia into seven national regions: Atlantic, North Eastern, North Western, Pacific, South Eastern, South Western, and Southern (Figure 1.6). The National Reporter System covers the appellate courts of all the states. The decisions of New York's highest court are reported in the *North Eastern Reporter* and the *New York Supplement.* The opinions of New York's lower courts, as well as those of the highest court, are reported in the *New York Supplement.* Similarly, California Supreme Court decisions appear in both the *Pacific Reporter* and the *California Reporter.* The opinions of California's lower courts, along with those of the California Supreme Court, are published in the *California Reporter.* The federal reporters published by West Group are also part of the National Reporter System.

Figure 1.6
West Group's
National Reporter
System

The reporters in the National Reporter System contain several special features. The advance sheets include a number of tables that later appear in the bound volume. The table that you will use most frequently is the Table of Cases Reported (Figure 1.7). If you are looking for a very recent case, you can search either Westlaw or the advance sheets. Remember that the Table of Cases Reported in the advance sheets is cumulative for each volume. That means you only have to check the table in the most recent advance sheet for that volume.

Take a few minutes to look at the special tables in the advance sheets in your library. You may one day need to find a listing of all judges sitting on a particular court or a listing of cases that cite the American Bar Association's Standards for Criminal Justice, for example. These tables can be found in the first few pages of each reporter following the Table of Cases Reported.

Cases from the regional reporters are also available on Westlaw in regional reporter databases, such as West's Atlantic Reporter database (ATL) (Figure 1.8). Decisions of every state are also online in state-specific databases. To search in a state case law database, use the state's two-letter postal abbreviation for that state followed by –CS (Figure 1.9). Coverage for state case databases varies, so you need to check the print *Westlaw Database Directory* or click the **Scope** button after you access a database. Scope tells you the type of documents available in a database and the scope of coverage for these documents.

Figure 1.7
A Table of Cases Reported
from an Advance Sheet

CASES REPORTED

62 F.3d

(Cases in bold type appear in this issue)

Call 1-800-562-2FAX to order full text cases by fax.

FIRST CIRCUIT
(Cases in this issue, pp. 1–37)

	Page		Page
Command Transp. Inc. v. B.J.'s Wholesale Club Inc.—C.A.1 (Mass.)	18	U.S. v. Barbioni—C.A.1 (Me.)	5
		U.S. v. Montoya (Two Cases)—C.A.1 (Mass.)	1
Jordan v. Hawker Dayton Corp.—C.A.1 (Me.)	29	U.S. v. Sturtevant—C.A.1 (Mass.)	33
		U.S. v. Villegas—C.A.1 (Mass.)	1
Northeast Erectors Ass'n of BTEA v. Secretary of Labor, Occupational Safety & Health Admin.—C.A.1 (Mass.)	37	U.S. Fidelity & Guar. Co. v. Baker Material Handling Corp.—C.A.1 (Mass.)	24
Nuccio v. Nuccio—C.A.1 (Me.)	14	U.S. on Behalf of Pittsburgh Tank & Tower, Inc. v. G & C Enterprises, Inc.—C.A.1 (Me.)	35
Pittsburgh Tank & Tower, Inc., U.S. on Behalf of, v. G & C Enterprises, Inc.—C.A.1 (Me.)	35	Violette v. Smith & Nephew Dyonics, Inc. (Two Cases)—C.A.1 (Me.)	8

Figure 1.8
Regional Reporter Databases on
Westlaw

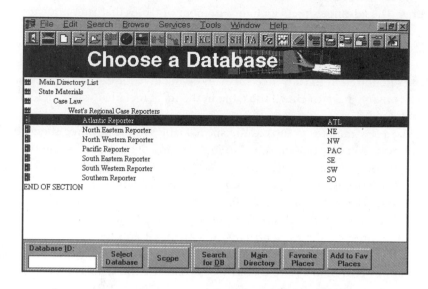

Figure 1.9
State Case Law Databases
on Westlaw

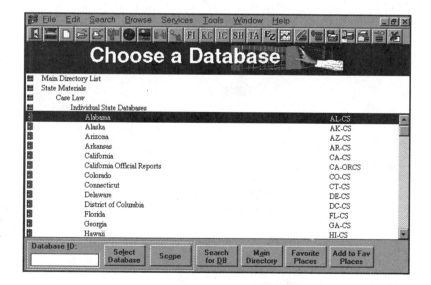

Deciphering a Case Citation

If someone hands you the legal citation of a case, you should be able to head to the correct volume and turn to the correct page without checking any indexes or asking for help. Cases that appear in reporters have a citation that consists of the name of the case, the volume of the reporter, the name of the reporter, the page number in the reporter on which the case begins, and the year the case was decided:

Halbman v. Lemke,	99	Wis.2d	241,	298	N.W.2d	562	(1980)
↓	↓	↓	↓	↓	↓	↓	↓
Case name	Volume	Official reporter	Page	Volume	West Group reporter	Page	Year

The citation may include a notation of the court deciding the case, or the court may be obvious from the reporter abbreviation, such as Wis.2d. A citation to a particular paragraph or sentence may also include the number of the page on which the quotation appears:

298 N.W.2d	562,	564
	↓	↓
	Page case begins	Page of quotation

Although books may be your first choice, when the volume that you are looking for is not available, access Westlaw and use the Find service. You do not need to access a database; simply click the **Find** button on the main button palette and type your citation in the *Citation* text box. For example, type **298 nw2d 562** in the *Citation* text box to find *Halbman v. Lemke.*

If a case appears only on Westlaw (a very recent opinion or an unpublished case), the citation will consist of a Westlaw citation. A Westlaw citation appears on the screen in the upper-left corner of slip opinions and unreported cases. Each Westlaw citation consists of four parts: the year of the decision, WL (identifying Westlaw as the place the document is located), a unique document number, and the jurisdiction in which the case was decided. You can use the Find service to retrieve slip opinions and unpublished cases on Westlaw. Type the Westlaw citation (excluding the jurisdiction notation) in the *Citation* text box. For example, you will retrieve the case shown in Figure 1.10 if you type **1998 wl 211749**.

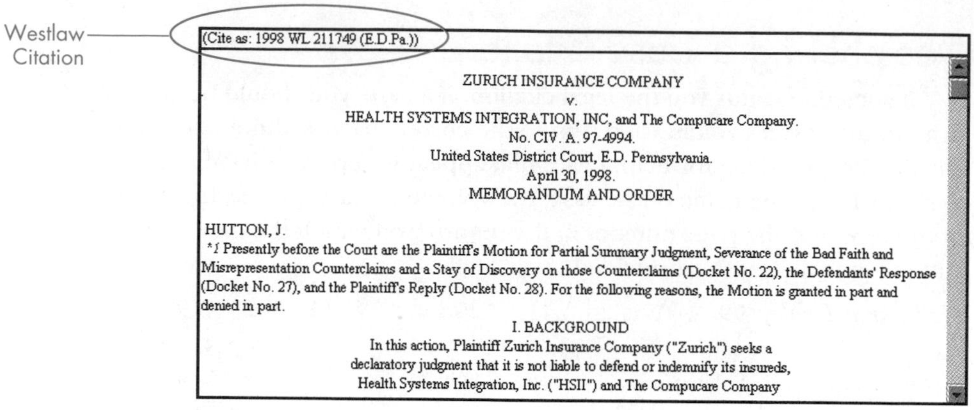

Figure 1.10
A Westlaw Citation
of an Unreported Case

Westlaw
Citation

(Cite as: 1998 WL 211749 (E.D.Pa.))

ZURICH INSURANCE COMPANY
v.
HEALTH SYSTEMS INTEGRATION, INC, and The Compucare Company.
No. CIV. A. 97-4994.
United States District Court, E.D. Pennsylvania.
April 30, 1998.
MEMORANDUM AND ORDER

HUTTON, J.
*1 Presently before the Court are the Plaintiff's Motion for Partial Summary Judgment, Severance of the Bad Faith and Misrepresentation Counterclaims and a Stay of Discovery on those Counterclaims (Docket No. 22), the Defendants' Response (Docket No. 27), and the Plaintiff's Reply (Docket No. 28). For the following reasons, the Motion is granted in part and denied in part.

I. BACKGROUND
In this action, Plaintiff Zurich Insurance Company ("Zurich") seeks a declaratory judgment that it is not liable to defend or indemnify its insureds, Health Systems Integration, Inc. ("HSII") and The Compucare Company

All of the rules for writing and deciphering legal citations appear in the *Bluebook* (Figure 1.11). For instance, if you are formally citing a very recent opinion available only on Westlaw, the *Bluebook* provides rules on the correct electronic citation format. The *Bluebook* has many shortcomings, however, and is sometimes more a hindrance than a help. Nevertheless, you will have to use the *Bluebook* during your entire legal career, so you should become acquainted with it now.

Parallel Citations

As we noted earlier, you will often find a string of citations after the case name:

In re Baby M,   109 N.J. 396,   537 A.2d 1227 (1988)
                        ↓   ↓
                Official reporter   Unofficial reporter

A citation to the same case published in a different reporter is called a *parallel citation*. Parallel citations are different citations to the same exact case, not to different stages of a case.

Figure 1.11
A Page from *The Bluebook:
A Uniform System of Citation*

Basic Citation Forms   55

Cases   10

Basic Citation Forms   10.1

A full case citation includes the name of the case (**rule 10.2**); the published sources in which it may be found, if any (**rule 10.3**); a parenthetical that indicates the court and jurisdiction (**rule 10.4**) and the year or date of decision (**rule 10.5**); and the subsequent history of the case, if any (**rule 10.7**). It may also include additional parenthetical information (**rule 10.6**) and the prior history of the case (**rule 10.7**). Special citation forms for pending and unreported cases (**rule 10.8.1**) and for briefs, records, motions, and memoranda (**rule 10.8.3**) are discussed in **rule 10.8**. **Rule 14.3** provides citation forms for administrative adjudications and arbitrations.

filed but not decided	Charlesworth v. Mack, No. 90-345 (D. Mass. filed Sept. 18, 1990).
unpublished interim order	Charlesworth v. Mack, No. 90-345 (D. Mass. Oct. 25, 1990) (order granting preliminary injunction).
published interim order	Charlesworth v. Mack, 725 F. Supp. 1395 (D. Mass. 1990) (order granting preliminary injunction).
unpublished decision	Charlesworth v. Mack, No. 90-345, slip op. at 6 (D. Mass. Dec. 4, 1990).
decision published in service only	Charlesworth v. Mack, 1990 Fed. Sec. L. Rep. (CCH) ¶ 102,342 (D. Mass. Dec. 4, 1990).
decision published in newspaper only	Charlesworth v. Mack, N.Y. L.J., Dec. 5, 1990, at 1 (D. Mass. Dec. 4, 1990).
decision available in electronic database	Charlesworth v. Mack, No. 90-345, 1990 U.S. Dist. LEXIS 20837, at *6 (D. Mass. Dec. 4, 1990).
published decision	Charlesworth v. Mack, 727 F. Supp. 1407, 1412 (D. Mass. 1990).
appeal docketed	Charlesworth v. Mack, 727 F. Supp. 1407 (D. Mass. 1990), *appeal docketed*, No. 90-567 (1st Cir. Dec. 20, 1990).
brief, record, or appendix	Brief for Appellant at 7, Charlesworth v. Mack, 925 F.2d 314 (1st Cir. 1991) (No. 90-567).
disposition on appeal	Charlesworth v. Mack, 925 F.2d 314, 335 (1st Cir. 1991).
disposition in lower court showing subsequent history	Charlesworth v. Mack, 727 F. Supp. 1407, 1412 (D. Mass. 1990), *aff'd*, 925 F.2d 314 (1st Cir. 1991).
petition for certiorari filed	Charlesworth v. Mack, 925 F.2d 314 (1st Cir. 1991), *petition for cert. filed*, 60 U.S.L.W. 3422 (U.S. Jan. 14, 1992) (No. 92-212).
petition for certiorari granted	Charlesworth v. Mack, 925 F.2d 314 (1st Cir. 1991), *cert. granted*, 60 U.S.L.W. 3562 (U.S. Jan. 21, 1992) (No. 92-212).

Source: © 1996 by The Columbia Law Review Association, The Harvard Law Review Association, the University of Pennsylvania Law Review, and The Yale Law Journal.

Figure 1.12
Four Ways of Finding
Parallel Citations

Official Citation

(a) A West Group Reporter

(b) A Digest

There are several ways to find a parallel citation if you know only one citation:

1. West Group's reporters (Figure 1.12a) and Westlaw provide the official citation if it is available. However, since the official reporters are generally slow to be published, the official citation is not usually available at the time the West Group reporter is published, unless the West Group reporter is the official reporter. Some of the official state reports not published by West Group cite to its reporters. The reporters of the U.S. Supreme Court cases published by West Group and Lexis Law Publishing both provide citations to the official *United States Reports* and to each other. The *United States Reports* does not supply any parallel citations.

2. If you know the name of the case, check the Table of Cases in the digest that covers the jurisdiction where your case was decided, and you will find all of the parallel citations (Figure 1.12b). Digests will be discussed in the next chapter.

3. You can easily find parallel citations by using either Shepard's citators or the KeyCite citation research service, which is part of Westlaw (Figure 1.12c). These services will be explained in a later chapter.

4. When you have the official citation and need the West Group citation, use the *National Reporter Blue Book*. Just look up the official citation, and you will find the parallel citation to the West Group reporter (Figure 1.12d).

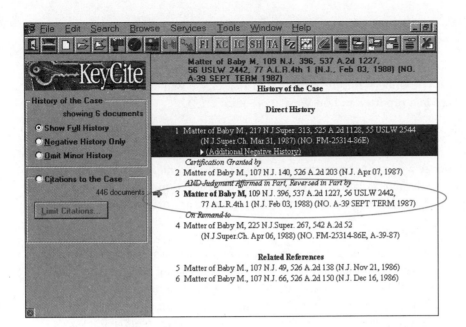

Figure 1.12
Four Ways of Finding
Parallel Citations (continued)

(c) KeyCite

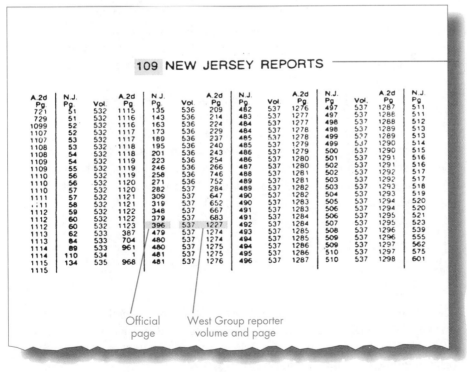

(d) *The National Reporter Blue Book*

Official volume

Official page

West Group reporter volume and page

Parts of a Case

Since you will be spending most of your waking moments, or at least your semiconscious moments, in law school reading cases, it is important that you understand the structure of a case. We will discuss the parts of a case in a reporter and on Westlaw (Figure 1.13).

Court

Particular reporters generally correspond to particular courts. When you choose a particular reporter, for instance, the *Federal Supplement,* you will be choosing particular courts or a particular jurisdiction, that is, cases from the federal district courts. Generally, the reporters are organized by jurisdiction.

Case Name or Title

Every case has a name. Most cases are named for the parties (usually two) involved in the lawsuit to indicate who is suing whom (e.g., *Bergman v. United States*). Some cases may have only one name with a Latin phrase attached (e.g., *In re Seiferth*). In a criminal case, since the state brings the action, the first party will often be the jurisdiction itself (e.g., *State v. Birditt*).

When a case begins in the trial court, the first name is the plaintiff, or the party bringing the suit, and the name after the *v.* is the defendant. On appeal, the name of the petitioner or appellant will be listed first; the name of the respondent or appellee will be listed second. Therefore, if the defendant in the trial court brings an appeal, his or her name may be listed first in the appellate case.

When you read a case in one of the reporters or on Westlaw, you will often find several plaintiffs, defendants, or cross-complainants. Correct citation form requires that only the first-named plaintiff and the first-named defendant be listed. The case name that appears at the top of each page in the reporters is not in correct citation format and should not be followed as an example of *Bluebook* format. For example, the following appears at the top of the page for the case at 441 F.2d 1061:

Local 13, Int. Longshoremen's & W.U. v. Pacific Mar. Ass'n

The correct *Bluebook* format for the case name would be *Local 13, Int'l Longshoremen's & Warehousemen's Union v. Pacific Maritime Ass'n.*

Docket Number

When a case is filed in the court clerk's office, it is assigned a docket number that remains with the case until it is decided. Typically, the first two numbers indicate the year that the case was filed. The docket number is printed below the name of the case.

Figure 1.13
Parts of a Case

(a) Parts of a Case on Westlaw

Citation ——————————————

Case Name or Title ——————————————

Docket Number ——————————————

Court ——————————————

Date ——————————————

Synopsis ——————————————

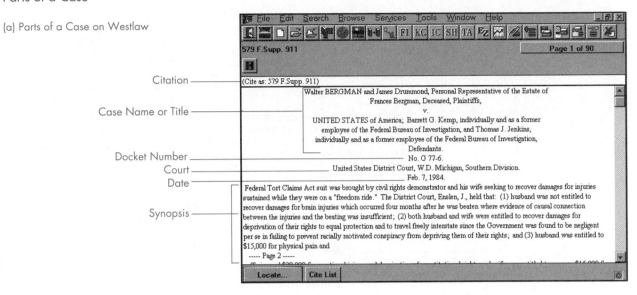

Headnote Number ——————————————

Topic ——————————————

Digest Classification
Hierarchy ——————————————

Key Line ——————————————

Headnote ——————————————

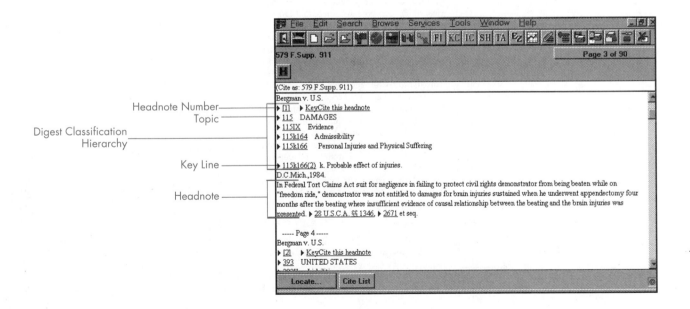

Figure 1.13
Parts of a Case (continued)

(b) Parts of a Case
in a West Group
Reporter

Citation ———————

Case Name or Title ———

Docket Number ———

Court ———

Date ———

Synopsis ———

Key Number ———
Topic ———

Headnote ———

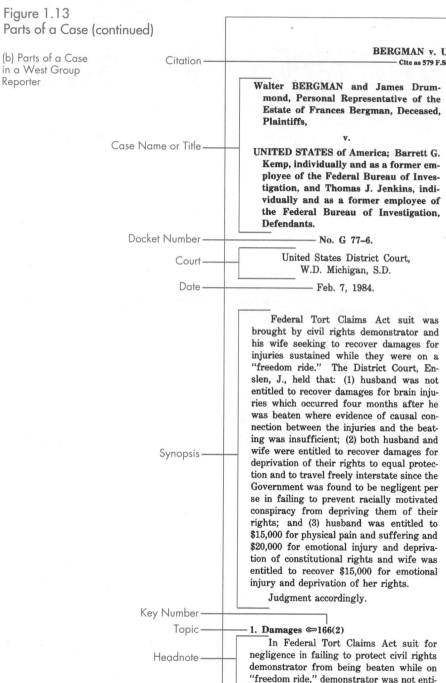

BERGMAN v. UNITED STATES   **911**
Cite as 579 F.Supp. 911 (1984)

Walter **BERGMAN** and James Drum-
mond, Personal Representative of the
Estate of Frances Bergman, Deceased,
Plaintiffs,

v.

UNITED STATES of America; Barrett G.
Kemp, individually and as a former employee of the Federal Bureau of Investigation, and Thomas J. Jenkins, individually and as a former employee of
the Federal Bureau of Investigation,
Defendants.

No. G 77–6.

United States District Court,
W.D. Michigan, S.D.

Feb. 7, 1984.

Federal Tort Claims Act suit was
brought by civil rights demonstrator and
his wife seeking to recover damages for
injuries sustained while they were on a
"freedom ride." The District Court, Enslen, J., held that: (1) husband was not
entitled to recover damages for brain injuries which occurred four months after he
was beaten where evidence of causal con-
nection between the injuries and the beating was insufficient; (2) both husband and
wife were entitled to recover damages for
deprivation of their rights to equal protection and to travel freely interstate since the
Government was found to be negligent per
se in failing to prevent racially motivated
conspiracy from depriving them of their
rights; and (3) husband was entitled to
$15,000 for physical pain and suffering and
$20,000 for emotional injury and depriva-
tion of constitutional rights and wife was
entitled to recover $15,000 for emotional
injury and deprivation of her rights.

Judgment accordingly.

1. Damages ⬅166(2)

In Federal Tort Claims Act suit for
negligence in failing to protect civil rights
demonstrator from being beaten while on
"freedom ride," demonstrator was not enti-

tled to damages for brain injuries sustained
when he underwent appendectomy four
months after the beating where insufficient
evidence of causal relationship between the
beating and the brain injuries was presented. 28 U.S.C.A. §§ 1346, 2671 et seq.

2. United States ⬅78(14), 110, 142

Under the Federal Tort Claims Act,
plaintiffs are entitled to compensatory
damages in accordance with state law, with
exception that United States may not be
held liable for prejudgment interest or pu-
nitive damages. 28 U.S.C.A. § 2674.

3. Damages ⬅52, 54
False Imprisonment ⬅34

In Alabama, damages for mental anguish in cases of assault, false imprisonment and negligence, include compensation
for insult and indignity, hurt feelings, mental suffering and fright.

4. Damages ⬅50

Under Alabama law, even where there
is no physical injury, plaintiff may recover
damages for mental anguish occasioned by
defendant's negligence.

5. Damages ⬅51

In Federal Tort Claims Act suit for
negligence in protecting civil rights demonstrator during "freedom ride," wife of
beaten demonstrator was entitled to recover damages for mental anguish even
though she herself was not beaten. 28
U.S.C.A. §§ 1346, 2671 et seq.

6. Damages ⬅48

In determining whether or not plaintiff
suffered mental anguish which can be com-
pensated under Alabama law, court is not
limited to direct testimony relating feelings
of indignity, mental suffering and fright;
mental anguish may properly be inferred
as natural and usual consequences from all
of the circumstances.

7. Damages ⬅49.10

In Federal Tort Claims Act suit for
negligence in protecting civil rights demonstrator during "freedom ride," demonstrators were entitled to damages for mental
anguish. 28 U.S.C.A. §§ 1346, 2671 et seq.

Date

A reporter or Westlaw will indicate the exact month, day, and year that the case was decided. For citation purposes, cite only the year.

Synopsis

Editors at West Group write a synopsis or brief description of each case that West Group publishes. You will find the synopsis below the date. Most synopses contain the following information: the facts of the case, the name and holding of the lower court judge, the holding of the court, and the name of the judge writing the opinion. If you have many cases to read, you can quickly scan the synopses to weed out the irrelevant cases, but be advised that the synopsis is not part of the opinion. It is a helpful editorial enhancement prepared by the publisher. If you are looking in a jurisdiction that has an official reporter in which the court writes a synopsis, you may get *two* synopses—one from West Group and one from the court.

Judge

The judge is listed both in the synopsis or syllabus of a case and on a separate line preceding the opinion. There is no manual index of judges' names that lists all cases decided by specific judges, but you can search for opinions written by a particular judge by using an online service. On Westlaw, you can retrieve cases in which a particular judge wrote the majority, dissenting, or concurring opinion.

Headnotes

Court decisions typically contain at least one legal issue. An issue is the question raised where the rules of law impinge on the facts of the case. West Group editors decipher the legal issues from cases and summarize each issue in a headnote. Each headnote is usually one sentence. Headnotes appear in the case in reporters and on Westlaw after the synopsis but before the opinion. A headnote in a reporter begins with a number in boldface type followed by a topic name and key number (Figure 1.14a). A headnote on Westlaw contains additional information showing the full digest classification hierarchy for a key number (Figure 1.14b).

Headnotes are numbered so you can use them as a table of contents to the case. Numbers corresponding to the headnote numbers appear in brackets in the text of the opinion. The number in brackets indicates that this text is covered by that particular headnote. On Westlaw, you can "jump" (using a hypertext link) from a headnote to the discussion of the point of law in the text of the opinion by clicking the headnote number.

Figure 1.14
Headnotes

(a) Headnote in a West Group Reporter

912   579 FEDERAL SUPPLEMENT

8. Conspiracy ⟜13

In Federal Tort Claims Act suit for negligence in protecting civil rights demonstrators during "freedom ride," demonstrators were entitled to damages for deprivation of their constitutional rights to equal protection and freedom of interstate travel where United States was found to be negligent per se under Alabama law in part because it violated its statutory duty to prevent racially motivated conspiracy from depriving freedom riders of equal protection. 42 U.S.C.A. § 1986.

9. Civil Rights ⟜13.17(5, 6)
  Damages ⟜130(1)

In Federal Tort Claims Act suit for negligence in protecting civil rights demonstrator from being beaten while on "freedom ride," demonstrator was entitled to damages of $15,000 for his physical pain and suffering, $20,000 for emotional injury and deprivation of constitutional rights. 28 U.S.C.A. §§ 1346, 2671 et seq.

OPINION ON DAMAGES

ENSLEN, District Judge.

Plaintiffs in this action under the Federal Tort Claims Act (FTCA) are Dr. Walter Bergman and the personal representative of the estate of his late wife, Frances Bergman. Both Walter and Frances Bergman were among the "freedom riders" who traveled by bus into the South in May, 1961 to test a recent pronouncement by the United States Supreme Court that the Constitution required racial equality in interstate transportation facilities. Their encounter with a conspiracy of violent racism in Alabama was described in detail by this Court in an earlier opinion. *Bergman v. United States*, 565 F.Supp. 1353 (W.D.MI. 1983). That decision followed upon trial of the United States' liability for the injuries plaintiffs suffered during their journey into Alabama.[1] I held that the federal Government was negligent in failing to take steps available to it to avoid the violence, and concluded that,

(b) Headnote on Westlaw

(Cite as: 579 F.Supp. 911)

Bergman v. U.S.

▸ [X]   ▸ KeyCite this headnote
▸ 91   CONSPIRACY
▸ 91I   Civil Liability
▸ 91I(A)   Acts Constituting Conspiracy and Liability Therefor
▸ 91k12   Persons Liable

▸ 91k13 k. In general.
D.C.Mich.,1984.
In Federal Tort Claims Act suit for negligence in protecting civil rights demonstrators during "freedom ride," demonstrators were entitled to damages for deprivation of their constitutional rights to equal protection and freedom of interstate travel where United States was found to be negligent per se under Alabama law in part because it violated its statutory duty to prevent racially motivated conspiracy from depriving freedom riders of equal protection. ▸ 42 U.S.C.A. § 1986.

The next part of the headnote after the number is a term or phrase, which is the broad topic under which West Group has classified that particular legal issue. After the topic in the West Group reporters is a key number. (On Westlaw the full digest classification hierarchy appears between the broad topic and the very specific key number.) The key number represents a specific aspect or subsection of the topic. For example, under the topic Conspiracy, key number 13 covers "Conspiracy—In general." West Group editors classify a case under all the applicable topics and key numbers. To find out what the key number stands for, consult either a West Group digest or the Key Number Service on Westlaw. Digests are books that group headnotes from cases under different topics of law; they are arranged by topics and key numbers. Once you find a relevant topic and key number, you can continue with the digests or search for the topic and key number on Westlaw (as explained in the next chapter). The lines of text in the digest are actually the headnote itself; that is, they are an annotation of one of the legal issues in the case.

Writing headnotes is an art, not a science. Two different editors will see different sets of legal issues in a case. As in the debate over whether Hank Aaron or Babe Ruth was the greater ballplayer, there is no "correct" answer. Look at the headnotes in each of the following two versions of a U.S. Supreme Court case and see how different they are (Figures 1.15a and b). The West Group reporter contains thirteen short headnotes while the Lexis Law Publishing reporter contains two longer headnotes and a set of references to other related materials. The official *United States Reports* does not contain any headnotes per se, but it does include a long synopsis of the case.

Topic

As we have just seen, topics are the main classifications for cases. In a library, you would look in a West Group digest volume for the topic that you need. Cases may be searched on Westlaw by digest topic.

Attorneys

Just preceding the text of the opinion you will find the names of the attorneys, including the city where each attorney practices. You can use this information to contact the attorneys for more details about the case. If the opinion indicates that one of the parties argued a point of law persuasively, for example, you may want to read the attorney's brief for an expanded discussion of that point. Westlaw contains briefs for the United States Supreme Court in the U.S. Supreme Court Briefs database (SCT-BRIEF), but the best source for briefs from other courts is often the attorneys who argued the case. Before contacting an attorney, you may want to search Westlaw for other cases the attorney has handled.

Figure 1.15
Variations in Headnotes

(a) Headnotes from West
Group's *Supreme Court
Reporter*

---

916   **108 SUPREME COURT REPORTER**   **485 U.S. 112**

not individually reviewed for substantive priority by higher supervisory officials and that civil service commission decided appeals from such decisions in some circumscribed manner that gave substantial deference to original decision maker were insufficient to support conclusion that supervisors were authorized to establish employment policy for city with respect to transfers and layoffs.

Reversed and remanded.

Justice Brennan filed opinion concurring in judgment in which Justices Marshall and Blackmun joined.

Justice Stevens filed dissenting opinion.

Justice Kennedy took no part in the consideration or decision of the case.

1. Federal Courts ⇐461

City's failure to timely object to jury instruction on municipalities' liability for their employees' unconstitutional acts did not deprive Supreme Court of jurisdiction to determine proper legal standard for im-

3. Civil Rights ⇐13.7

Municipalities may be liable under § 1983 only for acts for which municipality itself is actually responsible, that is, acts which municipality had officially sanctioned or ordered. (Per Justice O'Connor with the Chief Justice and two Justices concurring and three Justices concurring in the judgment.) 42 U.S.C.A. § 1983.

4. Civil Rights ⇐13.7

Only those municipal officers who have final policymaking authority may by their actions subject municipal government to § 1983 liability. (Per Justice O'Connor with the Chief Justice and two Justices concurring and three Justices concurring in the judgment.) 42 U.S.C.A. § 1983.

5. Civil Rights ⇐13.7

Whether particular official has final policymaking authority for purposes of § 1983 liability is question of state law. (Per Justice O'Connor with the Chief Justice and two Justices concurring and three Justices concurring in the judgment.) 42 U.S.C.A. § 1983.

(b) Headnote from Lexis Law
Publishing's *United States Supreme
Court Reports, Lawyers' Edition*

ST. LOUIS v PRAPROTNIK
(1988) 485 US 112, 99 L Ed 2d 107, 108 S Ct 915
HEADNOTES

Classified to U.S. Supreme Court Digest, Lawyers' Edition

Appeal § 1677; Civil Rights § 27; Trial § 165 — reversal — liability of city — retaliatory employment actions — supervisors — jury question

1a-1c. The United States Supreme Court will reverse a Federal Court of Appeals decision, which affirmed a Federal District Court judgment finding a city liable under 42 USCS § 1983 for the violation of a city employee's federal constitutional rights through retaliatory employee transfer and layoff actions taken by city agency supervisors in response to the employee's appeal of his suspension to the city's grievance review board, where (1) four Justices are of the opinion that the Federal Court of Appeals applied an incorrect legal standard in concluding that the supervisors were city "policymakers" whose actions could subject the city to liability under § 1983, in that (a) the identification of officials with such final policymaking authority is a question of state and local law, rather than a question of

Opinion

We are now to the actual text of the judge's decision, which is called the *opinion*. An opinion is a court's written explanation of why it did what it did. The structure of an opinion includes the nature of the case, a general statement of the issues presented, the facts, the errors assigned, and a dispositional section.

Opinions may be unanimous, which used to be good form, but today it is less frequent. This means that you may find other opinions after the majority's statement. A dissenting opinion is written by a single judge or a minority of judges who disagree with the result. There may also be concurring opinions when a judge or judges agree with the result of the main opinion but not with the reasoning. Because of the doctrine of precedent, this policy is important. In complex cases, a judge may concur in part and dissent in part. Especially in U.S. Supreme Court cases, sorting out all the separate opinions can be difficult.

You may also encounter a few other kinds of opinions. A *per curiam* opinion is an opinion written anonymously that includes the reasoning of the entire court. Such opinions are generally short and are weak precedent. Memorandum decisions report routine decisions.

In reading any opinion, remember that much of the opinion does not resolve the issues in dispute. Opinions may contain factual summaries, the judge's opinion on the state of civilization, or anything else. Judges can write what they like, but everything that does not resolve a legal issue is *dicta*. You will find that dicta, though not binding precedent, may be persuasive. That is, dicta may still be helpful to your case.

The last paragraph in a majority opinion is the mandate of the court. It states what action is being taken on appeal. For example, the court may indicate that the decision is affirmed, reversed, remanded, modified, or dismissed.

Conclusion

You should now feel familiar with cases. They are not really like the cryptic, heavily edited versions that lurk in your casebooks. In their fully reported form, they have editorial enhancements and other useful parts. In addition, they all follow a similar pattern, so you will find familiar aspects as you move from the federal court system to the state court system.

This chapter has explained how to locate a case in a reporter from a legal citation and how to find and use parallel citations. At this point, you should also be able to recognize and understand the parts of a case in a reporter volume and on Westlaw. Now that you understand the basics of reporters in print and on Westlaw, we will proceed to finding particular cases.

Finding Cases

Finding cases has been a challenge for lawyers for hundreds of years, and a variety of tools have been developed to help. In some ways every tool that you will encounter is designed to help you find cases. This chapter concentrates on print digests and the online Westlaw databases. Both the digests and Westlaw try to be comprehensive. This means that they do not offer access to cases on just one topic, but instead provide access to all cases—a full-tilt blunderbuss approach. Given that there are some three million cases with perhaps another 130,000 being added each year, it is no surprise that these tools need some special instruction. This chapter will explain them.

Digests

Digests are research tools that arrange abstracts of cases by subject. They are particularly useful for finding cases involving legal issues or concepts, such as ownership of property or various contract theories. Digests are built from headnotes, which were introduced in the last chapter. Every digest has two components: (1) a base of headnotes and (2) a subject arrangement that divides legal issues and the headnotes that discuss those issues into a logical structure.

Using digests is one way of locating a case by its subject. Often, you will get maximum results by using digests in conjunction with Westlaw, but for the time being, let's examine how to use a digest alone to find the information we need.

To give you an example of how a digest works, suppose a child has been injured by an unleashed pit bull in the state of Washington. The child's parents want you to file a claim against the dog's owner and against the local humane society for not enforcing the city's leash law. You need to find cases regarding injuries from pit bulls. The only clue you have is that you remember reading about a pit bull case that took place in the state of Washington. How can you use this clue to find the cases you need?

The traditional answer has been to use a digest*. A digest is a comprehensive subject index to cases. It contains a comprehensive list of legal topics, including some personal favorites of the authors, such as Hawkers and Peddlers. Each legal topic is subdivided into issues and each issue is assigned a digest classification number called a *key number*. Listed under each key number are headnotes from reported cases addressing the issue. As a result, headnotes from different cases that discuss the same point of law appear together. The paragraphs in the digests are basically the headnote paragraphs from the cases in the reporters rearranged according to subject (Figures 2.1a and b).

Understanding the relationship between the headnotes and the digests is crucial to using the digests. Remember that West Group editors create headnotes by isolating every issue of law that appears in the opinion. They then assign topics and key numbers to every headnote. Each headnote is assigned at least one key number, and some headnotes are assigned several. Consequently, the same headnote may appear in two or more places in the digest.

Figure 2.1
Headnote Paragraph in the Reporter and in the Digest

(a) Headnote in *Pacific Reporter*

1280 Wash.   **737 PACIFIC REPORTER, 2d SERIES**

5. Municipal Corporations ⊜723

Special relationship exception to public duty doctrine arises where relationship develops between individual and agents of entity performing governmental function, such that duty is created to perform mandated act for benefit of particular person or class of persons.

6. Municipal Corporations ⊜723

Before entity may be held liable under

₁₈₈₈John H. Loeffler, Olson, Loeffler & Landis, Spokane, for appellants.

Jonathan C. Rascoff, Spokane, for respondents.

MUNSON, Judge.

John and Roxie Champagne brought this action on behalf of their minor son, John, against the Spokane Humane Society for personal injuries resulting from the attack

9. Animals ⊜54

Although owner of pit bulls was negligent in allowing them to run loose, humane society, which had been contractually delegated authority to enforce animal regulations of city's ordinance, could be liable for its later negligence, if any, in failing to apprehend the pit bulls.

1. Mr. Mason subsequently disappeared and is

and to enforce the animal regulatory provisions of the Spokane city ordinances. Spokane city ordinance C13835₁₈₈₉provides in pertinent part:

Section 1. Dogs at Large. It shall be unlawful for any person to cause, permit, or allow any dog or dogs, owned, harbored, controlled or kept by him, in the

not a party to this action.

*The digests that we will discuss are published by West Group. Although other companies also publish digests, West Group has the largest system, the only one that covers all jurisdictions.

Figure 2.1
Headnote Paragraph in the
Reporter and in the Digest
(continued)

(b) Identical Headnote in
Washington Digest

1 Wash D 2d—515

ANIMALS 68

For references to other topics, see Descriptive-Word Index

value of use and occupation thereof. RCW 16.24.070.
    MacKenzie-Richardson, Inc. v. Allert, 272 P.2d 146, 45 Wash.2d 1.

Wash. 1927. To recover for dog bite, it must be shown that dog was wrongfully on sidewalk.
    Shelby v. Seung, 257 P. 838, 144 Wash. 317.

Recovery for injuries for dog bite held improperly allowed without showing dog was wrongfully on street.
    Shelby v. Seung, 257 P. 838, 144 Wash. 317.

Wash. 1906. The owner of a steer who has knowledge of its dangerous character is liable for injuries inflicted by the steer while running at large, irrespective of whether the owner was negligent in securing the steer.
    Harris v. Carstens Packing Co., 86 P. 1125, 43 Wash. 647, 6 L.R.A., N.S., 1164.

54. —— **Persons liable for injuries.**

Wash.App. 1987. Although owner of pit bulls was negligent in allowing them to run loose, humane society, which had been contractually delegated authority to enforce animal regulations of city's ordinance, could be liable for its later negligence, if any, in failing to apprehend the pit bulls.
    Champagne v. Spokane Humane Soc., 737 P.2d 1279, 47 Wash.App. 887, review denied.

Evidence that defendant was running in excess of 300 head of cattle on approximately 12,000 acres of leased pasture, that county road ran through the pasture for four miles, that there was no fence separating pasture from the road, that it was necessary for cattle to cross road to reach watering place, that cattle were frequently observed on the road with no herdsman tending them and that herdsman, who patrolled the entire tract, ordinarily made only one daily check of the road, warranted misdemeanor conviction of owner for permitting his cattle to run at large and not under the care of a herder. West's RCWA 16.13.010.
    State v. Dear, 638 P.2d 85, 96 Wash.2d 652.

58–66. *For other cases see the Decennial Digests and WESTLAW.*

Library references
    C.J.S. Animals.

66. **Personal injuries.**

Library references
    C.J.S. Animals §§ 170, 177.

67. —— **Domestic animals in general.**

Wash. 1980. Negligence cause of action against animal owner arises when there is ineffective control of an animal in a situation where it would reasonably be expected that an injury could occur and injury does proximately result from the negligence; amount of control required is that which would be exercised by a reasonable person based on the total situation at the time, including the past behavior of the

West Group organizes its digests according to the West Key Number System. In this system, the entire body of law has been broken down into general topics. Each topic has been further divided into a number of points of law. A separate number, the key number, is assigned to each point of law.

Animals 54

You must use both parts, the topic and the key number, in order to use the digests.

In the digests, the paragraphs under each key number are arranged by jurisdiction, and under each jurisdiction, they are arranged by date of decision. The cases are listed in reverse chronological order with the most recent at the beginning (Figure 2.2).

The beauty of the Key Number System is that the key number assigned is uniform throughout all West's digests. As a result, when you find a relevant case in the *Georgia Digest,* you can look under the identical key number in other jurisdictions and find relevant cases; however, a particular regional or state digest may not list cases under every topic and key number

Figure 2.2
Cases Arranged by Jurisdiction in
Reverse Chronological Order in
the *Federal Practice Digest*

13 F P D 4th—257   **CIVIL RIGHTS**   ☞112

For references to other topics, see Descriptive-Word Index

C.A.5 (Tex.) 1985. Negligent infliction of emotional distress is a state common-law tort; there is no constitutional right to be free from such distress and, thus, no liability for such distress under 42 U.S.C.A. § 1983.
> Grandstaff v. City of Borger, Tex., 767 F.2d 161, rehearing denied 779 F.2d 1129, certiorari denied 107 S.Ct. 1369, 480 U.S. 916, 94 L.Ed.2d 686, appeal after remand 846 F.2d 1016.

C.A.5 (Tex.) 1985. Section 1983 creates a distinct species of tort liability, not to be absorbed into ordinary common-law principles. 42 U.S.C.A. § 1983.
> Rankin v. City of Wichita Falls, Tex., 762 F.2d 444.

C.A.5 (Tex.) 1984. Civil rights statute neither provides a general remedy for alleged tort of state officials nor opens federal courthouse doors to relieve complaints of all who suffer injury at hands of state or its officers. 42 U.S.C.A. § 1983.
> Villanueva v. McInnis, 723 F.2d 414.

A conspiracy to deprive another of his civil rights is insufficient to prove actual deprivation of a constitutional right under civil rights statute. 42 U.S.C.A. § 1983.
> Villanueva v. McInnis, 723 F.2d 414.

arising out of tort law. U.S.C.A. Const.Amend. 14.
> Gumz v. Morrissette, 772 F.2d 1395, certiorari denied 106 S.Ct. 1644, 475 U.S. 1123, 90 L.Ed.2d 189.

C.A.7 (Wis.) 1985. General principles of tort liability govern the liability imposed under 42 U.S.C.A. § 1983.
> Hibma v. Odegaard, 769 F.2d 1147.

C.A.7 (Wis.) 1984. Conduct which merely engenders common-law tort liability, without infringing on constitutionally protected interests, is not a sufficient basis to support a cause of action under § 1983. 42 U.S.C.A. § 1983.
> Cameo Convalescent Center, Inc. v. Senn, 738 F.2d 836, certiorari denied Percy v. Cameo Convalescent Center, Inc., 105 S.Ct. 780, 469 U.S. 1106, 83 L.Ed.2d 775, certiorari denied 105 S.Ct. 780, 469 U.S. 1106, 83 L.Ed.2d 775, appeal after remand 800 F.2d 108.

D.C.Cal. 1985. A constitutional duty is to be distinguished from a normal tort duty, since not every injury in which a state official has played some part is actionable under § 1983. 42 U.S.C.A. § 1983.
> Escamilla v. City of Santa Ana, 606 F.Supp. 928, affirmed 796 F.2d 266.

because no related cases exist for that jurisdiction. When you see the statement "For other cases see the *Decennial Digest* and Westlaw" in a digest, you should follow this direction.

Figure 2.3 lists the digests published by West Group. As you can see, there are different digests, each designed to fill specific needs. Logically, you would retrieve federal cases (including Supreme Court cases) from one of the various federal digests, and you would use the Supreme Court digest to retrieve only Supreme Court cases. If you want all cases from all jurisdictions, use the American Digest System, which consists of the *Century Digest,* the *Decennial Digest,* and the *General Digest.* This system has enormous scope: it includes all reported American cases, state and federal, from 1658 to the present. To make this digest manageable, West Group has divided it into five- or ten-year periods. West Group updates the *Decennial Digest* with a series of bound volumes known as the *General Digest* (ninth series); a volume is published approximately every month.

If you are researching state law, you should select a state digest since it will provide you with the quickest way to determine case law in one state. A regional digest would be useful when you need cases from neighboring jurisdictions. A good rule of thumb is to always use the smallest possible digest.

Now that you have the correct digest for your jurisdiction, you need to learn how to use it.

West's Digests	
State	All states except Delaware, Nevada, and Utah. For Delaware, use the *Atlantic Digest;* for Nevada and Utah, use the *Pacific Digest.*
Regional	Only four current regional digests: *Atlantic, North Western, Pacific,* and *South Eastern.* Use the state digests for states not covered in the regional digests.
Federal (both lower federal courts and the Supreme Court)	*Federal Digest,* red, all cases prior to 1939 *Modern Federal Practice Digest,* green, 1939–1960 *Federal Practice Digest 2d,* blue, 1961–1975 *Federal Practice Digest 3d,* red, 1976–1988 *Federal Practice Digest 4th,* blue, 1989–present
Supreme Court only	*United States Supreme Court Digest,* 1790–date
American Digest System (all cases, both federal and state)	*Century Digest,* 1658–1896 *First–Tenth Decennial Digests,* 1897–1996 *General Digest 9th,* 1996–present

Figure 2.3
West's Digests

Finding a Case in a Digest

If you are lucky enough to know one relevant case, perhaps obtained from a classmate or a textbook, you should read the case and determine the key numbers that are relevant to your legal issue. Once you have relevant key numbers, you can go directly to the digest volume that indexes additional cases on point. For example, your client is charged with importing cocaine into the United States. He claims that the customs officer unlawfully searched his suitcase while it was in the baggage hold of the aircraft. A colleague suggests that you read the case *United States v. Franchi-Forlando*, 838 F.2d 585 (1st Cir. 1988). From this case, you can determine the appropriate topic and key numbers and head to the digest to retrieve other pertinent cases (Figures 2.4a and b). Legal research skills revolve around the finding of one good case, and you will encounter many methods of doing so.

Figure 2.4
Key Numbers from One Relevant
Case Can Lead to Others

(a) Key Numbers in a Case

---

586   **838 FEDERAL REPORTER, 2d SERIES**

1. Drugs and Narcotics ⇔74, 124

The Government did not have to prove that defendant knew that airplane en route from Colombia to Spain would stop in the United States in order for defendant to be convicted of unlawfully importing cocaine into the United States when airplane made scheduled stop in Puerto Rico and, in any event, evidence was sufficient for jury to find that defendant knew he would land in the United States. Comprehensive Drug Abuse Prevention and Control Act of 1970, § 1002(a), 21 U.S.C.A. § 952(a).

2. Customs Duties ⇔126(7)

Customs officer could lawfully search suitcase of passenger who was in transit from Colombia to Spain, while suitcase was in baggage hold during scheduled stop in Puerto Rico. Tariff Act of 1930, §§ 467, 496, 581(a), 19 U.S.C.A. §§ 1467, 1496, 1581(a).

3. Customs Duties ⇔126(7)

Customs regulation providing that customs officers are not to open baggage but are to detain it until owner opens or refuses to open it did not preclude search of suitcase which was not accompanying passenger through customs but which was in baggage hold of aircraft en route from Colombia to Spain, during scheduled stop in Puerto Rico.

6. Criminal Law ⇔200(1)

Convictions for both unlawfully importing cocaine into the United States and unlawfully possessing cocaine on an aircraft arriving in the United States without proper listing in the aircraft's documents did not violate double jeopardy, in that the applicable statutory provisions each required proof of a fact which the other did not, in that the undocumented importation offense applied to approved as well as unapproved controlled substances. Comprehensive Drug Abuse Prevention and Control Act of 1970, §§ 1002(a), 1005, 21 U.S.C.A. §§ 952(a), 955; U.S.C.A. Const. Amend. 5.

Rafael F. Castro–Lang, San Juan, P.R., by Appointment of the Court, for defendant, appellant.

Jose R. Gaztambide, Asst. U.S. Atty., with whom Daniel F. Lopez–Romo, U.S. Atty., Hato Rey, P.R., was on brief for appellee.

Before CAMPBELL, Chief Judge, TIMBERS,* Senior Circuit Judge, and BREYER, Circuit Judge.

BREYER, Circuit Judge.

The appellant, Orlando Franchi–Forlando, is an Italian citizen, living in Colombia. He was flying on Iberia Airlines from Co-

---

(b) Digest Entries Under a Key Number

---

36 F P D 4th—385   **CUSTOMS DUTIES ⇔126(7)**

For references to other topics, see Descriptive-Word Index

"Reasonable suspicion" standard for justifying an "extended border search" was not applicable to search of package at Pittsburgh airport, where package was searched while still under customs bond and prior to its delivery to addressee, even though package had stopped in New York and Chicago before reaching Pittsburgh.

U.S. v. Caminos, 770 F.2d 361.

C.A.1 (Puerto Rico) 1990. Search conducted by customs officials of baggage of aircraft passengers proceeding from Columbia to Europe was a "border search" irrespective of passengers' in-transit status or their lack of knowledge that stop would be made in the United States.

U.S. v. Garcia, 905 F.2d 557.

C.A.1 (Puerto Rico) 1988. Customs officer could lawfully search suitcase of passenger who was in transit from Colombia to Spain, while suitcase was in baggage hold during scheduled stop in Puerto Rico. Tariff Act of 1930, §§ 467, 496, 581(a), 19 U.S.C.A. §§ 1467, 1496, 1581(a).

U.S. v. Franchi–Forlando, 838 F.2d 585.

Customs regulation providing that customs officers are not to open baggage but are to detain it until owner opens or refuses to open it did not preclude search of suitcase which was not accompanying passenger through customs but which was in baggage hold of aircraft

intent to unlade and also includes planned stops of commercial airplanes whatever their passengers' final destinations. Tariff Act of 1930, § 496, 19 U.S.C.A. § 1496.

U.S. v. McKenzie, 818 F.2d 115.

C.A.6 (Tenn.) 1986. Customs officials have authority to conduct border-type search of aircraft pursuant to Anti-Smuggling Act where they are reasonably certain that aircraft entered from foreign country. Anti-Smuggling Act, § 3(a), 19 U.S.C.A. § 1703(a).

U.S. v. One (1) 1966 Beechcraft Baron, No. N242BS, 788 F.2d 384.

Customs officials had authority to conduct border-type search of abandoned aircraft, even though unidentified aircraft that crossed border while operating without navigation lights, which officials had been tracking on radar, evaded surveillance and disappeared and there was one-hour time lapse between disappearance of monitored aircraft and discovery of abandoned aircraft. Anti-Smuggling Act, § 3(a, c), 19 U.S.C.A. § 1703(a, c).

U.S. v. One (1) 1966 Beechcraft Baron, No. N242BS, 788 F.2d 384.

C.A.5 (Tex.) 1988. Border patrol agents' detention of defendant's suitcase for approximately an hour and a half after seizure of suitcase when agents could have employed more diligent, less intrusive investigatory techniques and when there was an absence of

Descriptive-Word Index

If you do not have one great case by which to find other cases, your gateway into the digest can be the Descriptive-Word Index (DWI). To find the pit bull cases, for example, you would use the *Washington Digest* and begin searching for cases by using the Descriptive-Word Index (Figure 2.5).

The DWI is a long list of everyday words, legal terms, and phrases. In a way, it is an index to the collected headnotes (this may sound odd, but don't worry—it is very useful). Under these DWI terms, you can find relevant topics and key numbers. Before you use the DWI, analyze your fact situation thoroughly in order to generate sufficient words to look up in the DWI. You cannot use the DWI effectively if you do not fully understand your fact situation; you may overlook important terms.

Let's return to our problem involving the pit bull. West Group suggests that before consulting a Descriptive-Word Index, you should analyze your problem and determine very specific words or phrases to be searched by breaking the problem down into the following elements common to every case:

1. The *parties* involved: in our case, the owner of the pit bull, the injured child, and the humane society.
2. The *places* where the facts arose and the *objects* or *things* involved: the facts took place in the city, and a pit bull or a vicious dog was involved.
3. The *acts* or *omissions* that form the *basis of action* or *issue*: the owner of the pit bull was negligent in allowing the dog to run loose, and the humane society was negligent in failing to apprehend the loose pit bull.
4. The *defense* to the action or issue: the humane society claims that it never saw the pit bull running loose.
5. The *relief* sought: the owner and the humane society are liable for personal injuries.

Beginning with the Descriptive-Word Index in the *Washington Digest*, you might look under the term *pit bulls*. You would find that *pit bulls* is not listed; this term is too restrictive and you must think of alternative terms. You should broaden your search term to *animals*. When you look under *Animals*, you will find the subtopic *Injuries—Running at large*. This entry will lead you to *Animals* key numbers 52–55 (Figure 2.6). Next you will pull the digest volume marked *Animals* off the shelf and turn to key numbers 52–55. You will then note that key number 54 is applicable.

Figure 2.5
The Descriptive-Word Index
in the *Washington Digest*

Figure 2.6
Using the Descriptive-Word Index
to Find Key Numbers

37 Wash D 2d—79

ANIMALS

References are to Digest Topics and Key Numbers

ANIMALS—Cont'd
DESTRUCTION of diseased animals. Anim 32
DETINUE, killing or injuring animals. Anim 44
DISEASES. Anim 28–37
   Lessee's liability for destruction of barn used for
      glandered horses. Land & Ten 134
   Vaccination by stockyards company. Wareh 8
DISTRAINING trespassing animals. Anim 95, 100(5)
DRIVING from range of pasture. Anim 14
DRIVING off trespassing animals. Anim 94
DUTIES of owners, stock laws. Anim 50(3)
ELECTIONS, stock law election. Anim 50(2)
ESTRAYS, see this index Estrays
EVIDENCE—
   Actions for—
      Damages caused by trespassing animals. Anim 100(4)
      Personal injuries caused by animals. Anim 74(3–5)
   Condition of animal. Evid 477(5)
   Damages for loss or injury. Damag 174(2)
   Judicial notice of—
      Phenomena of animal life. Evid 13
   Ownership. Anim 3, 10
   Value or market price. Evid 113(22)

ANIMALS—Cont'd
INJURIES by or to animals—Cont'd
   Railroads injuring animals, see this index Railroads
   Running at large. Anim 52–55
      Evidence, similar transactions. Evid 141
   Statutory regulations. Anim 79
   Street railroad injuring animals, see this index Street
      Railroads
   Trespassing animals. Anim 96
INSPECTION—
   Officers. Inspect 4
INSTRUCTIONS to jury—
   Personal injuries. Anim 74(7)
INSURANCE of livestock. Insurance 426
JUDGMENT in actions for injuries caused by tres-
      passing animals. Anim 100(9)
JUDICIAL notice—
   Phenomena of animal life. Evid 13
KEEPING and use, municipal regulations. Mun Corp 604,
      631(3)
KILLING. Anim 43–45
   Animals running at large. Anim 52
   Trespassing animals. Anim 96
   Vicious animals. Anim 73, 84

Topic Method

The digests can also be used in other ways. If you analyze your legal problem in terms of subject areas, such as animals, you could then go directly to the volume of the digest entitled *Animals*. Next you would read through the summary of contents or the analysis that appears at the beginning of the text of each topic until you find the appropriate entry (Figure 2.7). The topic approach is only useful for someone who knows the legal topics involved in the problem, however. As a beginning researcher, if you use the topic method, you probably will not select the proper topic and key numbers because you are not yet well acquainted with all of the subject possibilities.

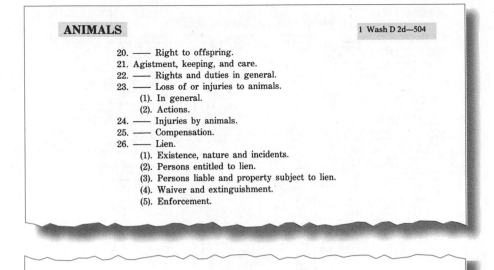

ANIMALS   1 Wash D 2d—504

20. —— Right to offspring.
21. Agistment, keeping, and care.
22. —— Rights and duties in general.
23. —— Loss of or injuries to animals.
    (1). In general.
    (2). Actions.
24. —— Injuries by animals.
25. —— Compensation.
26. —— Lien.
    (1). Existence, nature and incidents.
    (2). Persons entitled to lien.
    (3). Persons liable and property subject to lien.
    (4). Waiver and extinguishment.
    (5). Enforcement.

51. —— Impounding animals at large.
52. —— Killing or injuring animals at large.
53. —— Injuries by animals at large.
54. —— Persons liable for injuries.
55. —— Actions.
56. —— Penalties for violations of regulations.
57. —— Criminal prosecutions.
58. Estrays.

Figure 2.7
Using the Topic Method to
Find Key Numbers

Finding a Case by Its Name

If you know the name of the case you want to read, you have only to look in the Table of Cases in any digest. This table is easy to use and will lead you to the correct reporter and page number (Figure 2.8).

When you know the jurisdiction, use the Table of Cases volumes at the end of the digest for that jurisdiction. Every digest has its own Table of Cases. If you do not know the jurisdiction, but do know the approximate year, use the Table of Cases in the American Digest System, which consists of the *Decennial Digest* and the *General Digest.*

In addition to providing you with the correct citation to the case, the Table of Cases also lists key numbers under which that case has been classified. Note that the entry for *Champagne v. Spokane Humane Society* in the Table of Cases in Figure 2.8 lists Animals key number 54. Therefore, from the entry in the Table of Cases, you can go to the digest and find related cases under the appropriate topic and key number.

If the case was decided during the previous year, you may find the citation through the pocket parts to the Table of Cases in the digests, or you may have to check the Table of Cases Reported in the advance sheets to the reporter in which you expect the case to appear.

Figure 2.8
Finding a Case in the Table of Cases

40 Wash D 2d—87

CHAPMAN

References are to Digest Topics and Key Numbers

Chamberlain v. Cobb, Wash, 225 P 414, 129 Wash 549.—Bills & N 398.
Chamberlain v. Geer, Wash, 237 P 719, 135 Wash 340.—Bills & N 342, 378.
Chamberlain v. Piercy, Wash, 143 P 977, 82 Wash 157.—Bankr 3066(1), 3066(5); Corp 228, 259(7).
Chamberlain v. Winn, Wash, 24 P 446, 1 Wash 259.—Replev 91.
Chamberlain & Co. v. French, Wash, 230 P 837, 131 Wash 394. See Northern Cedar Co v. French.
Chamberlain & Co v. Gloyd 46 SCt 204, 270 US 625, 70 LEd 767. Mem.
Chamberlin v. Chamberlin, Wash, 270 P2d 464, 44 Wash2d 689, 68 ALR2d 457.—Divorce 145, 146, 151, 184(5); Pretrial Proc 713, 722, 724.
Chamberlin v. Winn, Wash, 24 P 446, 1 Wash 259. See Chamberlain v. Winn.
Chamberlin v. Winn, Wash, 20 P 780, 1 Wash 501, aff Chamberlain v. Winn, 24 P 446, 1 Wash 259.—Replev 69(4); Sales 147.
Chambers v. Calvin Philips & Co., Wash, 312 P2d 659, 50 Wash2d 413.—Corp 1.6(3); Trusts 167, 262.
Chambers v. Carlyon, Wash, 62 P2d 726, 188 Wash 352.—Corp 123(24); Plgs 56(4).
Chambers v. City of Mount Vernon, WashApp, 522 P2d 1184, 11 WashApp 357.—Health & E 25.15(10); Mun Corp 722; Nuis 85.
Chamness v. Marquis, Wash, 383 P2d 886, 62 Wash2d 509.—App & E 717, 1071.1(1); Brok 56(3), 84(1), 85(2), 86(4).
Chamness Realty v. Marquis 62 Wash2d 509, 383 P2d 886. See Chamness v. Marquis.
Champa v. Washington Compressed Gas Co., Wash, 262 P 228, 146 Wash 190.—Damag 62(1); Nuis 3(6), 4, 50(5), 54.
Champagne v. Birnot, Wash, 254 P 829, 143 Wash 187.—App & E 415; Chat Mtg 138(2).
Champagne v. Department of Labor and Industries, Wash, 156 P2d 422, 22 Wash2d 412.—Trial 182, 260(1); Work Comp 1853, 1911, 1929.
Champagne v. Hygrade Food Products, Inc., DCWash, 79 FRD 671.—Fed Civ Proc 1372.
Champagne v. McDonald, Wash, 251 P 874, 141 Wash 617.—Accord 8(1).
Champagne v. Spokane Humane Soc., WashApp, 737 P2d 1279, 47 WashApp 887, review den.—Anim 54; Judgm 181(33); Mun Corp 723, 751(1); Neglig 61(1).
Champ Arcade v. City of Seattle 86 Wash2d 395, 544 P2d 1242. See Bitts, Inc v. City of Seattle.
Champion v. Shoreline School Dist. No. 412 of King County, Wash, 504 P2d 304, 81 Wash2d 672.—Schools 63(1), 130, 147.34(1); Statut 181(1), 208, 223.-2(1).
Contracts 176(1); Damag 76, 78(1); Evid 80(1); Frds St of 130(1), 130(2); Impl & C C 81; Motions 51; Plead 34(1), 53(2), 214(2), 214(4), 354.
Chandler v. Gallemore, Wash, 43 P2d 968, 181 Wash 345.—Corp 80(12), 261, 263(2).
Chandler v. Humphrey, Wash, 31 P2d 1012, 177 Wash 402.—Corp 217; Lim of Act 2(1).
Chandler v. Miller, Wash, 19 P2d 1108, 172 Wash 252.—Corp 80(12), 247, 262(1), 262(2), 269(2); Plead 147.
Chandler v. Miller, Wash, 13 P2d 22, 168 Wash 563.—Corp 262(1), 563(2); Judgm 822(3).
Chandler v. Otto, Wash, 693 P2d 71, 103 Wash2d 268.—Mun Corp 159(5); Offic 70½.
Chandler v. Washington Toll Bridge Authority, Wash, 137 P2d 97, 17 Wash2d 591.—Bridges 5, 20(1), 20(2), 20(4), 20(5), 20(6); Contracts 4, 5, 187(1); Impl & C C 1, 2, 3, 4.
Chaney v. Chaney, Wash, 105 P 229, 56 Wash 145.—App & E 655(1), 1074(3); Divorce 161, 167.
Chantler v. Hubbell, Wash, 75 P 802, 34 Wash 211.—Fraud Conv 176(2); Trusts 96.
Chantry, In re, Wash, 524 P2d 909, 84 Wash2d 153.—Atty & C 61.
Chantry, In re, Wash, 407 P2d 160, 67 Wash2d 190.—Atty & C 32(2), 58.
Chaoussis' Estate, In re, Wash, 247 P 732, 139 Wash 479.—Ex & Ad 24.

What if you know only the defendant's name in a case? Check the Defendant-Plaintiff Table in the state and federal digests (Figure 2.9). The regional digests do not contain Defendant-Plaintiff Tables.

Searching for Cases Using Westlaw

Now that you understand how to find a case through the digests, let's look at how to find cases using Westlaw. There are two basic elements to successful online research: constructing a proper search request and choosing the right database. Mastering these elements may appear challenging at first. After all, Westlaw contains thousands of databases and allows you to formulate search requests several different ways. With a little practice, however, you will be surprised at how quickly Westlaw can help you locate the information you need.

In the rest of this chapter, we will explain how to compose effective search requests; how to access the right database; and how, after you've retrieved cases, to browse the cases online.

Composing Westlaw Search Requests

As with the West digests, Westlaw offers several different ways to find case law. The type and amount of information you have to begin with will help determine which way will work best for you. If you are looking for a specific case, you can formulate a Westlaw search request using the case reporter citation or the names of the parties. If you are looking for cases relevant to a particular issue, you can formulate your request using the words that describe the issue or using a topic and key number. This section will show you how to use any of these pieces of information to formulate an effective search request on Westlaw.

SPOKANE   41 Wash D 2d—404

References are to Digest Topics and Key Numbers

AND FOR—State, Wash, 177 P 654, 105 Wash 49.
SPOKANE COUNTY, SUPERIOR COURT OF WASHINGTON IN AND FOR—State, Wash, 174 P 646, 103 Wash 402.
SPOKANE COUNTY, SUPERIOR COURT OF WASHINGTON IN AND FOR—State, Wash, 147 P 436, 85 Wash 72.
SPOKANE COUNTY, SUPREME COURT OF—State, Wash, 34 P 930, 7 Wash 234.
SPOKANE COUNTY, TAXPAYERS OF—Spokane County, 85 Wash2d 216, 533 P2d 128.
SPOKANE COUNTY, TAXPAYERS OF—Spokane County, 84 Wash2d 475, 527 P2d 263.
SPOKANE COUNTY, TAXPAYERS OF, AND WITHIN, SCHOOL DIST. NO. 81 OF—School Dist. No. 81 of Spokane County, Wash, 225 P2d 1063, 37 Wash2d 669.
SPOKANE COUNTY, WASH.—Dodd, CAWash, 393 F2d 330.
SPOKANE CULVERT & FABRICATING CO.—Novenson, Wash, 588 P2d 1174, 91 Wash2d 550.
SPOKANE CYCLE & AUTO SUPPLY CO.—Maskell, Wash, 170 P 350, 100 Wash 16.
SPOKANE DAIRY PRODUCTS CO.—Royal Dairy Products Co., Wash, 225 P 412, 129 Wash 424.
SPOKANE DRUG CO.—Adams, CCWash, 57 F 888.
SPOKANE DRY GOODS CO.—Spokane Merchants' Ass'n, Wash, 299 P 371, 162 Wash 577.
SPOKANE DRY GOODS CO.—U.S., DCWash, 264 F 209.
SPOKANE, EACH AND EVERY LOT IN CITY OF—Spokane County, Wash, 13 P2d 1084, 169 Wash 355.
SPOKANE FALLS & N. RY.—Williams, Wash, 87 P 491, 44 Wash 363.
SPOKANE FALLS & N. RY. CO.—Fleutsch, Wash, 6 Wash 623, 34 P 150.
SPOKANE FALLS & N. RY. CO.—Flutsch, Wash, 6 Wash 623, 34 P 150.
SPOKANE FALLS & N. RY. CO.—Allend, Wash, 58 P 244, 21 Wash 324.
SPOKANE FALLS & N. RY. CO.—Dun-

SPOKANE FALLS & NORTHERN RY. CO.—Taylor, Wash, 73 P 499, 32 Wash 450.
SPOKANE FALLS & N. RY. CO.—Williams, Wash, 84 P 1129, 42 Wash 597.
SPOKANE FALLS & N. RY. CO.—Williams, Wash, 80 P 1100, 39 Wash 77.
SPOKANE FALLS, CITY OF—Curry, Wash, 27 P 477, 2 Wash 541.
SPOKANE FALLS, CITY OF—Spokane St. Ry. Co., CCWash, 46 F 322.
SPOKANE FALLS, CITY OF—Spokane Street Railway Co., Wash, 33 P 1072, 6 Wash 521.
SPOKANE FALLS, CITY OF—State, Wash, 25 P 903, 2 Wash 40.
SPOKANE FALLS, CITY OF—Town of Denver, Wash, 34 P 926, 7 Wash 226.
SPOKANE FALLS GASLIGHT CO.—Theis, Wash, 95 P 1074, 49 Wash 477.
SPOKANE FALLS GASLIGHT CO.—Theis, Wash, 74 P 1004, 34 Wash 23.
SPOKANE FUEL DEALERS CREDIT ASS'N—U.S., DCWash, 55 FSupp 387.
SPOKANE GAS & FUEL CO.—City of Spokane, Wash, 47 P2d 671, 182 Wash 475.
SPOKANE GAS & FUEL CO.—City of Spokane, Wash, 26 P2d 1034, 175 Wash 103.
SPOKANE GAS & FUEL CO.—Cole, Wash, 119 P 831, 66 Wash 393.
SPOKANE GAS & FUEL CO.—Jobe, Wash, 131 P 235, 73 Wash 1, 48 LRANS 931.
SPOKANE GRAIN CO.—Frederick & Nelson, Wash, 91 P 570, 47 Wash 85.
SPOKANE HARDWARE CO.—Conlan, Wash, 201 P 26, 117 Wash 378.
SPOKANE, HOME TEL. & TEL. CO. OF—Cavers, Wash, 201 P 20, 117 Wash 299.
SPOKANE, HOME TEL. & TEL. CO. OF—State, Wash, 172 P 899, 102 Wash 196.
SPOKANE HUMANE SOC.—Champagne, WashApp, 737 P2d 1279, 47 WashApp 887.
SPOKANE HYDRAULIC CO.—Cunningham, Wash, 52 P 235, 18 Wash 524.

SPOKANE INTERN. RY. CO.—Neitzel, Wash, 141 P 186, 80 Wash 30.
SPOKANE INTERN. RY. CO.—Neitzel, Wash, 117 P 864, 65 Wash 100, 36 LRA,NS, 522.
SPOKANE INTERN. RY. CO.—Pierce, Wash, 131 P2d 139, 15 Wash2d 431.
SPOKANE-INTERNATIONAL RY. CO.—Schaefer, Wash, 188 P 530, 110 Wash 316.
SPOKANE INTERN. RY. CO.—Walters, Wash, 108 P 593, 58 Wash 293, 42 LRA,NS, 917.
SPOKANE INTERN. R. CO.—McEwen, CAWash, 325 F2d 491.
SPOKANE INTERSTATE FAIR—Polk, Wash, 132 P 401, 73 Wash 610.
SPOKANE INTERSTATE FAIR ASS'N—Fidelity & Deposit Co. of Md., CCAWash, 8 F2d 224, 44 ALR 468.
SPOKANE JOBBERS' ASS'N—Hoffman, Wash, 102 P 1045, 54 Wash 179.
SPOKANE KNITTING MILLS—Jantzen Knitting Mills, DCWash, 44 F2d 656.
SPOKANE, LOCAL NO. 400 OF COOKS AND HELPERS, WAITERS AND WAITRESSES OF—Adams, Wash, 215 P 19, 124 Wash 564.
SPOKANE LODGE NO. 228, BENEV. AND PROTECTIVE ORDER OF ELKS—Local Joint Executive Bd. of Spokane, CAWash, 443 F2d 403.
SPOKANE MERCANTILE CO.—Burnham, Wash, 51 P 363, 18 Wash 207.
SPOKANE MERCHANTS' ASS'N—Fidelity & Deposit Co. of Maryland, Wash, 157 P 464, 91 Wash 170.
SPOKANE MERCHANTS' ASS'N—Kasper, Wash, 151 P 800, 87 Wash 447.
SPOKANE MERCHANT'S ASS'N—Kriegler, Wash, 189 P 1004, 111 Wash 179.
SPOKANE MILL CO.—U. S., DCWash, 206 F 999.
SPOKANE MORTG. CO.—Ellingson, WashApp, 573 P2d 389, 19 WashApp 48.
SPOKANE NAT. BANK—Grant, CCWash, 47 F 673.
SPOKANE NAT. BANK—Weber, CCA-Wash, 64 F 208, 12 CCA 93.
SPOKANE NAT. BANK—Weber, CCA-Wash, 50 F 735.

Figure 2.9
A Defendant-Plaintiff Table

Finding a Case on Westlaw by Its Citation

When you know the citation of a case, either a case reporter citation or a Westlaw citation, you can retrieve it on Westlaw using Find. Simply click the **Find** button on the main button palette and type the case citation in the *Citation* text box. For example, to retrieve *Champagne v. Spokane Humane Society,* 47 Wash.App. 887, 737 P.2d 1279 (1987), type either **47 wash app 887** or **737 p2d 1279.**

You can use Find from virtually anywhere on Westlaw, including the Westlaw Directory. There is no need to access a database. If you are not sure about the correct citation format, you can access a fill-in-the-blank template by clicking the **Find** button and then typing the publication abbreviation in the *Citation* text box. For example, to display the Find template for *Pacific Reporter 2d*, type **p2d**. For a complete list of publication abbreviations and formats that you can use with Find, click the **Pubs List** button at the Welcome to Find window.

You also can retrieve a case by citation by clicking the **Find By** button at the Terms and Connectors Query Editor or Natural Language Description Editor and choosing **Cite** from the drop-down list. Type the citation or the volume and page numbers in the appropriate blanks (Figure 2.10).

Figure 2.10
Find By Citation Template

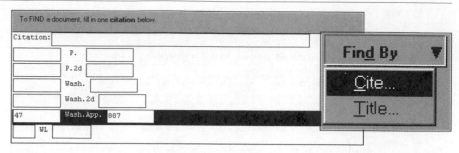

Finding a Case on Westlaw by Its Title

If you know the name of at least one of the parties to a case, you can easily retrieve the case on Westlaw. First, access the database for the jurisdiction in which the case was decided. For example, to retrieve the Washington case *Champagne v. Spokane Humane Society,* access the Washington Cases database (WA-CS). Then search for significant terms from the title in the title field (ti). At the Terms and Connectors Query Editor, type

ti(champagne & spokane)

You also can retrieve a case by title by clicking the **Find By** button at the Terms and Connectors Query Editor or Natural Language Description Editor and choosing **Title** from the drop-down list. A Find by Title dialog box is displayed in which you can enter the name(s) of one or more parties (Figure 2.11).

Figure 2.11
Find By Title Dialog Box

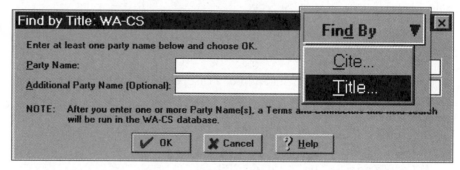

Searching for Cases on Westlaw by Subject

Often when you use Westlaw, you will not be looking for a specific case, but instead any case that supports your point of view on a particular legal issue. Westlaw offers two different search methods for retrieving cases by subject. One is called WIN (Westlaw is Natural); the other is called Terms and Connectors.

WIN, also called the Natural Language search method, allows you to describe your issue in plain English. Terms and Connectors requires you to formulate your search request using key terms from your issue and connectors to specify the relationship between these terms. Westlaw offers both search methods because each has its own unique advantages. Also, some databases (e.g., Dialog databases) can only be searched using Terms and Connectors. Though you may prefer WIN because it is easy to use, our advice is to become familiar with both search methods.

WIN—The Natural Language Search Method

If the idea of accessing a database and typing your issue in plain English sounds easy to you—it is! To use WIN, you simply access a database, click the **Search Type** button and choose **Natural Language** from the drop-down list. The Natural Language Description Editor is displayed (Figure 2.12). Type a description of your issue in plain English. For example, to find cases discussing whether a humane society that failed to enforce a city leash law is responsible for an injury to a child caused by a pit bull, type

is the humane society liable for not enforcing a city leash law

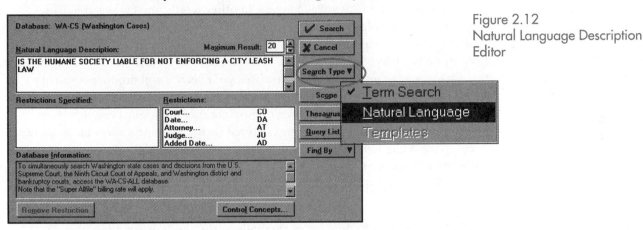

Figure 2.12
Natural Language Description Editor

Westlaw processes your description and displays the twenty cases that most closely match the concepts in your description (Figure 2.13).

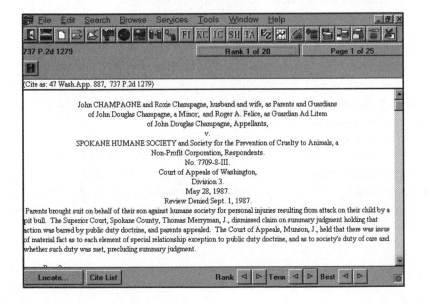

Figure 2.13
Case Retrieved Using Natural Language

When you run a search using WIN, the first case Westlaw displays is the one with the greatest likelihood of matching your description. Cases ranked further down the list are statistically less likely to match your description, so you may or may not find them to be relevant.

If you've looked through the twenty cases and want to see more, choose **Next 10 Documents** from the Browse menu to display the next ten cases.

If you want Westlaw to display the most recent cases first instead of displaying them in the order of statistical relevance, choose **Sort** from the Browse menu. Then select **Age** from the Sort dialog box and click **OK**.

By now you can see why WIN has created so much excitement among legal researchers. With the right description, you can retrieve relevant cases more easily than has ever been possible.

A word of caution, however: a few generations still stand between WIN and the computer on the *Starship Enterprise*. In other words, the famous adage of computer processing—garbage in, garbage out—still applies. So choose your search concepts carefully, modeling them on the language a court would use to describe the issue.

One way to improve the chances that your search will produce relevant results is to add related concepts to your description. With WIN, you simply type the related concept in parentheses to the right of your original concept. For example, in the description we just entered (is the humane society liable for not enforcing a city leash law) you can add *town* and *municipal* as alternatives to *city* by inserting those terms in this manner:

**is the humane society liable for not enforcing a
city (town municipal) leash law**

If you need help thinking of alternatives, use the Westlaw thesaurus. To access the thesaurus, type your description at the Natural Language Description Editor and click the **Thesaurus** button. Any related concepts you add using the thesaurus will be automatically inserted into your description.

When you add related concepts to your description, you are broadening your search. In some situations, however, restricting your search may also be necessary. For instance, you may want to retrieve cases within a certain date range or cases decided by a particular judge.

To restrict your WIN search, double-click a restriction in the *Restrictions* list box at the Natural Language Description Editor. A dialog box is displayed in which you can enter the appropriate date(s) or term(s).

You can further refine your search result by using Control Concepts. The Control Concepts feature allows you to specify which concepts must be included in or excluded from your Natural Language results. To access the Control Concepts dialog box, click the **Control Concepts** button at the Natural Language Description Editor. Then follow the on-screen directions.

The Terms and Connectors Search Method

The second search method available on Westlaw is called *Terms and Connectors*. Learning to use the Terms and Connectors search method requires slightly more effort than learning to use WIN, but it is not difficult.

In fact, the theory is quite simple. We begin with the assumption that a court opinion addressing a given issue or fact situation will contain key terms near each other. The Terms and Connectors search method is simply a way to specify the proximity of those terms in your search request.

For example, consider our hypothetical in which a pit bull bit a child. If this fact situation were ever addressed in a published court opinion, it is likely the term *pit bull* would appear near the term *child* in the opinion, perhaps in the same paragraph or sentence.

To retrieve cases in which *pit bull* appears in the same paragraph as *child*, you would type **"pit bull" /p child**. To retrieve cases in which *pit bull* appears in the same sentence as *child*, type **"pit bull" /s child**. The **/p** and **/s** are called *connectors* (now you see where the name Terms and Connectors comes from). Connectors specify proximity. Figure 2.14 lists the most common Westlaw connectors.

One important thing to remember when you are using the Terms and Connectors search method is that leaving a space between terms means *or*. In the example above, for instance, if you typed **pit bull** without quotation marks, Westlaw would interpret that to mean *pit* or *bull*. By using quotation marks around *pit bull*, however, Westlaw searches for it as a two-word phrase.

Though the Terms and Connectors search method is easy to grasp, it usually takes some practice to become familiar with the connectors and know which ones work best in a particular situation. Learning Terms and Connectors is well worth the effort, however, because it allows you to control exactly how Westlaw searches for information. The next section offers a good example of the control you gain using Terms and Connectors.

Connector	Function
/s	within same sentence
/p	within same paragraph
/n	within "n" number of terms, where "n" is a number
&	within same document
[leave space]	either term or both terms
[quotation marks around terms]	terms appear in same order as in quotation marks

Figure 2.14
Common Westlaw Connectors

Searching for Cases on Westlaw Using Fields

Almost all Westlaw documents are composed of several parts called fields. For example, the title, synopsis, headnotes, and names of the judge and attorneys in a case are each considered a separate field. You can narrow your search to look for terms in a specific field instead of in an entire case. To find out which fields are available for a specific database, scroll through the *Fields/Restrictions* list box at the Terms and Connectors Query Editor (Figure 2.15).

Figure 2.15
Fields in a Case Law Database

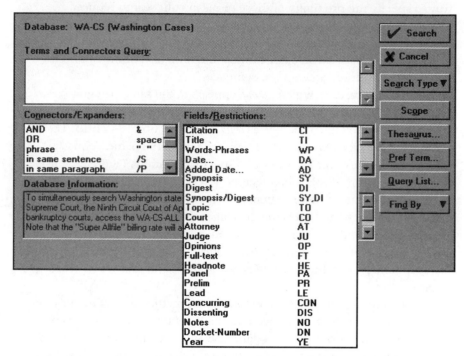

The format for typing a field-restricted search is the same for all fields: the field restriction (e.g., ti, sy, to) is followed immediately by the terms enclosed in parentheses. Instead of searching the entire case for those terms, Westlaw will only search the specified field. We will illustrate a few of the case law field restrictions:

▶ *Synopsis field:* West's editors write a synopsis for each case published in the West reporters. This information appears in the synopsis field (sy) on Westlaw. Generally, a synopsis includes a review of the facts presented in the case, the name and holding of the lower court judge, the holding of the court in the case, and the names of the dissenting and concurring judges. Since the synopsis summarizes the procedural issues of a case, use the synopsis field restriction when a procedural issue is important. For example, to retrieve Washington cases in which a particular trial court judge has been reversed, access the WA-CS database and type a query such as

sy(merryman & reversed)

Slip opinions, unreported cases, and cases not published by West Group generally do not have synopses. Synopses are added to West-reported cases on Westlaw within a few days to a few weeks. Therefore, if you wish to retrieve very recent opinions, do not use the synopsis field restriction—simply search in the database without using any field restrictions.

▶ *Topic field:* Headnotes for cases published by West Group are classified by its editors under as many digest topics as apply. When searching on Westlaw, you can retrieve all cases containing a headnote classified under a specific digest topic by restricting your search to the topic field (to). All digest topics on Westlaw are numbered. A list of the digest topics and their numerical equivalents is located in Appendix A of *Discovering Westlaw* and in the Key Number Service on Westlaw. You can use the topic number in a topic field restriction to retrieve all cases with a headnote on your topic. For instance, typing **to(28)** would retrieve all cases with a headnote addressing issues involving animals.

The topic field includes not only the West digest topic number, but also the topic name, the digest classification hierarchy, the key number, and the text of the key line for each key number (Figure 2.16). Consequently, topic field searches are effective when you are not certain which specific key number is relevant. You can still search language describing your specific legal issue to which a key number has been assigned. Within the topic field, combine a topic name or number with words describing your issue. For example, access the WA-CS database and type

to(28 /p injur! /p liab!)

You will retrieve Washington cases with headnotes classified under West digest topic number 28, the number for Animals, in which the topic field paragraph also contains forms of the terms *injure* and *liable*.

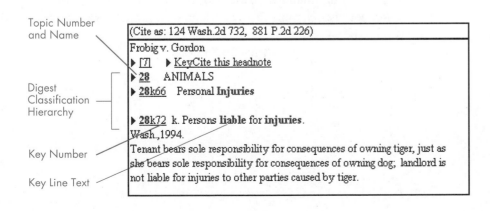

Figure 2.16
Elements Included in the Topic Field

▶ *Digest field:* You may also want to restrict your search to the most important of fields, the digest field. The digest field contains all of the information provided in the topic field plus the text of the headnotes. The digest field may contain several digest paragraphs, each of which appears on a separate Westlaw page. For searching purposes, each Westlaw page within the digest field is considered a paragraph.

A digest search is particularly useful when your search contains common words, such as *contracts*. By limiting your search to the digest field, you will avoid retrieving cases based on irrelevant occurrences of your search terms in the opinion.

Searching in the digest field also avoids the problems of judges who use idiosyncratic words or phrases. Since you use the computer to search for particular words, an unusual word usage by a judge can throw off your result. The editors at West Group use a standard vocabulary in the digest field to address this problem. For instance, if the judge refers to the *plaintiff* or *defendant* throughout a landlord-tenant opinion, West editors will use the words *landlord* or *tenant* in the headnotes.

Searching in the digest field at the same time that you search the synopsis field can be very effective because these two fields contain summaries of the useful issues in a case. For example, if you are searching for cases involving the legal theory of assumption of risk in regard to an injury from an animal, you should search in the digest field and the synopsis field by typing

sy,di(assum! /p risk /p animal)

▶ *Judge field:* On Westlaw, you can search for cases authored by a particular judge by using the judge field (ju). The only catch is that the judge must have written the majority opinion. A judge field search does not retrieve an opinion in which a judge dissented or concurred. To retrieve these opinions, search for the judge's name in the dissenting (dis) or concurring (con) field.

▶ *Attorney field:* If you are looking for cases that involve a particular attorney, you should search the attorney field (at). For example, to search for district court cases in which Griffin Bell represented a party, type

at(griffin /3 bell)

Searching for Cases on Westlaw by West Topic and Key Numbers

In the first part of this chapter, we explained how to use key numbers from the digests and other print resources to quickly pinpoint cases dealing with specific legal issues. Key numbers are also a powerful research tool on Westlaw. Once you find a topic and key number related to the legal issue or concept you are researching, you simply run a search on Westlaw using that topic and key number to retrieve cases dealing with the same legal issue or concept.

Headnote 9

Topic 28, Animals

Headnote Hierarchy

Key Number 54 Persons liable for injuries

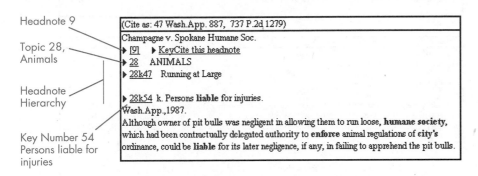

(Cite as: 47 Wash.App. 887, 737 P.2d 1279)
Champagne v. Spokane Humane Soc.
▶ [9]   ▶ KeyCite this headnote
▶ 28   ANIMALS
▶ 28k47   Running at Large

▶ 28k54   k. Persons **liable** for injuries.
Wash.App.,1987.
Although owner of pit bulls was negligent in allowing them to run loose, **humane society**, which had been contractually delegated authority to **enforce** animal regulations of city's ordinance, could be **liable** for its later negligence, if any, in failing to apprehend the pit bulls.

Figure 2.17
Headnote Hierarchy on Westlaw

For example, suppose you want to find New York cases discussing the same issue as in our Washington case, *Champagne v. Spokane Humane Society*, especially the matter summarized in headnote 9 (Figure 2.17). When you view that headnote on Westlaw, you can see the complete hierarchy of concepts used to classify the point of law to a specific key number. In this instance, headnote 9 has been classified under topic 28, Animals, and key number 54, Persons liable for injuries. Notice also that on Westlaw, the letter *k* replaces the familiar key symbol. To use this topic and key number to locate New York cases, access the New York Cases database (NY-CS) and type **28k54** (Figure 2.18).

In West reporters and West-reported cases on Westlaw, each case headnote is numbered; these numbered headnotes act as a guide to the discussion of the point of law in the text of the opinion. On Westlaw, to move directly from a headnote to related text in the opinion, click its headnote number.

You can also jump to the Key Number Service from a headnote. The Key Number Service is a convenient feature that helps you locate key numbers to add to your search. The service contains the entire West Digest System topic and key number outline, so you can view key numbers in their hierarchical context. Using this service, you can identify key numbers pertaining to your issue, or you can obtain related key numbers, which you can use to expand or narrow your search.

Figure 2.18
Result of a Topic and
Key Number Search

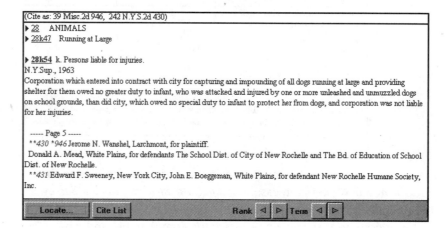

To jump from a headnote to the Key Number Service, click the Jump marker preceding the level of the headnote hierarchy you desire. The Key Search dialog box is displayed (Figure 2.19). Select **Explore the Key Number System**... and click **OK**. You will go directly to the point in the Key Number Service where the selected level is displayed (Figure 2.20).

Choosing a Westlaw Database

When we began our introduction to Westlaw research, we told you there were two basic elements to successful online research: constructing a proper search request and choosing the right database. Though we will spend less time discussing database selection than search requests, don't assume this second step is less important. Choosing the best database requires careful thought.

Keep in mind that a particular case may be available in several different databases. *Champagne v. Spokane Humane Society,* for example, is available in the following databases: Ninth Circuit Federal and State Cases (CTA9-ALL), Washington Cases (WA-CS), Washington State and Federal Cases (WA-CS-ALL), Washington Tort Law Cases (WATRT-CS), State Case Law (ALLSTATES), and Federal & State Case Law (ALLCASES).

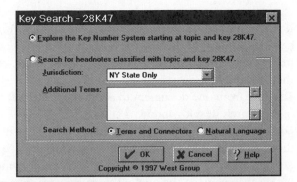

Figure 2.19
Key Search Dialog Box

Figure 2.20
Key Number Service

Generally, your search will take less time in a smaller database, so choose the smallest database for your needs. For instance, there is no reason to wait for Westlaw to sort through cases from all fifty states when you only need cases from one state.

Finally, it is never too early to become aware of database costs. As a law student you will pay little or nothing to use Westlaw, but keep in mind that practicing attorneys who subscribe to Westlaw are billed by the hour or by transaction. Knowing which databases can give you the answers you need for the least amount of money will be a valuable asset when you begin practice.

Browsing Cases on Westlaw

Once you retrieve cases on Westlaw, you must determine whether they are relevant to your issue. You can browse online in various ways.

▶ A quick way to determine whether the documents you retrieve are relevant is to scan the pages containing your highlighted search terms. Use the **Term** arrows to display these pages. The first page of each case is always displayed, whether or not it contains your search terms.

▶ You may choose to browse by page by using the scroll bar or by clicking your right mouse button and choosing **Next Page**.

▶ If you have used the WIN search method, you may browse your documents in best mode, stopping only at the portion of each case that most closely matches your description. To browse in best mode, click the **Best** arrows at the bottom of the Search Result window.

▶ To move from one document to another, click the **Rank** arrows at the bottom of the Search Result window.

▶ Locate allows you to browse your result for a particular term, whether or not the term appeared in your original search request. To use Locate, click the **Locate** button at the bottom of the Search Result window.

▶ Rather than viewing the text of the documents, you may want to print a list of the document citations. To do this, click the **Cite List** button at the bottom of the Search Result window. Since your library will likely contain the reporters and other legal materials that you retrieve on Westlaw, you may want to sign off the computer and turn to the books. It can be very expensive to read the full text of the materials online.

▶ You should be aware of a feature known as Star Paging. You may need to cite the exact page of the official *United States Reports,* even though you are using the unofficial *Supreme Court Reporter.* Star Paging is a device used to indicate the precise word or letter with which the next page begins. In the printed *Supreme Court Reporter,* the number of the page in the official *United States Reports* is in the margin, and an upside down "T" symbol appears in the text at the point where the page break occurs in the official reporter (Figure 2.21). Star Paging is also available on Westlaw where it allows you to view page numbers of cases as they appear in the bound volumes or the advance sheets of the National Reporter System and the *United States Reports* or official reports from many states. Page numbers will appear highlighted within the text exactly where page breaks occur in the printed volumes (Figure 2.22).

Figure 2.21
Star Paging in the
Supreme Court Reporter

1022   **105 SUPREME COURT REPORTER**   469 U.S. 559

eral labor regulation as applied to state railroad employees, 426 U.S., at 854, n. 18 [96 S.Ct., at 2475, n. 18], *National League of Cities* acknowledged that not all aspects of a State's sovereign authority are immune from federal control." 456 U.S., at 764, n. 28, 102 S.Ct., at 2153, n. 28.

tution itself. A unique feature of the United States is the *federal* system of government guaranteed by the Constitution and implicit in the very name of our country. Despite some genuflecting in the Court's opinion to the concept of federalism, today's decision effectively reduces the Tenth Amendment to meaningless rhetoric when

these cases.[3]

Whatever effect the Court's decision may have in weakening the application of *stare decisis*, it is likely to be less |560 important than what the Court has done to the Consti-

2. Justice O'CONNOR, the only new member of the Court since our decision in *National League of Cities*, has joined the Court in reaffirming its principles. See *Transportation Union v. Long Island R. Co.*, 455 U.S. 678, 102 S.Ct. 1349, 71 L.Ed.2d 547 (1982), and *FERC v. Mississippi*, 456

the Court that *it* —an unelected majority of five Justices—today rejects almost 200 years of the understanding of the constitutional status of federalism. In doing so, there is only a single passing reference to

U.S. 742, 775, 102 S.Ct. 2126, 2145, 72 L.Ed.2d 532 (1982) (O'CONNOR, J., dissenting in part).

3. As one commentator noted, *stare decisis* represents "a natural evolution from the very nature of our institutions." Lile, Some Views on the Rule of *Stare Decisis*, 4 Va.L.Rev. 95, 97 (1916).

Figure 2.22
Star Paging on Westlaw

(Cite as: 469 U.S. 528, *559, 105 S.Ct. 1005, **1022)
DISSENTING OPINION

also ▶ Oregon v. Kennedy, 456 U.S. 667, 691-692, n. 34, 102 S.Ct. 2083, 2097-2098, n. 34, 72 L.Ed.2d 416 (1982) (STEVENS, J., concurring in judgment). In the present cases, the five Justices who compose the majority today participated in National League of Cities and the cases reaffirming it. [FN2] The stability of judicial decision, and with it respect for the
----- Page 56 -----
authority of this Court, are not served by the precipitate overruling of multiple precedents that we witness in these cases. [FN3]

FN2. Justice O'CONNOR, the only new member of the Court since our decision in National League of Cities, has joined the Court in reaffirming its principles. See ▶ Transportation Union v. Long Island R. Co., 455 U.S. 678, 102 S.Ct. 1349, 71 L.Ed.2d 547 (1982), and ▶ FERC v. Mississippi, 456 U.S. 742, 775, 102 S.Ct. 2126, 2145, 72 L.Ed.2d 532 (1982) (O'CONNOR, J., dissenting in part).

FN3. As one commentator noted, stare decisis represents "a natural evolution from the very nature of our institutions." Lile, Some Views on the Rule of Stare Decisis, 4 Va.L.Rev. 95, 97 (1916).

Whatever effect the Court's decision may have in weakening the application of stare decisis, it is likely to be less *560 important than what the Court has done to the Constitution itself. A unique feature of the United States is the federal system

Conclusion

You have just learned how to find cases using digests and Westlaw. We discussed how digests are put together and how to use them. We also introduced West topics and key numbers. The same topics and key numbers that appear in cases are the subject access points in the digests. We noted that West Group has individual sets of digests for almost all states in addition to several regional and federal digests and the mammoth *Decennial Digest* and *General Digest.*

You also learned how to search on Westlaw by entering a case law citation using the Find service, entering a description of your issue with WIN Natural Language, or restricting your Terms and Connectors search to particular case law fields. You learned how to conduct a topic and key number search on Westlaw, using the advantages of the West digest indexing system online. Westlaw gives you enormous flexibility in getting the best results.

Updating Case Law Research

Finding the law is only half of the legal research battle. Updating it with citator services is the second, and equally important, half.

Because of the constant possibility of change in the law, systems have been created to help you determine the current status of any legal authority. These systems are known as *citator services*. The two citator services that will be discussed in this chapter are KeyCite and Shepard's Citations.

KeyCite

What Is KeyCite?

KeyCite is a citation research service developed by West Group and made available exclusively through Westlaw. KeyCite integrates all the case law on Westlaw, allowing you to

- trace the history of a case;
- retrieve a list of cases on Westlaw that cite a case; and
- track legal issues in a case.

Citing references from secondary sources on Westlaw, such as ALR annotations and law review articles, are covered by KeyCite as well. You can use these citing references to find case discussions by legal experts. In addition, KeyCite is completely integrated with the West Key Number System so that it provides the tools for navigating the case law databases on Westlaw.

KeyCite is as current as Westlaw itself. Direct history, which traces the same case through the appellate process, is added to KeyCite within one to four hours of receipt of an opinion at West Group. Citing cases are added to KeyCite as soon as they are added to Westlaw. KeyCite is also as comprehensive as Westlaw; it provides history for federal cases from 1754 to the present and history for state cases from 1879 to the present. All citing cases on Westlaw—including unpublished opinions—are included in KeyCite.

Why Use KeyCite?

The first reason to use KeyCite is to determine whether an authority—a U.S. Supreme Court decision, for example—on which you have been relying is still valid. Though the law is conservative, it does change at times; some of what was once *good law* is now *bad law*. Thousands of cases in the two-hundred-year history of American jurisprudence have been reversed or overruled by subsequent adjudications. These bad cases are still found in law books, and they are still in the online services.

You can find, for instance, the 1942 Supreme Court case of *Betts v. Brady* in any of the reporters for U.S. Supreme Court cases. The *Betts* case holds that the Sixth Amendment does not apply to the states and that there is no absolute right to counsel in a state criminal trial. Nothing in those reporters says, "This case has been overruled and is no longer good law." If you found *Betts* in the reporters and stopped researching at this point, you would be convinced that a state has no obligation to provide an attorney for an indigent defendant in a criminal trial. If you check *Betts v. Brady* on KeyCite, however, you will find that the case was overruled in 1963 by the Supreme Court in *Gideon v. Wainwright* (Figure 3.1).

Nothing is more damaging to your client's interests or your own professional reputation than to rest your arguments on bad law. The first reason to use a citator service like KeyCite is to avoid such damage.

Figure 3.1
KeyCite History of the Case

Citation to *Gideon*
(overruling *Betts*)

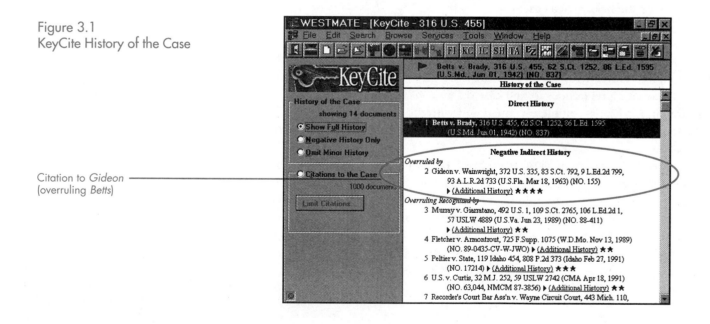

The second reason to use KeyCite is to determine how a case has been *treated by* other cases. Aside from the question of being good law or bad law, the value of a case may be strengthened or weakened by the interpretation subsequently given it by the same court or other courts. It may be that every court that has confronted a situation similar to the one in the cited case has chosen to construe that case narrowly. Although the case is still good law, subsequent interpretations of it may make it less compelling authority. The precedential value of a case greatly depends on the treatment it has received by later cases.

A third, and final, reason to use KeyCite is simply to find more cases. Because cases tend to cite the seminal case in a particular area of law, if you find the seminal case and check it in KeyCite, you are likely to discover numerous cases on the same issue.

Accessing KeyCite

You can access KeyCite by clicking the **KeyCite** button on the main button palette or choosing **KeyCite** from the Services menu and then entering a case citation. You can also access KeyCite by clicking the red or yellow case status flag or blue "H" from a displayed case, when available (Figure 3.2). If the case you are viewing on Westlaw has negative history that may affect its precedential value, you will see a red or yellow flag; if the case has some history but it is not known to be negative history, you will see a blue "H" (Figure 3.3).

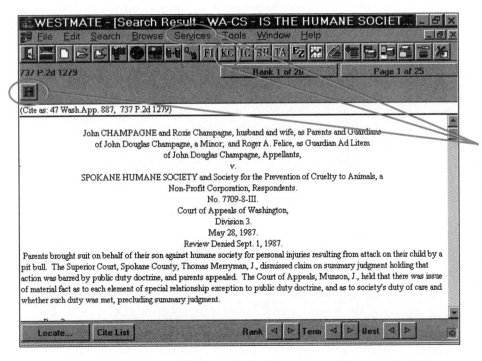

Figure 3.2
Accessing KeyCite

Access KeyCite in one of three ways.

Figure 3.3
Case Status Flags

 A red flag warns that the case is no longer good law for at least one of the points it contains.

 A yellow flag warns that the case has some negative history, but hasn't been reversed or overruled.

 A blue "H" indicates that the case has some history.

Viewing a KeyCite Result: History of the Case

Once you have accessed KeyCite, the History of the Case window is displayed (Figure 3.4). This history is divided into the following categories:

Direct History	traces the same case through the appellate process and includes both prior and subsequent history
Negative Indirect History	lists cases outside the direct appellate line that may have a negative impact on the precedential value of your case
Related References	lists cases that involve the same parties and facts as your case, whether or not the legal issues are the same

All direct and negative indirect history is assigned by West attorney-editors who read and analyze each and every case. The phrases they use to describe this history follow the exact language of the court as much as possible.

By clicking one of the buttons on the left side of the History of the Case window, you can customize your KeyCite result to display different types of case history. You can click **Show Full History** to show direct and negative indirect history, including related references. You can click **Negative History Only** and display only negative direct and indirect history. Or you can click **Omit Minor History** to exclude related references and minor procedural history, such as denials of rehearings.

You can go directly to a case listed in the History of the Case window by double-clicking the name of that case. The page on which a reference to your case first appears is displayed.

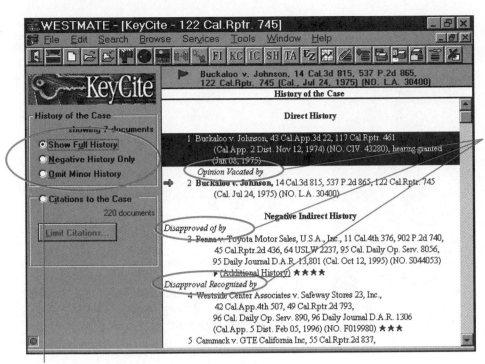

Figure 3.4
Reading Your KeyCite Result:
History of the Case

Phrases describing the historical relationship between the opinions or the treatment given to your case by other cases.

Click to display the Citations to the Case window to view cases and other materials citing your case.

Viewing a KeyCite Result: Citations to the Case

The Citations to the Case window displays all cases on Westlaw and secondary sources, such as law review articles and ALR annotations, that have cited your case. To access this window, click the **Citations to the Case** button from the History of the Case window.

The first portion of the Citations to the Case window lists all negative citing cases, followed by a list of all other cases citing your case (Figure 3.5). These cases are categorized by the depth of treatment they give to your case. Each depth of treatment category is represented by one to four stars. Within each depth of treatment category, cases are ordered first by court (federal, then state) and then by age (in reverse chronological order). For more information about each of the depth of treatment categories, see the chart on the following page.

Figure 3.5
Reading Your KeyCite
Result: Citations to the Case

Indicates the citing case
(in this instance,
LiMandri) directly quotes
the cited case (*Buckaloo*)

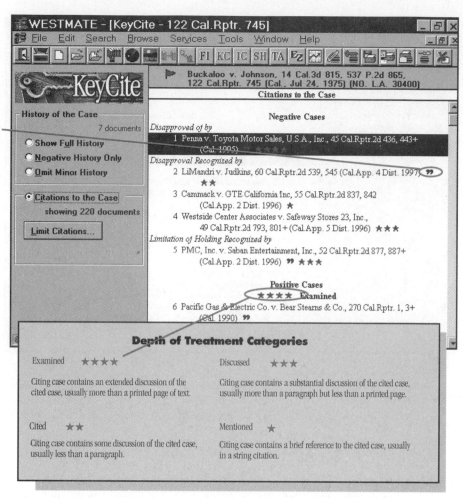

You will find some cases in your research that will be cited by hundreds, sometimes thousands, of cases and secondary sources. In order to reduce your Citations to the Case display to a manageable size, you can limit the citing references by topic, headnote, date, depth of treatment or other elements. Click the **Limit Citations** button to display the Limit Citations window.

Restricting Your Result by Topic and Headnote

The Limit Citations window shows you all the headnotes as they appear in the cited case (Figure 3.6). Read the headnotes and decide which are relevant to your research. Then use the *Headnotes* check boxes on the left side of the window to restrict the list of citing cases to those that discuss the points of law summarized in the relevant headnotes. As an alternative, you can restrict your list of citing cases to those that discuss points of law classified under specific topics.

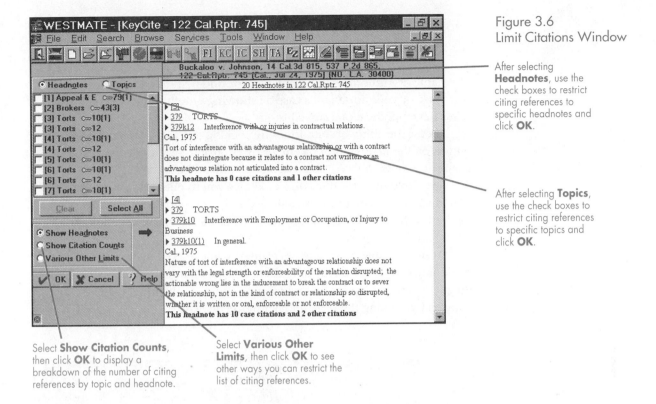

Figure 3.6
Limit Citations Window

After selecting **Headnotes**, use the check boxes to restrict citing references to specific headnotes and click **OK**.

After selecting **Topics**, use the check boxes to restrict citing references to specific topics and click **OK**.

Select **Show Citation Counts**, then click **OK** to display a breakdown of the number of citing references by topic and headnote.

Select **Various Other Limits**, then click **OK** to see other ways you can restrict the list of citing references.

Restricting Your Result Using Various Other Limits

From the Limit Citations window, select **Various Other Limits**, then click **OK**. The Various Other Limits window is displayed, which allows you to restrict the list of citing references in additional ways. You can restrict the citing references to one or more depth of treatment categories, e.g., *examined*; to a specific jurisdiction or West publication; to cases decided before or after a given date; or to cases added to Westlaw after a given date. You can also choose to include citations to or exclude citations from ALR articles, law review articles, and other secondary sources.

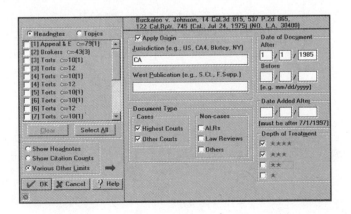

Figure 3.7
Various Other Limits Window

Table of Authorities

In conjunction with KeyCite, you can use the Table of Authorities service, which lists the cases *cited by* a case. (KeyCite lists cases *citing* a case.) The Table of Authorities is a useful tool for finding hidden weaknesses in your case or your opponent's case by showing whether the cases on which it relies have significant negative history.

Access the Table of Authorities by clicking the **Table of Authorities** button on the main button palette or by choosing **Table of Authorities** from the Services menu. Then enter a citation and click **OK**.

The Table of Authorities display allows you to determine at a glance which cited cases merit investigation. Cited cases with negative history are marked with a red or yellow flag. All cited cases are marked with depth of treatment stars (Figure 3.8).

From the Table of Authorities display, you can go directly to the beginning of a cited case by double-clicking its citation. You can also go to the page of the citing case on which a reference to the cited case first appears by clicking the page number in the display.

Figure 3.8
Table of Authorities

Double-click to display the cited case (*Allen*).

Click to display the page of the citing case (*Buckaloo*) on which a reference to the cited case (*Allen*) first appears.

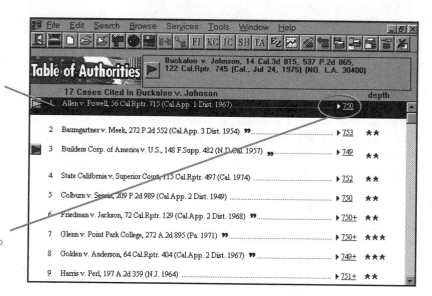

Shepard's Citations

Shepard's Citations lists, in tabular form, all authority citing a specific authority. For case authority, it lists all cases (the *citing* cases) that have cited a specific case (the *cited* case). Figure 3.9 shows part of the table listing all cases that have cited the Supreme Court decision at 411 U.S. 1.

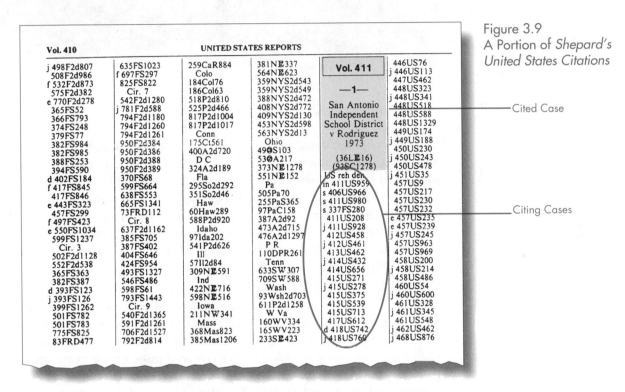

Figure 3.9
A Portion of *Shepard's United States Citations*

— Cited Case

— Citing Cases

Figure 3.10
A Wide Variety of Citators

Using Print Volumes of Shepard's Citations

The first step when using Shepard's is to make sure that you have the appropriate set of volumes to find the authority you need. A library collection of Shepard's citators contains literally hundreds of different volumes (Figure 3.10). They all have the same dark red bindings. You must read the titles carefully to find the correct set. This sounds simple, but novice users frequently start with the wrong set by accident. If you have a case from the *North Eastern Reporter,* you need to find *Shepard's Northeastern Reporter Citations;* even though *Shepard's Northwestern Reporter Citations* looks similar, it won't do the job.

It is also possible to use Shepard's for the same case in more than one citator set, and the citing authority that you find will be different depending on the set that you use. For example, a state supreme court case can be in either a Shepard's state citator or a Shepard's regional reporter citator. In the state citator, the citing authority will include (1) federal cases, (2) state cases from that state, and (3) selected law review articles. The regional reporter citator has as citing authority (1) federal cases, (2) state cases *from all states,* but (3) *no* law review articles. The title page of every Shepard's volume lists the sources of citing authority for that set (Figure 3.11).

The second step in the process is gathering all the volumes in the appropriate set of citators. Some sets of citators, such as *Shepard's United States Citations,* may have several volumes, beginning with the initial hard-copy volumes, followed by several supplements, and ending with a current advance sheet. To be comprehensive in your Shepard's research and to be as up-to-date as possible, you must have *all* the volumes of a particular Shepard's set.

Figure 3.11
Title Pages from a State Citator
and a Regional Citator

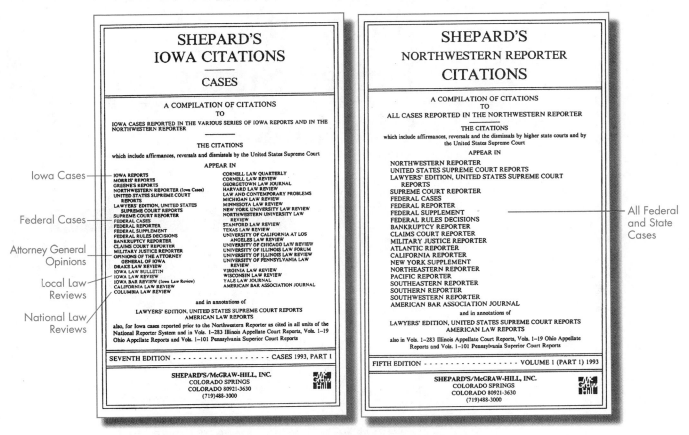

Source: © 1993 by Shepard's. Shepard's Iowa Citations. Shepard's Northwestern Reporter Citations. Reproduced by permission of Shepard's. Further reproduction of any kind is strictly prohibited.

The easiest way to make sure that you have all volumes in a citator set is to begin with the most recent advance sheet in the set. Normally (though not always), this will be a monthly *red* pamphlet or a fortnightly *blue* pamphlet, and it will have an edition date (Figure 3.12). On the cover of this pamphlet will be a guide to "WHAT YOUR LIBRARY SHOULD CONTAIN." Make sure that you have all the volumes that you need. (A corollary to Murphy's Law says that if you are missing one volume, it will be the one that includes a citing case that has overruled the case that you are researching.)

Learning the Language of Shepard's

Assume that you now have the right set of citators and all the volumes in the set. Next you must learn the very concise language of Shepard's.

Figure 3.12
An Advance Sheet for *Shepard's United States Citations*

VOL. 94   JULY 1, 1995   NO. 13

Shepard's

United States

Citations

Case Edition
Part 1—United States Reports
Semiannual Cumulative Supplement

(USPS 605470)

WHAT YOUR LIBRARY SHOULD CONTAIN

The 1994 Revision of *Shepard's United States Citations, Case Edition*, consists of three subsets, each corresponding to one of the three publishers of Supreme Court cases: *United States Reports; United States Supreme Court Reports, Lawyers' Edition;* and *Supreme Court Reporter*. This part supplements the *United States Reports* subset, volumes 1.1–1.8, of *Shepard's United States Citations, Case Edition*. Your library should contain the following hardbound and softcover volumes.

Hardbound Books
Volumes 1.1–1.8, and 4 (1994)

Softcover Books
July 1, 1995 Semiannual Cumulative Supplement
(Vol. 94, No. 13, Part 1)

NOTICE: If you have not purchased the 1994 revised edition, please see page vi of the preface.

DESTROY ALL OTHER ISSUES

RECYCLE YOUR OUTDATED SUPPLEMENTS

When you receive new supplements and are instructed to destroy the outdated versions, please consider taking these paper products to a local recycling center to help conserve our nation's natural resources. Thank you

SHEPARD'S
M c G R A W - H I L L

Source: © 1995 by Shepard's. Shepard's United States Citations. Reproduced by permission of Shepard's. Further reproduction of any kind is strictly prohibited.

First, you must become familiar with Shepard's abbreviations (Figure 3.13). Shepard's uses its own citation form; it does not use the *Bluebook* citation form. For example, Shepard's designation for the *Federal Supplement* is FS, not F.Supp. A table of these abbreviations appears at the beginning of every volume of Shepard's. Note also that the page numbers in a Shepard's list are to the page of the citing case on which the citation occurs, not to the starting page of the case (Figure 3.14).

REPORTER ABBREVIATIONS

A2d–Atlantic Reporter, Second Series
AB–American Bankruptcy Reports
ABST–Abstracts
AbD–Abbott's Court of Appeals Decisions (N.Y.)
AbN–Abstracts, New Series
ABn–American Bankruptcy Reports, New Series
AbP–Abbott's Practice Reports (N.Y.)
AbPn–Abbott's Practice Reports, New Series (N.Y.)
AC–American Annotated Cases
AD–American Decisions
ADC–Appeal Cases, District of Columbia Reports

Bradf–Bradford's Surrogate's Court Reports (N.Y.)
Bray–Brayton's Reports (Vt.)
Breese–Breese's Reports (Ill.)
Breese App–Breese Appendix
BRW–Bankruptcy Reporter (West)
BTA–United States Board of Tax Appeals Reports
Bur–Burnett's Reports (Wis.)
C2d–California Supreme Court Reports, Second Series
C3d–California Supreme Court Reports, Third Series
C4th–California Supreme Court Reports, Fourth Series

Figure 3.13
Shepard's Reporter Abbreviations

Source: © 1994 by Shepard's. Shepard's United States Citations. Reproduced by permission of Shepard's. Further reproduction of any kind is strictly prohibited.

Figure 3.14
Page Numbers in Shepard's

Page on which citation occurs, not initial page of the case

Source: © 1994 by Shepard's. Shepard's United States Citations. Reproduced by permission of Shepard's. Further reproduction of any kind is strictly prohibited.

Shepard's also uses a second set of abbreviations, known as *history* and *treatment* abbreviations. Shepard's editors read the citing cases to determine their relationship to the cited case and assign analytical abbreviations that describe the relationship. The *history* of the case is its direct procedural history. For example, on appeal the case may have been affirmed or reversed by a higher court. The *treatment* of the case is the way other cases (those not within the direct procedural history) have treated it. The Shepard's editors may, in their editorial judgment, find a citing case to have *explained* or *followed* or *distinguished* the cited case. A list of history and treatment abbreviations is also found at the beginning of each volume (Figure 3.15).

Another aspect of Shepard's you must become familiar with is the use of superscript numbers that refer to the headnote of the *cited* case. In the example in Figure 3.16, the superscript "8" means that the citing case has cited that portion of the cited case summarized by its eighth headnote. (You might want to re-read that sibilant sentence slowly. It does make sense— really.) As puzzling as this sounds, once you understand the function of these little numbers, you will find they are very timesaving. If you are Shepardizing a famous case that has been frequently cited, such as *Miranda v. Arizona,* and you are interested in only one aspect of the case, using the headnote numbers is an excellent way to winnow a very long list of citing cases into a much shorter one. If you are just interested in cases citing *Miranda* for the legal issue summarized in its second headnote, you only need to read the cases that have that particular headnote reference number in the Shepard's display. Remember, however, that the same case is often published in more than one reporter and by more than one publisher. Different publishers write different headnotes. In order to use the Shepard's headnote numbers correctly, you must Shepardize with the citator that corresponds to the reporter volume you are reading. Thus, if you are Shepardizing a Supreme Court case as you read it in the *Supreme Court Reporter* (S.Ct.), you must use the Shepard's table for S.Ct. citations.

Of course, a case may have been overruled or otherwise weakened as precedent since the publication of the most current Shepard's advance sheet. Only by using an up-to-date online service such as KeyCite can you be sure that your case is still good law.

HISTORY AND TREATMENT ABBREVIATIONS

Abbreviations have been assigned, where applicable, to each citing case to indicate the effect the citing case had on the case you are Shepardizing. The resulting "history" (affirmed, reversed, modified, etc.) or "treatment" (followed, criticized, explained, etc.) of the case you are Shepardizing is indicated by abbreviations preceding the citing case reference. For example, the reference "f434F2d872" means that there is language on page 872 of volume 434 of the *Federal Reporter*, Second Series, that indicates the court is "following" the case you are Shepardizing. Instances in which the citing reference occurs in a dissenting opinion are indicated in the same manner. The abbreviations used to reflect both history and treatment are as follows.

History of Case

a	(affirmed)	The decision in the case you are Shepardizing was affirmed or adhered to on appeal.
cc	(connected case)	Identifies a different case from the case you are Shepardizing, but one arising out of the same subject matter or in some manner intimately connected therewith.
m	(modified)	The decision in the case you are Shepardizing was changed in some way.
p	(parallel)	The citing case is substantially alike or on all fours, either in law or facts, with the case you are Shepardizing.
r	(reversed)	The decision in the case you are Shepardizing was reversed on appeal.
s	(same case)	The case you are Shepardizing involves the same litigation as the citing case, although at a different stage in the proceedings.
S	(superseded)	The citing case decision has been substituted for the decision in the case you are Shepardizing.
US reh den		Rehearing denied by the U.S. Supreme Court.
US reh dis		Rehearing dismissed by the U.S. Supreme Court.
v	(vacated)	The decision in the case you are Shepardizing has been vacated.

Treatment of Case

c	(criticized)	The citing case disagrees with the reasoning/decision of the case you are Shepardizing.
d	(distinguished)	The citing case is different either in law or fact, for reasons given, from the case you are Shepardizing.
e	(explained)	The case you are Shepardizing is interpreted in some significant way. Not merely a restatement of facts.
f	(followed)	The citing case refers to the case you are Shepardizing as controlling authority.
h	(harmonized)	An apparent inconsistency between the citing case and the case you are Shepardizing is explained and shown not to exist.
j	(dissenting opinion)	The case is cited in a dissenting opinion.
L	(limited)	The citing case refuses to extend the holding of the case you are Shepardizing beyond the precise issues involved.
o	(overruled)	The ruling in the case you are Shepardizing is expressly overruled.
q	(questioned)	The citing case questions the continuing validity or precedential value of the case you are Shepardizing.

Figure 3.15
Shepard's History and
Treatment Abbreviations

Figure 3.16
Headnote Numbers in Shepard's

Vol. 93			SUPREME COURT REPORTER		

Court

Parallel Citations

History/Treatment of Case

Headnote Number

Source: © 1994 by Shepard's. Shepard's United States Citations. Reproduced by permission of Shepard's. Further reproduction of any kind is strictly prohibited.

Conclusion

After some practice, you will find that updating your research with KeyCite or Shepard's is really quite simple. If, after you have worked with KeyCite or Shepard's, you still do not understand the procedure or the result, ask a reference librarian for help, or consult *Discovering Westlaw* or the applicable Shepard's documentation.

Whichever citator service you use, updating your research is an essential part of every research assignment. It is a good practice to start in law school.

Legislation

If you suspect your issue involves a statute, you should begin your research with a check of the statutory codes. A practicing attorney is more likely to need a statute than a case, though this can vary from one legal specialty to another. Although you may become acquainted with the Uniform Commercial Code in Contracts and a few scattered constitutional provisions elsewhere, your first year of law school may not provide a systematic introduction to the legislative process and its resultant publications. This is changing as more courses concentrate on the legislative process, but case law still tends to receive more attention in law school. In this chapter, we will introduce you to the common forms of legislative publications, with a special focus on federal materials. Learn this and you will be ahead of the game.

Federal Laws

A federal law first appears in the information stream as a bill introduced in Congress by a representative or a senator. A bill is assigned its own unique number depending on the side of the legislature in which it originates and the order in which it is introduced. Then it is referred to the appropriate House or Senate committee. For example, an amendment to the Truth in Lending Act passed in 1980 began life as H.R. 4986, which means that it came from the House of Representatives (H.R.) and was the 4986th bill introduced in the House during that Congress. Once a bill is introduced and sent to the appropriate committee, it can meet several fates. Most bills sink from sight never to be seen again. Others are passed by the House but die in the Senate, or vice versa. Sometimes both the House and Senate pass a bill, but in different versions due to the process of amendment; in that case, a conference committee, with members from each house, is appointed to try to hammer out a compromise that can then be passed by each house. If both the House and Senate pass the same version of the bill, this process can be skipped, but in either case, the final version is sent to the president who can sign it into law or veto it and send it back to the house where it started. The House and Senate can then try to override the president's veto by mustering a two-thirds vote in each house (Figure 4.1).

Figure 4.1 The Legislative Process and Accompanying Documents

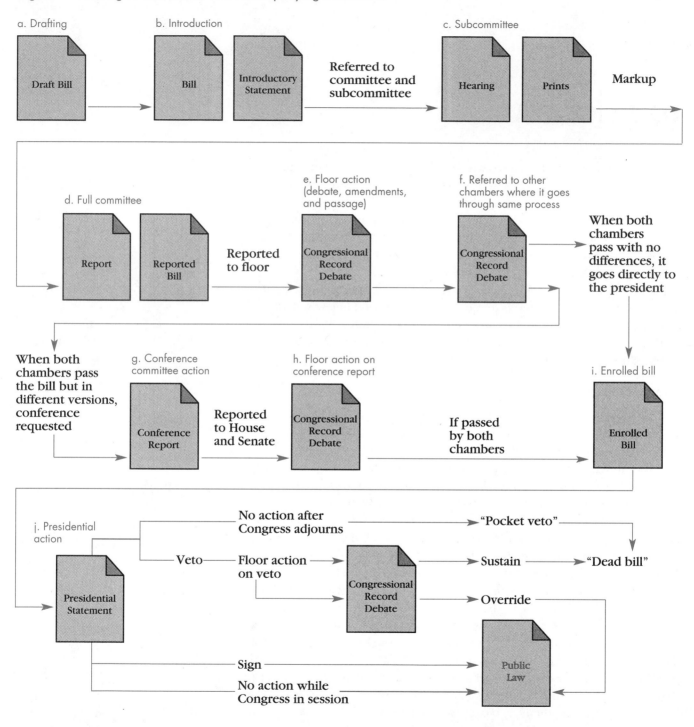

Source: Figure 4.1 is adapted from *A Research Guide to Congress: How to Make Congress Work for You, Second Edition* by Judith Manion, Joseph Meringolo, and Robert Oakes and used with permission of Legi-Slate, Inc.

Later in your career you may have to do a legislative history, a process that is as enjoyable as root canal work. Tracking amendments to related bills through each stage of the legislative process can be tricky, particularly when a controversial or high-profile issue generates a host of bills on the same issue. And because each step can be repeated, the relatively direct path illustrated by Figure 4.1 can evolve into a labyrinth. If you are lucky, a professionally compiled legislative history for the law you are researching may already exist (see *Sources of Compiled Legislative Histories* by Nancy P. Johnson). If you must go it alone, however, do not be daunted. The laws themselves are not difficult to use. In fact, once you learn to use the research tools that private publishers add to their editions of the laws, you may find the entire process—if not exactly enjoyable—quite straightforward.

A law, also called a *statute* or an *act*, is identified by a public law number, which is composed of the number of the Congress in which it passed, followed by a number that reflects the order in which the bill was enacted; for example, P.L. 101–12 refers to the twelfth law passed in the 101st Congress. As soon as they are enacted, federal laws are published separately in pamphlet form as *slip laws*. Slip laws include valuable information in the headings and margin notes. From them, you can learn when the law was approved, the number of the bill that was enacted into law, and the short title or popular name of the law. The reference to the *United States Code* (U.S.C.) will tell you where the provision will be codified in the U.S.C. The *U.S. Statutes at Large* citation will tell you the initial page of the law in the permanent bound volume. At the end of the slip law, you will find references to House and Senate reports as well as citations to the congressional debates. These legislative history references will tell you where you can find congressional materials that may help you determine the intent of the language of the law (Figure 4.2).

Although slip laws sound rather useful, you will not find them in most libraries. They are messy and hard to keep organized. But fear not, the slip laws are compiled into several much more useful formats, which will be discussed shortly. You also can access slip copy versions of public laws on Westlaw in the United States Public Laws database (US-PL).

At the end of each session of Congress, all of the slip laws for that year are compiled in numerical order and published in bound volumes. These laws are generically called *session laws* because they are compiled for each session of Congress. On Westlaw, session laws for the past session of Congress are moved from the US-PL database to the US-PL-OLD database. Therefore, to retrieve P.L. 101–625, the Cranston-Gonzalez National Affordable Housing Act, enter the search **ci(101-625)** in the US-PL-OLD database or use Find (click the **Find** button on the main button palette and type **us pl 101–625** in the *Citation* text box). You can also retrieve the same act by searching for terms from the act's name, which is included in the caption field (ca). Type **ca(affordable)** at the Terms and Connectors Query Editor after accessing the US-PL-OLD database.

Figure 4.2
A Slip Law: Headings, Margin
Notes, and Legislative History
References

Public Law Number ——————
Bill Number ——————
Date Approved ——————
Short Title ——————

Where It Will Appear in the U.S.C. ——————

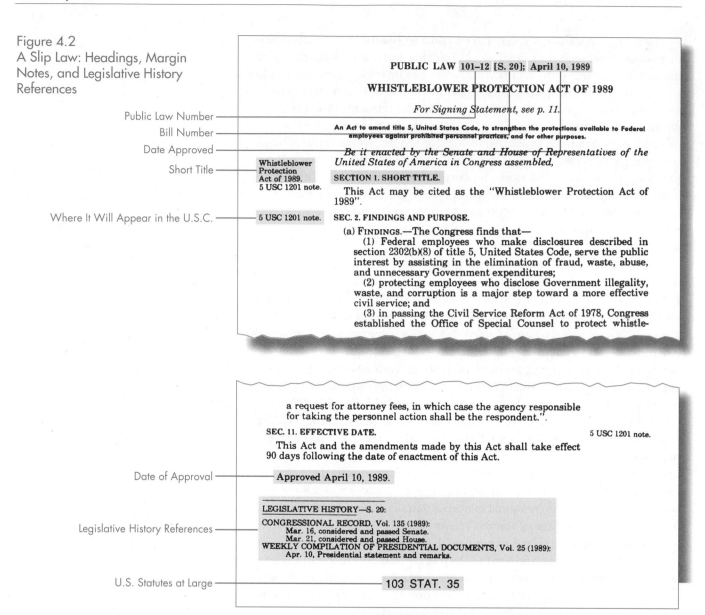

PUBLIC LAW 101–12 [S. 20]; April 10, 1989

WHISTLEBLOWER PROTECTION ACT OF 1989

For Signing Statement, see p. 11.

An Act to amend title 5, United States Code, to strengthen the protections available to Federal employees against prohibited personnel practices, and for other purposes.

Be it enacted by the Senate and House of Representatives of the United States of America in Congress assembled,

Whistleblower
Protection
Act of 1989.
5 USC 1201 note.

SECTION 1. SHORT TITLE.

This Act may be cited as the "Whistleblower Protection Act of 1989".

5 USC 1201 note.

SEC. 2. FINDINGS AND PURPOSE.

(a) FINDINGS.—The Congress finds that—

(1) Federal employees who make disclosures described in section 2302(b)(8) of title 5, United States Code, serve the public interest by assisting in the elimination of fraud, waste, abuse, and unnecessary Government expenditures;

(2) protecting employees who disclose Government illegality, waste, and corruption is a major step toward a more effective civil service; and

(3) in passing the Civil Service Reform Act of 1978, Congress established the Office of Special Counsel to protect whistle-

a request for attorney fees, in which case the agency responsible for taking the personnel action shall be the respondent.".

SEC. 11. EFFECTIVE DATE.   5 USC 1201 note.

This Act and the amendments made by this Act shall take effect 90 days following the date of enactment of this Act.

Date of Approval ——————

Approved April 10, 1989.

Legislative History References ——————

LEGISLATIVE HISTORY—S. 20:

CONGRESSIONAL RECORD, Vol. 135 (1989):
    Mar. 16, considered and passed Senate.
    Mar. 21, considered and passed House.
WEEKLY COMPILATION OF PRESIDENTIAL DOCUMENTS, Vol. 25 (1989):
    Apr. 10, Presidential statement and remarks.

U.S. Statutes at Large ——————

103 STAT. 35

The law as it is passed by Congress and as it appears in the session laws is useful if you are looking for the original version of an act, before it has been codified by its subject areas or amended, or if you require the language of a particular amendment. You will also use the session laws if you need to find a law that has been repealed and deleted from the code. For example, assume that your client committed a crime for which she received a sentence and a fine. If the crime was committed in 1986, before the date on which a new law on the topic became effective, you would have to look for the language of the repealed law that has been deleted from the code. When new laws are printed in the session laws, they have a preamble that may explain what the law is designed to do. This preamble can be helpful in determining the legislative intent of the act.

Note: Although session laws serve specific purposes, you cannot safely use the session law version of a statute to determine the *present* text of a law, since the original law may have been repealed or amended. You will find the present text of a law in a code, as explained later in this chapter.

Federal session laws can be located in three sources: *United States Statutes at Large* (Stat.) published by the U.S. Government Printing Office; *U.S. Code Congressional and Administrative News* (U.S.C.C.A.N.) published by West Group; and advance pamphlets to *United States Code Service* (U.S.C.S.) published by Lexis Law Publishing (Figure 4.3). The *United States Statutes at Large* is the official session law publication produced by the U.S. Government Printing Office for federal laws. *Statutes at Large* is found in every law library, but, as is frequently true of government publications, it is very slow to arrive, lagging three to four years behind the end of the session covered.

One of the titles that publishes session laws also contains valuable information pertaining to the history of those laws. *U.S. Code Congressional and Administrative News* (U.S.C.C.A.N.), published by West Group, includes selected legislative history material. It lists the citations for the House, Senate, and conference committee reports and reprints the report or reports that it determines to be the most closely related to the public law. To determine the meaning of a statute, you may need to refer to these congressional committee reports. For example, assume that you represent plaintiffs from the petroleum industry. Their case revolves around the meaning of the term *well* in three statutory provisions. By reading the congressional reports for the various acts, you may be able to determine the exact meaning of the term. It is this type of information that is gleaned from the legislative history materials.

U.S.C.C.A.N. does not reprint all the congressional materials, such as the hearings and debates, but the legislative history table does list the citations to the bills, reports, and debates in the *Congressional Record*. U.S.C.C.A.N. is updated monthly in separate softbound pamphlets that are later published in bound volumes. To obtain the most current laws, check the latest pamphlets. On Westlaw, the Legislative History–U.S. Code database (LH) contains House, Senate, and conference committee reports as set forth in U.S.C.C.A.N. from 1948 through 1989 as well as all congressional committee reports on pending legislation from January 1990 to the present. If you want to access the congressional debates as reported in the *Congressional Record* on Westlaw, you can search the Congressional Record database (CR).

Figure 4.3
The Three Sources of Session Laws

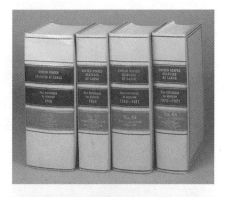

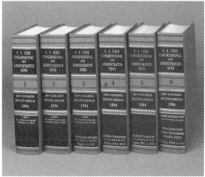

Figure 4.4
The Three Sources of Federal
Codes

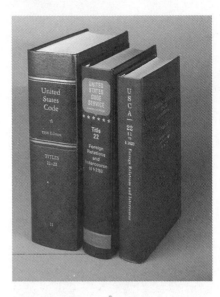

Federal Codes

Laws are classified, or codified, by subject or topic in volumes called *codes*. These codes not only group the laws by subject, but also show all subsequent amendments. This makes life much simpler. Most often you will use one of the codes (actually, you will use an annotated code, but that's discussed later in this section) when you try to locate federal statutes with all of their amendments and deletions.

Codes are easy to use and are effective research tools if used correctly. To locate laws efficiently, you need a basic understanding of how the codes are organized. Federal laws are collected and organized by subject matter into fifty titles and compiled into a code. There is no magic to the number fifty. Codes can be built around any subject arrangement. Some states use lots of topics, some only a few. The federal government decided on fifty topics in the 1920s and has retained the same arrangement ever since, even though a few of the topics are never used. For example, laws pertaining to age discrimination will be classified under Title 29, which is the title designated to laws concerning labor. Each title of the *U.S. Code* is further divided into subdivisions called chapters and sections. For age discrimination, the chapter would be 14, Age Discrimination in Employment, and the section would be 623, Prohibition of age discrimination. The citation to the code would read 29 U.S.C. § 623; you omit the chapter number in the citation and retain the section number. Recall that in addition to placing similar laws together under topics, codes also incorporate amendments and indicate repeals. Some laws may apply to more than one subject, so you may have to check more than one place in the code.

There are three federal codes: the *United States Code* is the official code for federal laws, while the *United States Code Annotated* and the *United States Code Service* are both unofficial annotated codes (Figure 4.4). Each of the codes is useful for certain purposes.

United States Code

The *United States Code* (U.S.C.) is published by the U.S. Government Printing Office. The whole set is recompiled every six years, using the same fifty subject categories or titles. Congress has deemed the U.S.C. prima facie evidence of the actual text, which means simply that the U.S.C. is sort of official. Ask your legal research instructor why we say "sort of."

The U.S.C. contains only the text of the law. It does not give citations to the cases that have interpreted the statutes; this information can only be found in one of the annotated codes. The U.S.C. is also very cumbersome to use. Although you can find material in the U.S.C. by checking the multi-volume index, the material may not be as current as you need. As we noted, the U.S.C. is reissued every six years, with cumulative annual supplements between the new editions. In reality, the annual cumulative supplements do not appear in the library until eight months to two years have passed.

Therefore, if you rely only on the U.S.C., you will miss the current laws, amendments, and deletions.

The reason that you may need to use the U.S.C. at all is that the *Bluebook* says to "cite to U.S.C. if therein." Therefore, the U.S.C. has the advantage of being official, but the two unofficial codes are much more helpful research tools than the U.S.C.

Annotated Codes

Annotated codes are more useful versions of the U.S.C. Not only do they contain the text of the U.S.C., they also refer to the cases that have interpreted the federal laws. For any statutory research, you will want to use one of the annotated codes—they are universally accepted. Both of the annotated codes—West Group's *United States Code Annotated* (U.S.C.A.) and Lexis Law Publishing's *United States Code Service* (U.S.C.S.)—contain basically the same text and title and section numbers as the official U.S.C. Both annotated codes contain references to cases that have construed the statutes, to administrative regulations, and to secondary sources. The annotated codes also contain cross-references to related sections within the code and refer to the research tools provided by their respective publishers. You may have a preference for one publisher's materials, or you may simply use whichever is available at the time that you need it.

United States Code Annotated

The *United States Code Annotated* (U.S.C.A.) is an excellent example of West Group's publishing philosophy. West Group believes in providing as much information as possible, leaving it to the researcher to sift through the information and discard what is not relevant. Following this philosophy, U.S.C.A. occupies well over two hundred volumes and provides researchers with citations to cases and a wide variety of other references as well (Figure 4.5). If you like receiving as much information as possible, you will prefer using the U.S.C.A.

In essence, by enhancing the statutory text with notes and references to other research materials, West allows you to use the U.S.C.A. as an entryway to a statutory research system. In the U.S.C.A., directly following the text of the statute, you will find the history of the statute. It indicates, in parentheses, when the law was originally passed and when it was amended or repealed. It provides citations to the *U.S. Statutes at Large* origin of the text as well as to amendments. The historical notes provide detail on specific word changes. This information can be extremely helpful when a law has gone through several revisions. Cross-references to related and qualifying laws are included to prevent oversights. Other references indicate where the legislative history can be located in the *U.S. Code Congressional and Administrative News* (U.S.C.C.A.N.). You will also find citations to the *Code of Federal Regulations* (C.F.R.), which contains administrative regulations (Figure 4.6).

Figure 4.5
Information Available
in the U.S.C.A.

Cross References

Executive Orders

Cross References

West Topics and Key Numbers

Library References

C.J.S. Reference

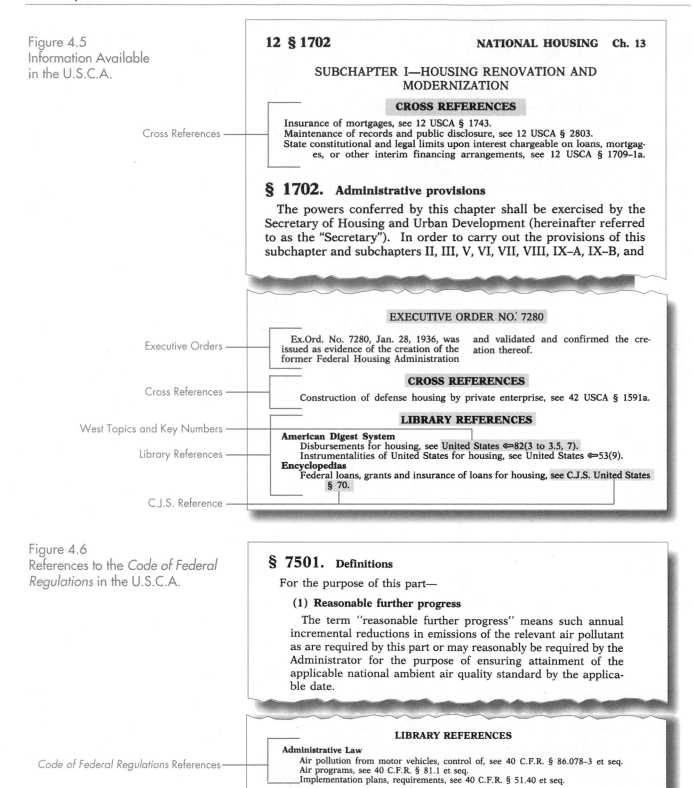

12 § 1702   **NATIONAL HOUSING   Ch. 13**

SUBCHAPTER I—HOUSING RENOVATION AND
MODERNIZATION

CROSS REFERENCES

Insurance of mortgages, see 12 USCA § 1743.
Maintenance of records and public disclosure, see 12 USCA § 2803.
State constitutional and legal limits upon interest chargeable on loans, mortgages, or other interim financing arrangements, see 12 USCA § 1709–1a.

§ 1702. Administrative provisions

The powers conferred by this chapter shall be exercised by the Secretary of Housing and Urban Development (hereinafter referred to as the "Secretary"). In order to carry out the provisions of this subchapter and subchapters II, III, V, VI, VII, VIII, IX–A, IX–B, and

EXECUTIVE ORDER NO. 7280

Ex.Ord. No. 7280, Jan. 28, 1936, was issued as evidence of the creation of the former Federal Housing Administration and validated and confirmed the creation thereof.

CROSS REFERENCES

Construction of defense housing by private enterprise, see 42 USCA § 1591a.

LIBRARY REFERENCES

American Digest System
Disbursements for housing, see United States ☞82(3 to 3.5, 7).
Instrumentalities of United States for housing, see United States ☞53(9).
Encyclopedias
Federal loans, grants and insurance of loans for housing, see C.J.S. United States § 70.

Figure 4.6
References to the *Code of Federal Regulations* in the U.S.C.A.

Code of Federal Regulations References

§ 7501. Definitions

For the purpose of this part—

(1) Reasonable further progress

The term "reasonable further progress" means such annual incremental reductions in emissions of the relevant air pollutant as are required by this part or may reasonably be required by the Administrator for the purpose of ensuring attainment of the applicable national ambient air quality standard by the applicable date.

LIBRARY REFERENCES

Administrative Law
Air pollution from motor vehicles, control of, see 40 C.F.R. § 86.078–3 et seq.
Air programs, see 40 C.F.R. § 81.1 et seq.
Implementation plans, requirements, see 40 C.F.R. § 51.40 et seq.

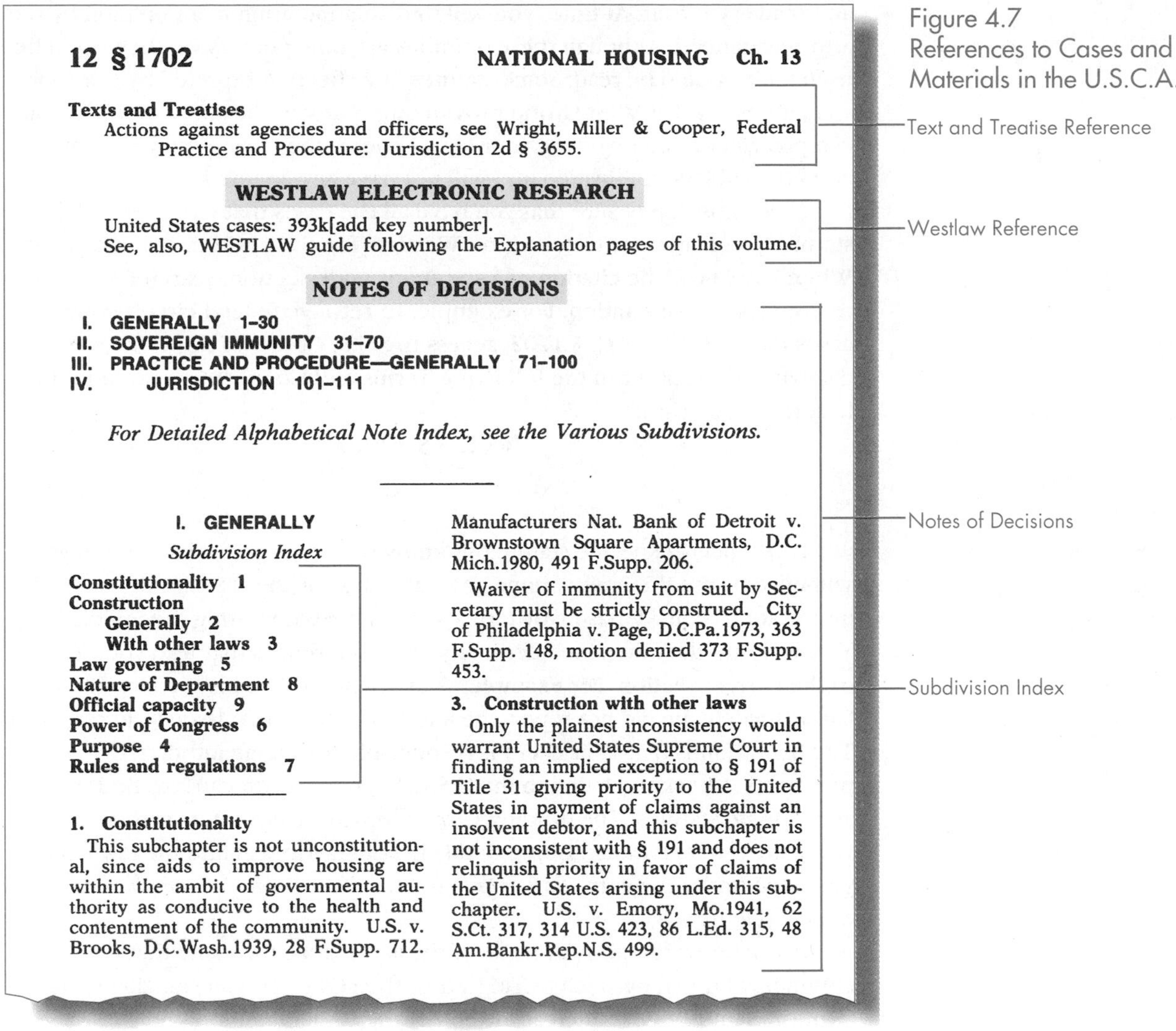

12 § 1702   **NATIONAL HOUSING**   **Ch. 13**

Texts and Treatises

Actions against agencies and officers, see Wright, Miller & Cooper, Federal Practice and Procedure: Jurisdiction 2d § 3655.

WESTLAW ELECTRONIC RESEARCH

United States cases: 393k[add key number].

See, also, WESTLAW guide following the Explanation pages of this volume.

NOTES OF DECISIONS

- I.   GENERALLY   1–30
- II. SOVEREIGN IMMUNITY   31–70
- III. PRACTICE AND PROCEDURE—GENERALLY   71–100
- IV.   JURISDICTION   101–111

For Detailed Alphabetical Note Index, see the Various Subdivisions.

I. GENERALLY

Subdivision Index

Constitutionality 1
Construction
    Generally 2
    With other laws 3
Law governing 5
Nature of Department 8
Official capacity 9
Power of Congress 6
Purpose 4
Rules and regulations 7

---

1. Constitutionality

This subchapter is not unconstitutional, since aids to improve housing are within the ambit of governmental authority as conducive to the health and contentment of the community. U.S. v. Brooks, D.C.Wash.1939, 28 F.Supp. 712.

Manufacturers Nat. Bank of Detroit v. Brownstown Square Apartments, D.C. Mich.1980, 491 F.Supp. 206.

Waiver of immunity from suit by Secretary must be strictly construed. City of Philadelphia v. Page, D.C.Pa.1973, 363 F.Supp. 148, motion denied 373 F.Supp. 453.

3. Construction with other laws

Only the plainest inconsistency would warrant United States Supreme Court in finding an implied exception to § 191 of Title 31 giving priority to the United States in payment of claims against an insolvent debtor, and this subchapter is not inconsistent with § 191 and does not relinquish priority in favor of claims of the United States arising under this subchapter. U.S. v. Emory, Mo.1941, 62 S.Ct. 317, 314 U.S. 423, 86 L.Ed. 315, 48 Am.Bankr.Rep.N.S. 499.

Figure 4.7
References to Cases and Other Materials in the U.S.C.A.
— Text and Treatise Reference
— Westlaw Reference
— Notes of Decisions
— Subdivision Index

The Library References section gives the applicable West topics and key numbers and citations to *Corpus Juris Secundum* (C.J.S.), a West Group legal encyclopedia. West's topics and key numbers give you access points into the West Group digests. The U.S.C.A. also contains references to other relevant materials published by West Group, such as West Group's *Federal Forms* and *Federal Practice Manual*.

As we observed earlier, the U.S.C.A. is known for its abundance of annotations of court and administrative decisions (Figure 4.7). Annotations are one-sentence summaries, written by West editors, that indicate if, and how, courts or administrative bodies have interpreted a law. The case citation appears at the end of each annotation so that you can find the case and read it yourself. At times you will find an annotation to an opinion by the attorney general. Although these opinions are only persuasive, they could be useful and should be read. Some statutes have been interpreted by the courts so many times that West Group provides an index to the annotations so you can preselect cases involving your legal issue. Some statutes may not have been the subject of litigation and will not have any annotations.

To be absolutely sure that you have all the cases that cite a federal statute, you may want to search on Westlaw for code references in case law. When you know the citation of a statute or code section, search for references to that citation. For example, to retrieve federal circuit court cases that cite 12 U.S.C. § 1702, access the U.S. Courts of Appeals Cases database (CTA) and run the following Terms and Connectors search in the headnote field (he):

he(12 +5 1702)

How to Use the U.S.C.A.

If you need a specific statute but know only the subject of the law, you will need to use the multivolume general index for the U.S.C.A. It is very important to consider as many terms as possible when using the index. You will find the index includes many cross-references that lead you to the correct section. For example, your client has lost his credit card. Unfortunately, he did not report the loss to the bank that issued the card. The bank claims that your client is responsible for the unauthorized purchases. Check the index to the U.S.C.A. under credit cards to find the appropriate statutes. The heading *Credit Cards and Plates* refers you to *Consumer Credit Protection*. Going to this heading, you will find the laws that you need under the entry *Loss or theft, liability of cardholder for unauthorized use in event of* (Figure 4.8).

If you know the popular name of the act, that is, the name that it is commonly known by, such as Title VII or the FOIA Act, you can check the Popular Name Table located at the end of the General Index. We use *popular* in a special sense here—it is not as if these laws have been on MTV. The popular name of an act is sometimes just the author of the act—for example, the Gramm-Rudman-Hollings Act named after the authors of the act in the U.S. Senate.

If you approach the U.S.C.A. with either the public law number or the *Statutes at Large* citation, you can check the volume labeled Tables at the end of the set. These tables translate the public law number and the *Statutes at Large* citation, broken down into its component section numbers, into the corresponding U.S.C.A. citation (Figure 4.9).

Figure 4.8
Using the U.S.C.A. Index

CREATIVE 1042

CREATIVE ORGANS
Veterans, wartime disability compensation, loss of one or more, effect on rates, **38 § 1114**

CREATIVE WRITING
National Foundation on the Arts and the Humanities, generally, this index

CREDIT (PAYMENT OF INDEBTEDNESS)
—Cont'd
Regional Agricultural Credit Corporations, generally, this index
Small business loan securitization, study and report, SEC and Board of Governors of Federal Reserve, **15 § 78b nt**
Transfer domestically or internationally, per-

Farm credit,
  Agricultural Credit, generally, this index
  Farm Credit Administration, generally, this index
  Farm Credit Banks, generally, this index
  Farm Credit System, generally, this index
  Farm Credit Administration, generally, this index
Federal credit reform, budget and fiscal operations. Congress, generally, this index

Protection, generally, this index
Short title, **18 § 1001 nt**

CREDIT CARDS AND PLATES —————————— Cross-Reference
Accounts receivable, sales, depository institutions, notice, etc., FDIC, **12 § 1821**
Consumer Credit Protection, this index
Credit billing. Consumer Credit Protection, this index
Fair credit billing. Consumer Credit Protec-

CONSUMER 656

CONSUMER CREDIT PROTECTION
—Cont'd
Credit cards and plates—Cont'd
Fraud—Cont'd
  Telecommunications instrument, hardware, software, etc., unauthorized use, **18 § 1029**
Fraudulent use, **15 § 1644**
General information without specific term, applications and solicitations, disclosure requirements, **15 § 1637**
Issuance, **15 § 1642**
Issuers, access to open end consumer credit plans, disclosure requirements, **15 § 1637**
Liability of cardholder, **15 § 1643**
Liability of issuer, violation of disclosure requirements, **15 § 1640**
Limits on liability of cardholder, **15 § 1643**
Loss or theft, liability of cardholder for unauthorized use in event of, **15 § 1643**
Other laws or agreement with issuer, liability imposed by, **15 § 1643**
Penalty,
  Fraud, access devices, **18 § 1029**

CONSUMER CREDIT PROTECTION
—Cont'd
Credit reporting agencies—Cont'd
Annual salary in excess of certain amounts, employment at, disclosure of obsolete information prohibited, exception, **15 § 1681c**
Charges for disclosures, **15 § 1681j**
Civil liability,
  Negligent noncompliance, **15 § 1681o**
  Noncompliance, **15 § 1681n**
Compliance procedures, **15 § 1681e**
Conditions of disclosure to consumers, notice, **15 § 1681h**
Congressional findings and statement of purpose,
  Defined, **15 § 1681a**
  Disclosures, conditions, **15 § 1681h**
Consumer dispute in subsequent consumer reports, notification of, **15 § 1681i** —————————— Reference to the Statute
Consumer report, defined, **15 § 1681a**
Consumer reporting agency,
  Defined, **15 § 1681a**
  Disclosure to consumer, **15 § 1681g**
  Federal claims, disclosure of mailing ad-

Figure 4.9
Finding the U.S.C.A. Citation from the Tables

1968   **STATUTES AT LARGE**

1968—90th Cong.—82 Stat.   **U S C A**

Apr.	P.L.	Sec.	Page	Tit.	Sec.	Status
29	90–296	1	109	28	1407	
		2	110	28	prec. 1391	
	90–297	1	110	42	1958	Rep.
		2, 3	111	42	1958 nts	Elim.
	90–298	—	111	46	817	
May						
3	90–299	1	112	47	223	
		2	112	47	153	
4	90–300	—	113	12	355	
7	90–301	1(a)	113	38	1810	
		1(b)	113	38	1811	
		2(a)	113	38	1810	
		2(b)	113	38	1822	Rep.
		3(a)	113	12	1709—1	Rep.
		3(b)	114	12	1713	
		3(c)	114	12	1715e	
		3(d)	114	12	1715v	
		3(e)	114	12	1715y	
		4	114	12	1709—1 nt	
		5(a)	116	38	1827	
		5(b)	116	38	prec. 1801	
8	90–302	1	117	42	1752, 1752 nt	
		2(a)	117	42	1755	
		2(b)	117	42	1758	
		3	117	42	1761	
		4	119	42	1776	
		5	119	42	1773	
17	90–308	—	123	25	331 nt	
	90–309	2	123	25	396f nt	
18	90–311	1 to 3	124	43	615 to 615e nt	Elim.
	90–312	—	125	33	59f	
22	90–313	1–7	126–129	49	1653 nt	
23	90–314	—	129	22	2589	
24	90–318	—	131	16	1132 nt	
29	90–321	1, 101	146	15	1601 nt	
		102	146	15	1601	
		103	147	15	1602	
		104	147	15	1603	
		105	148	15	1604	
		106	148	15	1605	
		107	149	15	1606	
		108	150	15	1607	
		109	150	15	1608	
		110	151	15	1609	Rep.
		111	151	15	1610	
		112	151	15	1611	
		113	151	15	1612	
		114	151	15	1613	
		115	—	15	1614	Rep.
		121	152	15	1631	
		122	152	15	1632	
		123	152	15	1633	
		124	152	15	1634	
		125	152	15	1635	
		126	153	15	1636	Rep.
		127	153	15	1637	
		128	155	15	1638	
		129	156	15	1639	Rep.
		130	157	15	1640	
		131	157	15	1641	
		132	—	15	1642	
		133	—	15	1643	
		134	—	15	1644	
		135	—	15	1645	
		136	—	15	1646	
		141	158	15	1661	
		142	158	15	1662	
		143	158	15	1663	
		144	158	15	1664	
		145	159	15	1665	
		146	—	15	1665a	
		161	—	15	1666	
		162	—	15	1666a	
		163	—	15	1666b	

310

Public Law Number

Public Law Section Number and U.S.C.A. Citation

Updating the U.S.C.A.

The constant possibility of change in legislation makes it *mandatory* for you to check for the very latest amendments to a law. Always check the publication date (copyright date on the back of the title page) of the hard-copy volume of the U.S.C.A. to determine if your law needs updating. To check for amendments, deletions, and new annotations that have appeared since the bound volume was published, check the supplementary pamphlets inserted in the back of each volume; these are called *pocket parts* because they fit into pockets in the cover of each volume. *Always, always, check the pocket part.* Do you catch our drift? Check it. The pocket parts are arranged by the same section numbers as the bound volume.

Because pocket parts to the U.S.C.A. appear only once a year, there are many times when a new law or amendment is not yet included. To fill this gap, the U.S.C.A. issues bimonthly noncumulative pamphlets that contain the newest laws and amendments arranged in U.S.C.A. classification form. All of the new annotations also appear in these pamphlets. Usually, two additional pamphlets, as needed, will also be issued. These are the *U.S.C.A. Statutory Supplements* containing all amendments to the code through the last law of the session signed by the president. These two pamphlets are not arranged in U.S.C.A. classification form, but are in public law form. Late in any given year, you will have to check the main U.S.C.A. volume, the pocket part, and each of the year's pamphlets. An amazing number of people forget to check the pamphlets. Don't be one of them.

When we discussed the West Group publication U.S.C.C.A.N., we noted that the bound volumes were supplemented on a monthly basis. You can also use the softbound monthly supplements to U.S.C.C.A.N. to update the code. The laws in U.S.C.C.A.N. are arranged in chronological order as they were passed by Congress. Remember that you can also update the code by checking the United States Public Laws database (US-PL) on Westlaw. Public laws are on Westlaw within a few days of approval by the president. Using the Update service on Westlaw is a particularly easy method for updating the U.S.C.A.

United States Code Service

The *United States Code Service* (U.S.C.S.) is published by Lexis Law Publishing. Like the U.S.C.A., the U.S.C.S. provides the researcher with references to authority, historical notes, cross-references, and case annotations. The U.S.C.S. also has a multivolume general index. The set is updated with annual pocket parts and quarterly cumulative supplements. The U.S.C.S. differs from the U.S.C.A. in that it is selective in its notes of case decisions. Therefore, the U.S.C.S. excludes case annotations that the editors deem to be obsolete, repetitive, or insignificant. On the other hand, the U.S.C.S. includes more notes of administrative decisions than the U.S.C.A. does. Therefore, if you are working on a subject area that is highly regulated, like occupational health and safety, you may want to check the U.S.C.S. (Figure 4.10), as well as administrative decision sources on Westlaw.

Figure 4.10
Citations to Decisions in the U.S.C.S.

OCCUPATIONAL SAFETY AND HEALTH   29 USCS § 661

Employer discharged employees as retaliation for filing safety charges, despite contention they were fired for taking extended lunch breaks, where there was no prior enforcement of tardiness rules and employees were not issued warnings. Donovan v Peter Zimmer America, Inc. (1982, DC SC) 557 F Supp 642.

Employer's proffered reason for discharging

plained to OSHA about health conditions in her workplace did not establish violation of nondiscrimination provisions (29 USCS § 660(c)), where no direct evidence of retaliation or employer animus was introduced and employer produced evidence that (1) it had taken actions to accommodate employee in resolving her complaint, (2) restructuring was bona fide, and (3)

§ 661.   Occupational Safety and Health Review Commission

(a) Establishment; membership; appointment; Chairman. The Occupational Safety and Health Review Commission is hereby established. The Commission shall be composed of three members who shall be appointed by the President, by and with the advice and consent of the Senate, from among persons who by reason of training, education, or experience are qualified to carry out the functions of the Commission under this Act. The President shall designate one of the members of the Commission to serve as Chairman.

(b) Terms of office; removal by President. The terms of members of the Commission shall be six years except that (1) the members of the Commission first taking office shall serve, as designated by the President at the time of appointment, one for a term of two years, one for a term of four years, and one for a term of six years, and (2) a vacancy caused by the death, resignation, or removal of a member prior to the expiration of the term for which he was appointed shall be filled only for the remainder of such unexpired term. A member of the Commission may be removed by the President for inefficiency, neglect of duty, or malfeasance in office.

[(c)](d) Principal office; hearings or other proceedings at other places. The principal office of the Commission shall be in the District of Columbia.

243

Figure 4.10
Citations to Decisions in the
U.S.C.S. (continued)

OCCUPATIONAL SAFETY AND HEALTH   29 USCS § 661, n 1

Law Review Articles:

Bangser, An Inherent Role for Cost-Benefit Analysis in Judicial Review of Agency Decisions: A New Perspective on OSHA Rulemaking. 10 Boston College Environmental Affairs L Rev 365, 1982.

Pleading and Practice Before the Occupational and Safety and Health Review Commission. 24 Labor LJ 779 (1973).

INTERPRETIVE NOTES AND DECISIONS

I. OSHRC

1. Judicial authority
2. Action by majority
3. Continuing jurisdiction of proceedings
4. Remand jurisdiction
5. Construction of rules and pleadings
6. Information subject to disclosure
7. Summary judgment
8. Evidence
9. Scope of review
10. —Final orders
11. —Constitutionality of Act
12. —Issues not raised before hearing examiner
13. —Withdrawal of citation
14. Assessment of attorneys' fees and costs
15. Disposition of proposed settlements
16. —Employee challenges
17. Statement of grounds for decision
18. Notice to respondent
19. Appearance in appellate court

II. ADMINISTRATIVE LAW JUDGE

20. Duties
21. Action after final disposition
22. Approval of settlement agreement
23. —Employee challenges
24. Enforcement of disclosure procedures
25. Order on withdrawal of notice of contest
26. Evidence
27. Acceptance of stipulations
28. When report is "made"
29. Required notice to respondent
30. Reopening hearing

I. OSHRC

1. Judicial authority

Commission's function is to act as a neutral arbiter and determine whether the Secretary's citations should be enforced over employee or union objections, and its authority does not extend to overturning the Secretary's decision not to issue or to withdraw a citation. Cuyahoga V.R. Co. v United Transp. Union (1985) 474 US 3, 88 L Ed 2d 2, 106 S Ct 286, on remand (CA6) 783 F2d 58.

Congress intended that occupational safety and health review commission would have nor-

mal complement of adjudicatory powers possessed by traditional administrative agencies such as Federal Trade Commission. Brennan v Gilles & Cotting, Inc. (1974, CA4) 504 F2d 1255, 27 ALR Fed 925 (disagreed with by Marshall v Sun Petroleum Products Co. (CA3) 622 F2d 1176) and (disagreed with by Marshall v Occupational Safety & Health Review Com. (CA6) 635 F2d 544) and (disagreed with by Oil, Chemical & Atomic Workers International Union v Occupational Safety & Health Review Com., 217 App DC 137, 671 F2d 643, 33 FR Serv 2d 1223, 65 ALR Fed 580) and (disagreed with by Donovan v A. Amorello & Sons, Inc. (CA1) 761 F2d 61) and (disagreed with by United Steelworkers of America, etc. v Schuylkill Metals Corp. (CA5) 828 F2d 314, 13 BNA OSHC 1393, 1987 CCH OSHD ¶ 28059) and (disagreed with by Re Perry (CA1) 882 F2d 534, 14 BNA OSHC 1113, 1989 CCH OSHD ¶ 28625).

Decision on general contractor's joint responsibility for subcontractors' workmen is vested in occupational safety and health review commission, guided by "economic realities" in interpreting terms "employer" and "employee" in manner to achieve statutory objectives. Brennan v Gilles & Cotting, Inc. (1974, CA4) 504 F2d 1255, 27 ALR Fed 925 (disagreed with on other grounds Marshall v Sun Petroleum Products Co. (CA3) 622 F2d 1176, cert den 449 US 1061, 66 L Ed 2d 604, 101 S Ct 784) and (disagreed with by Donovan v Oil, Chemical, etc. Local 4-23 (CA5) 718 F2d 1341) and (disagreed with by Donovan v United Transp. Union (CA6) 748 F2d 340) and (disagreed with by Marshall v Occupational Safety & Health Review Com. (CA6) 635 F2d 544) and (disagreed with by Oil, Chemical & Atomic Workers International Union v Occupational Safety & Health Review Com., 217 App DC 137, 671 F2d 643, 33 FR Serv 2d 1223, 65 ALR Fed 580) and (disagreed with by Donovan v A. Amorello & Sons, Inc. (CA1) 761 F2d 61) and (disagreed with by United Steelworkers of America, etc. v Schuylkill Metals Corp. (CA5) 828 F2d 314, 13 BNA OSHC 1393, 1987 CCH OSHD ¶ 28059) and (disagreed with by Re Perry (CA1) 882 F2d 534,

247

Federal Codes on Westlaw

You may prefer the convenience of accessing the codes on computer rather than searching in the printed materials. Fortunately, the federal statutes in codified form are available on Westlaw in the United States Code database (USC) and the United States Code Annotated database (USCA). To check the currentness of the statutes, use Scope. The statutes are current through a specific public law number.

You can retrieve the text of a code section by using the Find service with the citation to the code section. Click the **Find** button on the main button palette and type, for example, **20 usca 60** in the *Citation* text box. You can also access the USCA database and type **ci(20 +5 60)**; the "**+5**" is an instruction to the computer to locate *60* within five terms of *20*. If you are researching case law online and you see a citation to a code section, you can go directly to that section by clicking its citation. After reading the statutory language, you can return to the case by clicking the **Close Window** button on the main button palette.

Generally speaking, the bound codes have good print indexes, but at times those indexes just don't seem to have the access points that you had expected. Then a full-text search of the USC or USCA database on Westlaw can be especially helpful. Likewise, when you are searching for the interpretation of a particular word or phrase or want to see all of the occurrences of that word or phrase throughout the code, the print indexes may be of little use, and a Westlaw search will be essential.

State Codes

At times when you are using the federal codes, you will also need to refer to the state codes. For example, although most aspects of labor law are subject to extensive federal law, some matters are not covered by federal law but are regulated by comprehensive state statutes. For instance, federal law specifically covers picketing by employees during labor controversies, but many states have comprehensive statutes regulating violent conduct during picketing. It is this kind of link between federal law and state law that may lead you to compare the two.

Using Westlaw makes this research easier. You can begin by looking for the applicable federal law in the United States Code database (USC). As with case law research on Westlaw, you can use either the WIN Natural Language or the Terms and Connectors search method. Run the following Terms and Connectors query:

picket! & violen! crim! & employ! labor

This query retrieves several documents, including 18 U.S.C. § 1231 (Figure 4.11).

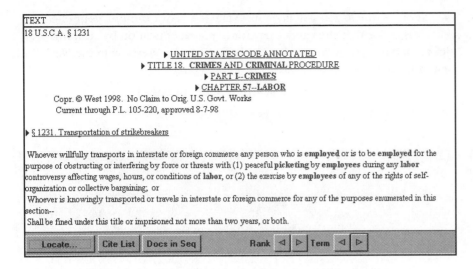

Figure 4.11
Document Retrieved Using the USC
Database

Next run the same search in the State Statutes–Unannotated database (STAT-ALL): click the **Change Database** button on the main button palette, select **Run query in different database** and type **stat-all** in the *New Database Identifier* text box. You will retrieve more than eighty documents from more than thirty states (Figure 4.12).

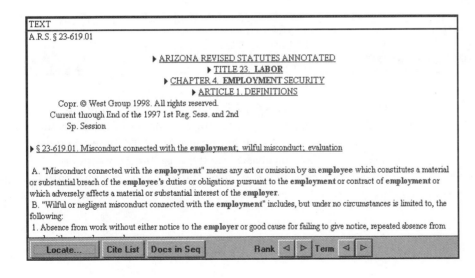

Figure 4.12
Document Retrieved Using the
STAT-ALL Database

At other times, you will need just state law. For example, your client feels it is unfair that she cannot pay for her legal education by scalping tickets at concerts. If you research this problem on Westlaw in the New York Statutes–Unannotated database (NY-ST) by typing

ticket /s scalp! resell! speculat!

you will retrieve statutes on this issue (Figure 4.13).

Figure 4.13
Retrieving a State Statute on
Westlaw

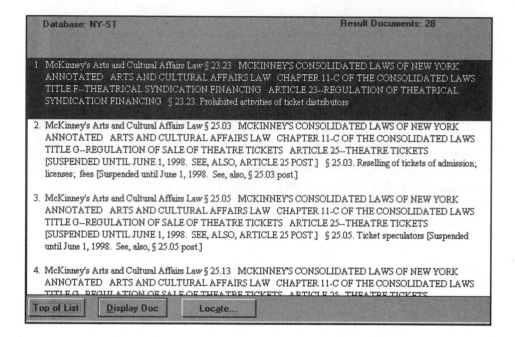

All state statutes can be searched on Westlaw in either an annotated or an unannotated database. If you want to see the summaries of the cases that interpret the statute, you should search in the annotated databases. You can also search in the unannotated databases and then use the Annotations service to retrieve the annotations. The unannotated databases focus on specific legislative terminology and narrow your search considerably.

When you search annotated statutory databases, it is most efficient to use a field restriction when you use the Terms and Connectors search method. The fields are the same for both the U.S.C.A. and the annotated state codes. When searching by subject, restrict your search to the prelim (pr) and caption (ca) fields. For example, type

pr,ca(ticket /s scalp! resell! speculat!)

in the NY-ST-ANN database. This restricts your search to the prelim field (which includes the title, subtitle, chapter, and subchapter headings of each section) and the caption field (which includes the section number, followed by terms that generally describe its contents). Figure 4.14 shows the result of your search.

In addition to searching laws from an individual state, you can search laws from many states simultaneously. Use either ST-ANN-ALL, for the annotated statutes from all states, or STAT-ALL, for the unannotated statutes from all states. For example, assume you are searching for legislation on the placement of smoke or heat detectors in hotels. To retrieve statutes from all states containing specific language on smoke detectors in hotels, access the STAT-ALL database and type

fire heat smok! /5 detect! & hotel motel lodg!
"public accommodation"

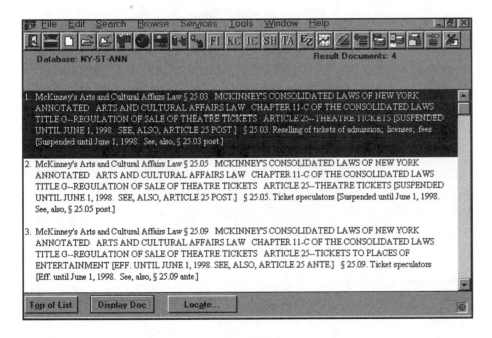

Figure 4.14
The Result of a Search Using the Prelim and Caption Fields

Figure 4.15
Documents Retrieved by
Searching All State
Statutes Simultaneously

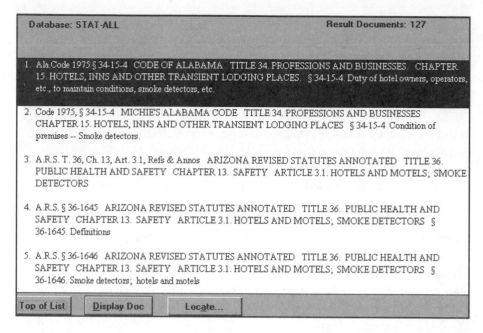

Figure 4.15 shows the result of your search. Once you have retrieved the statute you want, read the statute and use Documents in Sequence to view the documents following or preceding the displayed document (click the **Docs in Seq** button, then the **Doc** arrows).

Finally, remember that when you know a statute's citation, Find is the easiest method for retrieving the statute. Click the **Find** button and type, for example, **az st s 36–1646** in the *Citation* text box to retrieve section 36-1646 from *Arizona Revised Statutes Annotated*. Figure 4.16 shows the result of your search.

Figure 4.16
Retrieving a Statute When
You Know the Citation

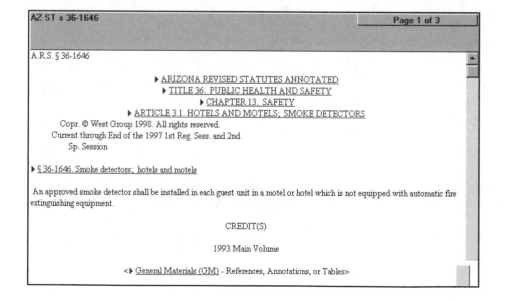

Print Publications

What we said earlier about the publication of federal legislation is also true for state legislation. Most states publish their statutes initially in a slip law format. Many states publish slip laws in the form of advance sheets, which are softbound supplements to a code. All states publish bound session laws. Most states publish a bound official code, and at least one annotated code is published for every state. Court rules and constitutions, along with the laws, are usually included in state codes. State codifications may be called codes, revisions, compilations, or consolidations, and their format and numbering systems will vary from state to state.

When you practice law, however, you will find that online access to the full text of state laws is an enormous advantage since your law firm is unlikely to have the codes from all of the states.

Updating State Statutes

Statutes databases are being added to or expanded all the time. On Westlaw, you can check Scope for current coverage information. You can also check the *Current through* line at the beginning of each statutory document.

The most important step in using state statutes on Westlaw, however, is using the Update service. This service allows you to quickly determine whether a statute or rule on Westlaw has been amended or repealed. When you retrieve a statute on Westlaw, it will contain an Update message if legislation amending or repealing it is available online. To display this legislation, click the *UPDATE* Jump marker in the message. Use the Update service to retrieve legislation that has been enacted after the last compilation of statutes in the statutes database. Eventually, material in the Update service is incorporated into the statutory databases. The Update service does not retrieve slip copy versions of laws or legislation enacting a new statute or covering a topic that will not be incorporated into the statutes. To retrieve these documents, run a search in a legislative service database.

The legislative service databases contain laws passed in the current or recent legislative sessions. These materials are eventually incorporated into the statutory databases. Legislative service databases are useful if you recently learned about a new law and want to view it online. We also recommend that you run searches you previously ran in a statutes database in a legislative service database to ensure that you have the most current information.

Constitutions

The U.S. Constitution is the foundation of our judicial system. As you will learn in your course on constitutional law, the wording of the U.S. Constitution is very general. Consequently, most of the law in this area has been made by the courts, especially by decisions of the U.S. Supreme Court. Finding the Constitution is easy and keeping up with the amendments is not a problem, but locating the cases can be a trial, no pun intended. You can locate the Constitution in the *U.S. Code* and as separate volumes of the two annotated versions, U.S.C.A. and U.S.C.S. The two annotated codes are perhaps the easiest way to find citations to cases that have interpreted the Constitution. Most parts have been interpreted so frequently, however, that you will need more help than the cases alone can provide. Fortunately, there are many other materials that you can use, including treatises, encyclopedias, and periodicals.

The U.S.C.A. provides extensive coverage by including annotations to both the federal and state decisions regarding each article or amendment to the Constitution. Over four thousand annotations to the Fourth Amendment alone are listed in the U.S.C.A. The digests, either the one devoted to the U.S. Supreme Court or the federal digests, will also prove useful in locating cases that interpret the Constitution.

Additionally, Westlaw can be useful in retrieving case law that interprets the Constitution. You can search by a particular section, by an amendment, or perhaps, by the citation combined with relevant terms. Westlaw also has specific First Amendment databases. For example, to obtain Supreme Court cases concerning a city's right to display religious scenes on public grounds, you can access the Federal First Amendment–Supreme Court Cases database (FCFA-SCT) and type a Terms and Connectors search such as

religio** nativity christmas hanukkah chanukah /s display scene

or, as a WIN search, you can simply ask

can a city display religious scenes on public grounds

These searches will retrieve cases, such as *County of Allegheny v. ACLU*, 492 U.S. 573, 109 S.Ct. 3086 (1989), that discuss the issue (Figure 4.17).

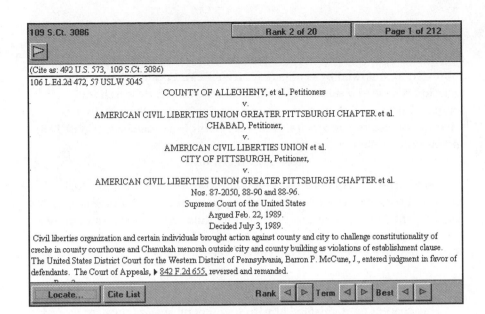

Figure 4.17
Retrieving Case Law That
Interprets the Constitution

State constitutions also have provisions that parallel the basic rights guaranteed by the U.S. Constitution. There is an interrelationship between the state and federal constitutions that protects all of us regardless of our residence. State constitutions can usually be found in the state codes. The constitutions for most states are available on Westlaw in the state statutes databases.

Court Rules

Court rules guide the operation of courts in solving legal controversies. Court rules typically cover such matters as court selection, action commencement, pleadings, discovery, jury selection, the trial, and the judgment. The various federal court rules may be found in a variety of practitioners' manuals, rules services, and formbooks. The two most accessible sources are the two annotated codes, U.S.C.A. and U.S.C.S. Both of these annotated codes have special volumes containing the federal court rules, including the Federal Rules of Civil Procedure, Criminal Procedure, Appellate Procedure, and Evidence. In the U.S.C.A., you will find these rules in special volumes accompanying Title 28, Judiciary and Judicial Procedure, and Title 18, Crimes and Criminal Procedure. These forms of statutory publication are crucial parts of the research process. You should come to understand how they are created and organized—they are the real world.

On Westlaw, the Federal Rules database (US-RULES) contains rules from the *United States Code Annotated*. State court rules are in the state rules databases. For an individual state, type the state's two-letter postal abbreviation, followed by **–rules** (e.g., **ny-rules**). You use the same techniques to search state rules databases that you use to search state statutes databases. For example, to retrieve California rules that discuss selecting a mediator, access the California Court Rules database (CA-RULES) and enter the following query:

select! /s mediator

Documents in Sequence is useful when you are viewing a rule that contains a reference to a nearby rule that you want to read. In the search result for the preceding query, for example, Rule 1633 contains a reference to Rule 1632. To view this rule, click the **Docs in Seq** button at the bottom of the window and then click the left **Doc** arrow twice.

Conclusion

This chapter has explained how to find federal laws as they are passed by Congress and then as they appear in a codified form. We discussed several titles and formats, including online databases, each of which is suited to a different purpose. We also discussed state legislative materials, with a special emphasis on state law on Westlaw. Once you have taken a few legislative courses, you will want to review this chapter since you may not have the opportunity to use federal or state legislative materials during your first year.

Administrative Law

Legislatures, including the U.S. Congress, pass broadly written laws that need to be enforced. To make such broad and often highly technical laws work, the legislature has to delegate some of its power to administrative agencies. These agencies, which are part of the executive/administrative branch of government, are responsible for writing specific rules and regulations (these terms have the same meaning) that enforce the statutes that are written by the legislatures. Think of the Federal Aviation Administration (FAA). Congress knows that it wants to enforce rules to govern air travel, but it also knows that it needs people with technical expertise to do it. Hence, Congress turns to the FAA.

Federal agencies regulate key areas of the economy: communications (Federal Communications Commission), the securities markets (Securities and Exchange Commission), labor relations (National Labor Relations Board), competitive trade practices (Federal Trade Commission), etc. The regulations issued by these agencies are just as binding as statutes and, from a practical viewpoint, affect the lives of everyone. A violation of a regulation may be as serious as a violation of a statute.

In addition to writing rules and regulations, agencies conduct hearings and issue orders, licenses, and advisory opinions. These functions are called *quasi-judicial* because the administrative agencies act like courts. If you take a course in administrative law, you will learn the procedures through which the government officials exercise their power and the checks the other branches of government have on the administrative branch.

We are concerned here not so much with procedure as with what the agencies do, an aspect of the law that is often ignored in law school. In this chapter, we will try to give you a brief look at administrative materials. We will examine the materials of federal agencies, their rules that implement legislation, and their power to adjudicate disputes concerning parties they regulate. The president's lawmaking actions will also be noted. State materials will be discussed briefly at the end of the chapter.

The *Federal Register* in Print Format

The U.S. Government Printing Office issues two publications that provide you with federal administrative regulations: the daily *Federal Register*

Figure 5.1
The *Federal Register*

and the annual *Code of Federal Regulations*. You need to understand both publications as well as the relationship between the two. In our examination of these publications, we will discuss both the print versions and the online versions.

Federal regulations are published chronologically in the *Federal Register* (Fed. Reg.) on a daily basis (Figure 5.1). In addition to publishing rules and regulations, the *Federal Register* publishes presidential documents, that is, presidential proclamations and executive orders. The *Federal Register* also publishes proposed rules. People are given the opportunity to comment on these proposed regulations before they are either adopted or rejected by federal agencies. The largest section of the *Federal Register* is the notice section, which contains information about agencies including orders, opinions, agency changes, and notices of meetings. The *Federal Register* may fill as many as fifty thousand pages a year. It will look boring and confusing at first, but if you practice law in a heavily regulated area, you will come to realize its utility.

Because the *Federal Register* (published since 1936) consumes an enormous amount of shelf space, you will be able to find it with ease in your library. Its size and fineness of print are reminiscent of a big city telephone directory. Because of its size and its newsprint paper, many libraries have the historical volumes of the *Federal Register* on microfiche.

The *Code of Federal Regulations* in Print Format

Figure 5.2
The *Code of Federal Regulations*

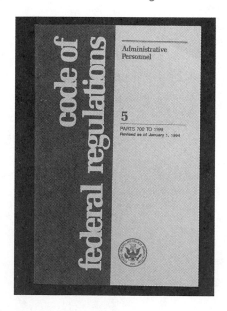

The same regulations that appear in the *Federal Register* are arranged by subject in the *Code of Federal Regulations* or C.F.R. (Figure 5.2). The C.F.R. includes only regulations that are currently in force. The entire C.F.R. is recompiled annually with any new amendments added. Regulations that have been withdrawn are deleted. If a proposed regulation is never adopted, it will not appear in the C.F.R.—it will only appear as a proposed regulation in the *Federal Register*.

The C.F.R. is organized by title, each of which represents a broad topic. Therefore, when you need to find all the federal regulations on electronic banking, you will look in the C.F.R. because it is arranged by subject. You will find that electronic banking is included in Title 12, which is dedicated to banking regulations. Using the *Federal Register* to find all of the regulations on a particular subject would be extremely difficult and time-consuming because the *Federal Register* is arranged chronologically. Therefore, you would have to search through approximately sixty years of the publication, page by page.

Within each title of the C.F.R., regulations are divided into chapters, each of which is devoted to the regulations of a particular agency. The chapters are further divided into parts, consisting of a body of regulations on a particular topic or agency function. Parts are divided into sections, the basic unit of the C.F.R., and, if further breakdown is necessary, into paragraphs (Figure 5.3).

Figure 5.3
The Organization of the C.F.R.

Federal Reserve System — Agency (and Chapter Heading)

Part 205

(g) *Reciprocal arrangements.* Finally, while a depository institution may enter into an arrangement with an unaffiliated third party wherein the third party agrees to stand ready to purchase time deposits held by the depository institution's customers, the Board will regard a reciprocal arrangement with another depository institution for purchase of each other's time deposits as a circumvention of the early withdrawal penalty rule and the purposes it is designed to serve.

[52 FR 47697, Dec. 16, 1987]

§ 204.132 **Treatment of Loan Strip Participations.**

(a) Effective March 31, 1988, the glossary section of the instructions for the Report of Condition and Income (FFIEC 031-034; OMB No. 7100-0036; available from a depository institution's primary federal regulator) ("Call Report") was amended to clarify that certain short-term loan participation arrangements (sometimes known or styled as "loan strips" or "strip participations") are regarded as borrowings rather than sales for Call Report purposes in certain circumstances. Through this interpretation, the Board is clarifying that such transactions should be treated as deposits for purposes of Regulation D.

(b) These transactions involve the sale (or placement) of a short-term loan by a depository institution that has been made under a long-term commitment of the depository institution to advance funds. For example, a 90-day loan made under a five-year revolving line of credit may be sold to or placed with a third party by the depository institution originating the loan. The depository institution originating the loan is obligated to renew the 90-day note itself (by advancing funds to its customer at the end of the 90-day period) in the event the original participant does not wish to renew the credit. Since, under these arrangements, the depository institution is obligated to make another loan at the end of 90 days (absent any event of default on the part of the borrower), the depository institution selling the loan or participation in effect must buy back the loan or participation at the maturity of the 90-day loan sold to or

funded by the purchaser at the option of the purchaser. Accordingly, these transactions bear the essential characteristics of a repurchase agreement and, therefore, are reportable and reservable under Regulation D.

(c) Because many of these transactions give rise to deposit liabilities in the form of promissory notes, acknowledgments of advance or similar obligations (written or oral) as described in § 204.2(a)(1)(vii) of Regulation D, the exemptions from the definition of "deposit" incorporated in that section may apply to the liability incurred by a depository institution when it offers or originates a loan strip facility. Thus, for example, loan strips sold to domestic offices of other depository institutions are exempt from Regulation D under § 204.2(a)(1)(vii)(A)(*1*) because they are obligations issued or undertaken and held for the account of a U.S. office of another depository institution. Similarly, some of these transactions result in Eurocurrency liabilities and are reportable and reservable as such.

[53 FR 24931, July 1, 1988]

PART 205—ELECTRONIC FUND TRANSFERS — Part

Sec. — Section
205.1 Authority, purpose, and scope.
205.2 Definitions and rules of construction.
205.3 Exemptions.
205.4 Special requirements.
205.5 Issuance of access devices.
205.6 Liability of consumer for unauthorized transfers.
205.7 Initial disclosure of terms and conditions.
205.8 Change in terms; error resolution notice.
205.9 Documentation of transfers.
205.10 Preauthorized transfers.
205.11 Procedures for resolving errors.
205.12 Relation to State law.
205.13 Administrative enforcement.
205.14 Services offered by financial institutions not holding consumer's account.

Appendix A—Model Disclosure Clauses

Supplements I and II—Official Staff Interpretations

Authority: Pub. L. 95-630, 92 Stat. 3730 (15 U.S.C. 1693b). — Authority Note

107

Prefacing each part of the C.F.R. are notes provided by the agency that outline the statutory (legislative) authority under which the regulations are issued. Remember that regulations are adopted to implement specific pieces of legislation. The *authority note* is useful when you want to trace the

Figure 5.4
Authority and Source Notes in
the C.F.R.

Authority Note

Source Note

§ 205.1   12 CFR Ch. II (1-1-90 Edition)

§ 205.1 Authority, purpose, and scope.

(a) *Authority.* This regulation, issued by the Board of Governors of the Federal Reserve System, implements title IX (Electronic Fund Transfer Act) of the Consumer Credit Protection Act, as amended (15 U.S.C. 1601 *et seq.*).

(b) *Purpose and scope.* In November 1978, the Congress enacted the Electronic Fund Transfer Act. The Congress found that the use of electronic systems to transfer funds provides the potential for substantial benefits to consumers, but that the unique characteristics of these systems make the application of existing consumer protection laws unclear, leaving the rights and liabilities of users of electronic fund transfer systems undefined. The Act establishes the basic rights, liabilities, and responsibilities of consumers who use electronic money transfer services and of financial institutions that offer these services. This regulation is intended to carry out the purposes of the Act, including, primarily, the protection of individual consumers engaging in electronic transfers. Except as otherwise provided, this regulation applies to all persons who are financial institutions as defined in § 205.2(i).

(Information collection requirements contained in this regulation have been approved by the Office of Management and Budget under the provisions of 44 U.S.C. 3501 *et seq.* and have been assigned OMB number 7100-0200)

[44 FR 18480, Mar. 28, 1979, as amended at 49 FR 40797, Oct. 18, 1984]

§ 205.2 Definitions and rules of construction.

For the purposes of this regulation, the following definitions apply, unless the context indicates otherwise:

(a)(1) "Access device" means a card, code, or other means of access to a consumer's account, or any combination thereof, that may be used by the consumer for the purpose of initiating electronic fund transfers.

(2) An access device becomes an "accepted access device" when the consumer to whom the access device was issued:

(i) Requests and receives, or signs, or uses, or authorizes another to use, the access device for the purpose of transferring money between accounts or obtaining money, property, labor or services;

(ii) Requests validation of an access device issued on an unsolicited basis; or

(iii) Receives an access device issued in renewal of, or in substitution for, an accepted access device, whether such access device is issued by the initial financial institution or a successor.

(b) "Account" means a demand deposit (checking), savings, or other consumer asset account (other than an occasional or incidental credit balance in a credit plan) held either directly or indirectly by a financial institution and established primarily for personal, family, or household purposes.

(c) "Act" means the Electronic Fund Transfer Act (Title IX of the Consumer Credit Protection Act, 15 U.S.C. 1601 et seq.).

(d) "Business day" means any day on which the offices of the consumer's financial institution are open to the public for carrying on substantially all business functions.

(e) "Consumer" means a natural person.

(f) "Credit" means the right granted by a financial institution to a consumer to defer payment of debt, incur debt and defer its payment, or purchase property or services and defer payment therefor.

(g) "Electronic fund transfer" means any transfer of funds, other than a transaction originated by check, draft, or similar paper instrument, that is initiated through an electronic terminal, telephone, or computer or magnetic tape for the purpose of ordering, instructing, or authorizing a financial institution to debit or credit an account. The term includes, but is not limited to, point-of-sale transfers, automated teller machine transfers, direct deposits or withdrawals of funds, and transfers initiated by telephone. It includes all transfers resulting from debit card transactions, including those that do not involve an electronic terminal at the time of the transaction. The term does not include payments made by check, draft, or similar paper instrument at an electronic terminal.

108

regulation back to its statutory authority. A *source note,* which lists the volume, page, and date of the *Federal Register* in which the regulation was published, follows the authority note (Figure 5.4). These two notes make up the administrative history of the regulation.

The C.F.R. is published each year in four installments as follows:

- Title 1 through Title 16—through January 1
- Title 17 through Title 27—through April 1
- Title 28 through Title 41—through July 1
- Title 42 through Title 50—through October 1

Because of these staggered dates, you must be careful to check the soft-bound cover of each title to determine the date of revision.

Fortunately, the U.S. Government Printing Office uses distinct colors for the covers of the C.F.R.—for example, 1995 is green, 1996 blue, 1997 magenta, and 1998 brown. These boldly colored covers make it easy for you to see whether you have the correct year.

Finding Regulations in the Print Version of the *Federal Register* and the C.F.R.

Obviously, the easiest way to find a regulation is to get the citation to the *Federal Register* or the C.F.R. from a secondary source, such as a law review article. If you do not already have the *Federal Register* or the C.F.R. citation, you can either use the print indexes or access Westlaw. The *Federal Register* has its own index. Each daily index contains a table of contents arranged by agency. There are also monthly and quarterly indexes and an annual index. These indexes are set up primarily by agency rather than by subject (Figure 5.5).

The C.F.R. publishes a single volume called *Index and Finding Aids,* which is revised once a year. However, this index suffers from several shortcomings—the main one being that it is not really a subject index. It is basically an agency index with a few subject terms interspersed (Figure 5.6).

To see how the index works, consider the following situation: Assume that your client, Jim, bought a car from a dealer. The first time Jim washed his car, some of the paint rubbed off. Upon closer inspection, Jim discovered that the car had been in a wreck and had been painted to conceal the damage. Armed with a signed statement that the car was free from defect, Jim stormed into the dealer's office. The dealer claimed that she did not know that the car had been damaged. Furthermore, the dealer told Jim that since he did not receive a written warranty, he was out of luck.

Will a federal agency be able to help with this problem? To find out, you would look in the *Index and Finding Aids* under the subject Warranties. (If you were aware that the Federal Trade Commission is involved with warranties, you could look under that agency.) Looking under Warranties leads you to the Magnuson-Moss Warranty Act, which then refers you to 16 C.F.R. § 700 (Figure 5.7).

Fortunately for Jim, under section 700.3(a) is a footnote stating that "a 'written warranty' is also created by a written affirmation of fact or a written

Figure 5.5
The *Federal Register* Index

NIH

NOTICES
Auto theft and comprehensive insurance premiums, Federal regulation; public review and comment on report, 30786
Fuel economy program, automotive; annual report to Congress, 11484
Fuel economy standards; exemption petitions, etc.:
Officine Alfieri Maserati, S.p.A., 22879, 25767
Grants and cooperative agreements; availability, etc.:
National occupant protection and impaired driving prevention programs, 7622
School bus safety projects; assistance to States, 32554
School bus safety; State matching of planning and administration costs, 40975
Highway safety analysis; police traffic accident reports; critical automated data reporting elements; list, 18220, 27327
Highway safety program; breath alcohol testing devices:
Evidential devices; model specifications and conforming products list, 6865, 32343
Highway traffic safety improvement; priority plan 1990-1992; availability, 47824
Meetings:
International Harmonization of Safety Standards, 13690
Motor Vehicle Safety Research Advisory Committee, 1764; 34639, 43060
National Driver Register Advisory Committee, 15096, 38186
Rulemaking, research, and enforcement programs, 9818, 25920, 40977, 41782
Motor vehicle defect proceedings; petitions, etc.:
Center for Auto Safety, 10570
Ditlow, Clarence M., III, 21140
Faircloth, Harvey G., et al., 6865
Fujimori, Warren W.T., 47600
Institute for Injury Reduction, Public Citizen, et al., 42144
Jarvis, Brian, 17348
Rand, M. Kristen, 42301
Roupinian, Paul, 21140
Skreba, Leonard T., 30072
Stewart, Gloria Jean, 20674
Sweeney, Harry M., 20382
Toyota Motor Co., 17349
Motor vehicle safety standards:
Nonconforming vehicles—
Final determinations, 32988
Importation eligibility; tentative determinations, 17518, 47418
Rear seat lap/shoulder belt retrofit kits, 35241
Motor vehicle safety standards; exemption petitions, etc.:
Automobiles Peugeot, 20382
Bridgestone (U.S.A.) Inc., 3297, 12617
Budd Co., 8632
Cadillac Plastic & Chemical Co., 11497, 28340
Cantab Motors, 11714, 21141
Consulier Industries, Inc., 5712, 12982
Cooper Tire & Rubber Co., 47823
Ferrari S.p.A., 3785
General Motors Corp., 21297, 34639, 40977
Goodyear Tire & Rubber Co., 2915
Hella, Inc., 37601
Marmon Motor Co., 7404
Mazda Motor Corp., 7404

Agency —

Mazda Motor Corp. of Japan, 28341
Mazda Research & Development of North America, Inc., 26528, 49365
Officine Alfieri Maserati S.p.A., 78, 7405
Supreme Corp., Inc., 38186
Takata-Gerico Corp., 28341
Uniroyal Goodrich Tire Co., 40506
Motor vehicle theft prevention standard; exemption petitions, etc.:
American Honda Motor Co., Inc., 4746, 22004, 46126
General Motors Corp., 17854
New car assessment program:
Crash test results and analysis; deformable moving barrier, 40595
Passenger motor vehicle theft data, 7406, 18794, 41149

National Institute for Occupational Safety and Health

See Centers for Disease Control

National Institute of Corrections

NOTICES
Grants and cooperative agreements; availability, etc.:
Program plan/academy training schedule (1991 FY), 32980
Meetings:
Advisory Board, 5086, 24672, 39747

National Institute of Justice

NOTICES
Body armor users workshop, 17681
Drug program evaluations; special initiative, 7387
Grants and cooperative agreements; availability, etc.:
Boot camps for juvenile offenders; constructive intervention and early support, 28718, 32980
Discretionary programs (1990 FY), 10146
Technology assessment program information center, 31908

National Institute of Standards and Technology

RULES
Manufacturing technology transfer; regional centers establishment transfer, 38274
Organization, functions, and authority delegations:
National Institute of Standards and Technology, 38314
PROPOSED RULES
Manufacturing technology transfer; centers establishment transfer, 18124
NOTICES
Grants and cooperative agreements; availability, etc.:
Advanced structural ceramics, 20620
Fire research program, 29877
Manufacturing technology transfer; regional centers, 38280
Precision measurement program, 48665
Standard reference data program, 47789
Information processing standards, Federal:
COBOL, 1243, 2733
Computer output microform formats and reduction ratios, 7516, 9824
Database language SQL, 3627
Electronic data interchange (EDI), 28274, 29146

Family of input/output interface standards, 10272
Government Open Systems Interconnection Profile (GOSIP), 27666, 32451
Graphical kernel system (GKS), 10273, 12444
Interface between data terminal equipment (DTE) and data circuit-terminating equipment (DOE) for operation with packet-switched data networks, or between two DTEs by dedicated circuit, 10276
POSIX; portable operating system interface for computer environments, 11424, 12778, 23959
POSIX shell and utility application interface for computer operating system environments, 23959
Programming language C, 19768
Programming language MUMPS, 10278
Laboratory Accreditation Program, National Voluntary:
Airborne asbestos analysis, 38734
Directory of accredited laboratories; supplement, 32452
Meetings:
Advanced Technology Visiting Committee, 5644, 7019, 23455, 27667, 33948, 47504
Broadband Integrated Services Digital Network (B-ISDN) users and implementors workshop, 5046
Computer courseware standards, architectural proposals; discussion, 20620
Computer System Security and Privacy Advisory Board, 5045, 32452, 46093
Eighth North American ISDN Users' Forum, 5046
FORTRAN programming language standard test suit; workshop, 6676
Intergrated Services Digital Network (ISDN) users and implementors workshop, 27668
International Laboratory Accreditation Conference, 33741
International standards activities, U.S. participation, 12252
Malcolm Baldrige National Quality Award's Board of Overseers, 49558
Malcolm Baldrige National Quality Award's Panel of Judges, 6035, 23456, 28080, 33948, 49325
OSI Implementors workshop, 2256
Weights and Measures National Conference, 1245, 27294
National Fire Codes:
Fire safety standards, 3991, 32679
Technical committee reports, 3991, 32678
Senior Executive Service:
General and Limited Performance Review Boards; membership, 29878

National Institutes of Health

NOTICES
Committees; establishment, renewal, termination, etc.:
AIDS and Related Research Study Sections et al., 2705
American Stop Smoking Intervention Study (ASSIST) Committee, 40945
Biological and Clinical Aging Review Committee et al., 15021
Genome Research Review Committee, 26265
Human Genome Research National Advisory Council, 17309

January—November 1990, FEDERAL REGISTER INDEX

95

promise that the product is defect free." It appears that he is not out of luck.

Commercial indexes are also available that are vastly superior to those of the C.F.R. and the *Federal Register*. Congressional Information Service has published an *Index to the Code of Federal Regulations* since 1981 and a *Federal Register Index* since 1984. With these publications, you can locate regulations by subject, agency, industry, geographic area, or authorizing legislation.

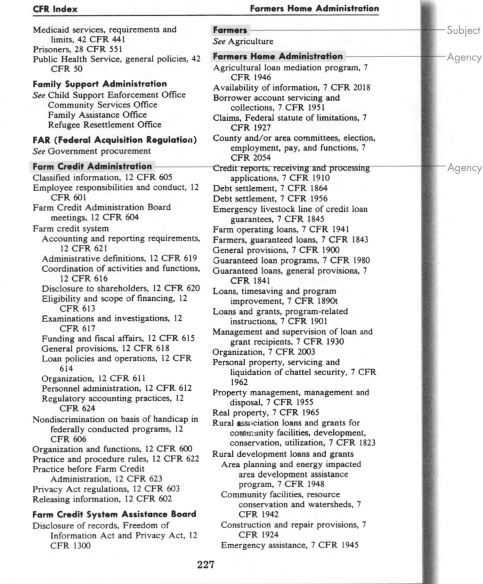

Figure 5.6
The C.F.R. *Index and Finding Aids*

CFR Index

Medicaid services, requirements and
    limits, 42 CFR 441
Prisoners, 28 CFR 551
Public Health Service, general policies, 42
    CFR 50

Family Support Administration
See Child Support Enforcement Office
    Community Services Office
    Family Assistance Office
    Refugee Resettlement Office

FAR (Federal Acquisition Regulation)
See Government procurement

Farm Credit Administration ———————— Subject
Classified information, 12 CFR 605
Employee responsibilities and conduct, 12
    CFR 601
Farm Credit Administration Board
    meetings, 12 CFR 604
Farm credit system
    Accounting and reporting requirements,
        12 CFR 621
    Administrative definitions, 12 CFR 619
    Coordination of activities and functions,
        12 CFR 616
    Disclosure to shareholders, 12 CFR 620
    Eligibility and scope of financing, 12
        CFR 613
    Examinations and investigations, 12
        CFR 617
    Funding and fiscal affairs, 12 CFR 615
    General provisions, 12 CFR 618
    Loan policies and operations, 12 CFR
        614
    Organization, 12 CFR 611
    Personnel administration, 12 CFR 612
    Regulatory accounting practices, 12
        CFR 624
Nondiscrimination on basis of handicap in
    federally conducted programs, 12
    CFR 606
Organization and functions, 12 CFR 600
Practice and procedure rules, 12 CFR 622
Practice before Farm Credit
    Administration, 12 CFR 623
Privacy Act regulations, 12 CFR 603
Releasing information, 12 CFR 602

Farm Credit System Assistance Board
Disclosure of records, Freedom of
    Information Act and Privacy Act, 12
    CFR 1300

Farmers Home Administration

Farmers ———————————————— Agency
See Agriculture

Farmers Home Administration
Agricultural loan mediation program, 7
    CFR 1946
Availability of information, 7 CFR 2018
Borrower account servicing and
    collections, 7 CFR 1951
Claims, Federal statute of limitations, 7
    CFR 1927
County and/or area committees, election,
    employment, pay, and functions, 7
    CFR 2054
Credit reports, receiving and processing ——— Agency
    applications, 7 CFR 1910
Debt settlement, 7 CFR 1864
Debt settlement, 7 CFR 1956
Emergency livestock line of credit loan
    guarantees, 7 CFR 1845
Farm operating loans, 7 CFR 1941
Farmers, guaranteed loans, 7 CFR 1843
General provisions, 7 CFR 1900
Guaranteed loan programs, 7 CFR 1980
Guaranteed loans, general provisions, 7
    CFR 1841
Loans, timesaving and program
    improvement, 7 CFR 1890t
Loans and grants, program-related
    instructions, 7 CFR 1901
Management and supervision of loan and
    grant recipients, 7 CFR 1930
Organization, 7 CFR 2003
Personal property, servicing and
    liquidation of chattel security, 7 CFR
    1962
Property management, management and
    disposal, 7 CFR 1955
Real property, 7 CFR 1965
Rural association loans and grants for
    community facilities, development,
    conservation, utilization, 7 CFR 1823
Rural development loans and grants
    Area planning and energy impacted
        area development assistance
        program, 7 CFR 1948
    Community facilities, resource
        conservation and watersheds, 7
        CFR 1942
    Construction and repair provisions, 7
        CFR 1924
    Emergency assistance, 7 CFR 1945

227

You may recall that in our discussion of the federal annotated codes in Chapter 4, we noted that both U.S.C.A. and U.S.C.S. list citations to the C.F.R. in the annotations after each section. Actually, if you are already working with a federal law, the easiest way to locate the regulations that will implement the law is to use one of the annotated codes. For example, the federal laws on warranties can be located in 15 U.S.C.A. § 2301. This section of the U.S.C.A. refers you to the governing regulations in 16 C.F.R. § 700.1 (Figure 5.8).

Figure 5.7
Using the C.F.R. *Index and Finding Aids*

Look Under Warranties ———

Find the Magnuson-Moss Warranty Act ———

16 C.F.R. § 700 ———

CFR Index	Waste treatment and disposal

Tobacco products and cigarette papers and tubes
  Exportation without payment of tax or with drawback of tax, 27 CFR 290
  Importation, 27 CFR 275
Wholesaling and warehousing industry in Puerto Rico, 29 CFR 683
Wine production and sales, 27 CFR 240

Warranties
Acquisition regulations
  Agriculture Department, 48 CFR 446
  Defense Department, 48 CFR 246
  Environmental Protection Agency, 48 CFR 1546
  General Services Administration, 48 CFR 546
  National Aeronautics and Space Administration, 48 CFR 1846
  State Department, 48 CFR 646
  Transportation Department, 48 CFR 1246
  United States Information Agency, quality assurance, 48 CFR 1946
Advertising of warranties and guarantees, guides, 16 CFR 239
Federal Acquisition Regulation, quality assurance, 48 CFR 46
Flammable Fabrics Act
  Flammability standards, clothing textiles, 16 CFR 1610
  General rules and regulations, 16 CFR 1608
Fur Products Labeling Act, rules and regulations, 16 CFR 301
Magnuson-Moss Warranty Act
  Informal dispute settlement procedures, 16 CFR 703
  Interpretations, 16 CFR 700
  Pre-sale availability of written warranty terms, 16 CFR 702
  Written consumer product warranty terms and conditions, disclosure, 16 CFR 701
Manufactured home consumer manual requirements, 24 CFR 3283
Motor vehicles and motor vehicle engines, air pollution control, 40 CFR 85
Textile Fiber Products Identification Act, rules and regulations, 16 CFR 303
Wool Products Labeling Act of 1939, rules and regulations, 16 CFR 300

Washington, D. C.
See District of Columbia

Waste treatment and disposal
See also Hazardous waste
      Recycling
      Sewage disposal
Air pollution control, performance standards for incinerators, 40 CFR 60
Alcohol fuels, biomass energy and municipal waste projects, loan guarantees for energy projects, 10 CFR 799
Army Department, environmental protection and enhancement, 32 CFR 650
Grants, State and local assistance, 40 CFR 35
Mines Bureau grant programs, procedures for solid waste disposal grants, 30 CFR 651
National Environmental Policy Act, Council on Environmental Quality requirements procedures implementation, 40 CFR 6
Panama Canal, sanitary requirements, vessel wastes, garbage, ballast, 35 CFR 125
Rural development loans, community facilities, resource conservation and watersheds, 7 CFR 1942
Solid wastes
  Citizen suits, prior notice, 40 CFR 254
  Criteria for classification of solid waste disposal facilities and practices, 40 CFR 257
  Identification of regions and agencies for solid waste management, 40 CFR 255
  Land disposal guidelines, 40 CFR 241
  Medical waste, standards for tracking and management, 40 CFR 259
  National pollutant discharge elimination system, criteria and standards, 40 CFR 125
  Residential, commercial, and institutional solid wastes, source separation for materials recovery guidelines, 40 CFR 246
  Residential, commercial, and institutional solid wastes, storage and collection guidelines, 40 CFR 243

753

If you are not using the U.S.C.A., you can check the C.F.R. *Index and Finding Aids* for its useful Parallel Table of Authorities and Rules. This table allows you to locate the C.F.R. citation if you already have the U.S.C. citation (Figure 5.9).

Figure 5.8
Finding Citations to the C.F.R.
in the U.S.C.A.

COMMERCE AND TRADE

15 § 2301
Note 1a

CHAPTER 50—CONSUMER PRODUCT WARRANTIES

LAW REVIEW COMMENTARIES

Concept of warranty duration: A tangled web. Max E. Klinger, 89 Dick.L.Rev. 935 (1985).

Effect of warranty disclaimers on revocation of acceptance under the Uniform Commercial Code. Manning Gilbert Warren III and Michelle Rowe, 37 Ala.L.Rev. 307 (1986).

New Mexico's "Lemon Law": Consumer protection or consumer frustration? Joseph Goldberg, 16 New Mexico L.Rev. 251 (1986).

Overview of the Magnuson–Moss Warranty Act and the successful consumer-plaintiff's right to attorneys' fees. Robert A. Riegert, 95 Com. L.J. 468 (1990).

§ 2301. Definitions

FEDERAL PRACTICE AND PROCEDURE

Jurisdictional amount in controversy, see Wright, Miller & Cooper: Jurisdiction § 3701 et seq.

CODE OF FEDERAL REGULATIONS

Interpretations, see 16 CFR 700.1. ——————————————— C.F.R. Citation

LAW REVIEW COMMENTARIES

A comparative analysis of three lemon laws. Anne V. Swanson, 75 Ill.B.J. 436 (1987).

An informal resolution model of consumer product warranty law. Jean Braucher, Wis. L.Rev. 1405 (1985).

Beyond the Uniform Code. Gerald T. McLaughlin and Neil B. Cohen, 210 N.Y.L.J. 3 (Dec. 8, 1993).

Consumer leases under Uniform Commercial Code Article 2A. Fred H. Miller, 39 Ala.L.Rev. 957 (1988).

Examining restraints on freedom to contract as an approach to purchaser dissatisfaction in the computer industry. Comment, 74 Cal. L.Rev. 2101 (1986).

Illinois lemon car buyer's options in a breach of warranty action. Lisa K. Jorgenson, 20 John Marshall L.Rev. 483 (1987).

Implied warranty and the Used Car Rule. Comment, 46 La.L.Rev. 1239 (1986).

Is revision due for Article 2? Fairfax Leary, Jr. and David Frisch, 31 Vill.L.Rev. 399 (1986).

Legislative responses to plight of new car purchasers. Richard L. Coffinberger and Linda B. Samuels, 18 UCC L.J. 168 (1985).

Product quality laws and the economics of federalism. David A. Rice (1985) 65 Boston U.L.Rev. 1.

Seller beware: Computer buyers' theories of liability. Marc S. Friedman and Mary J. Hildebrand, 120 N.J.L.J. 389 (1987).

Squeezing consumers: Lemon law, consumer warranties, and a proposal for reform. Joan Vogel, Ariz.State L.J. 1985, p. 589.

NOTES OF DECISIONS

Commercial buyer 7
Consumer 3
Normally 5
Purposes of resale 6
Service contract 4a
State regulation or control 1a
Supplier 8
Written warranty 4

---

1. Law governing

If state law requires vertical privity to enforce an implied warranty and there is none, there can be no recovery under this chapter. Feinstein v. Firestone Tire and Rubber Co., D.C.N.Y.1982, 535 F.Supp. 595.

Under this chapter, it is state law which governs arising of implied warranty against supplier. Miller Auto Leasing Co. v. Weinstein, 1983, 461 A.2d 174, 189 N.J.Super. 543, affirmed 473 A.2d 996, 193 N.J.Super. 328, certification denied 483 A.2d 192, 97 N.J. 676.

1a. State regulation or control

Sections of Minnesota's "lemon law" requiring automobile manufacturers to participate in informal dispute resolution, including oral hearings at consumer's option, and permitting charge to consumers for their use was not preempted by Magnuson-Moss Warranty Act, where Congress intended state regulation to operate with Warranty Act in mutually supplementary manner, compliance with both Minnesota law and federal law was possible, and compliance with Minnesota law did not frustrate purposes of federal law. Automobile Importers of America, Inc. v. State of Minn., C.A.8 (Minn.) 1989, 871 F.2d 717, certiorari denied 110 S.Ct. 201, 493 U.S. 872, 107 L.Ed.2d 154, dissenting opinion 110 S.Ct. 261, 493 U.S. 901, 107 L.Ed.2d 210, rehearing denied 110 S.Ct. 1515, 494 U.S. 1050, 108 L.Ed.2d 651.

Magnuson-Moss Act authorization of attorney fees to prevailing plaintiffs did not preempt state statutes allowing for attorneys fees to prevailing parties including defendants. Deadwyler v. Volkswagen of America, Inc., W.D.N.C.1990,

Figure 5.9
The C.F.R. Parallel Table of
Authorities and Rules

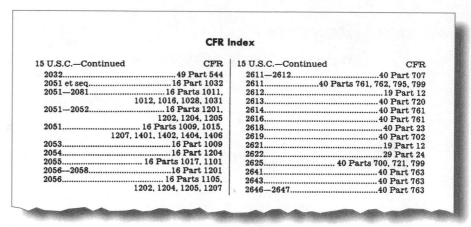

U.S.C. Citation ——

C.F.R. Citation ——

Finding Regulations on Westlaw

Fortunately, the full text of the *Federal Register* and the C.F.R. are on Westlaw and other online services. On Westlaw, the *Federal Register* is in the Federal Register database (FR), and the C.F.R. is in the Code of Federal Regulations database (CFR).

The FR database on Westlaw dates from July 1980. The full text of *Federal Register* documents are generally available online on the day of publication. You would use the FR database when you are looking for recent documents, ones that are not yet included in the CFR database.* For example, in an area such as rule making by the Environmental Protection Agency, which promulgates rules on almost a daily basis, you would want to search the daily FR database. Type

**"environmental protection agency" & "final rule"
& da(aft 2/2/1999)**

*The CFR database on Westlaw is more current than the print version. Check the *Current through* date at the Query Editor or in Scope.

and you will retrieve documents in the *Federal Register* issued after the *Current through* date for the CFR database, e.g., February 2, 1999. You may also format a search in the FR database using Natural Language.

You would also use the FR database to search for material that is not included in the C.F.R., such as proposed regulations (those never adopted by an agency) and agency notices. For example, suppose you want to locate the Department of Transportation's proposed rule of June 13, 1986, dealing with replacement lighting equipment. Because this proposed rule was never adopted, it will only appear in the *Federal Register*. Figure 5.10 shows the result of the following search in the FR database:

replac! /p light! & da(6/13/1986)

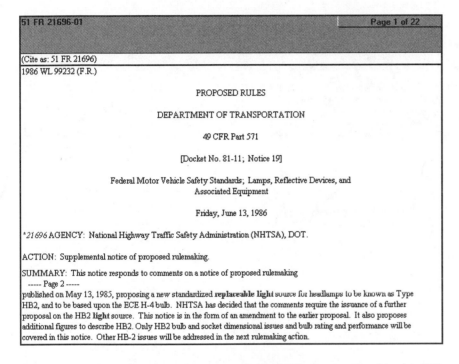

Figure 5.10
Finding a Proposed Regulation
on Westlaw

On Westlaw, the current version of the C.F.R. is contained in the CFR database. To illustrate how you can search this database, let us return to our warranty problem involving the car that was painted to conceal the damage. Access the CFR database and type the following Terms and Connectors query:

magnuson-moss & writ! /s warrant!

(As with the Federal Register database, the CFR database can also be searched with Natural Language.) This query retrieves twenty-two documents. Click the **Cite List** button to view a list of document citations. While scanning the list, you can read the applicable regulation, "700.3 Written warranty," by highlighting its entry in the list and clicking the **Display Doc** button (Figure 5.11).

Figure 5.11
Searching the CFR
Database on Westlaw

(a) List of Document Citations

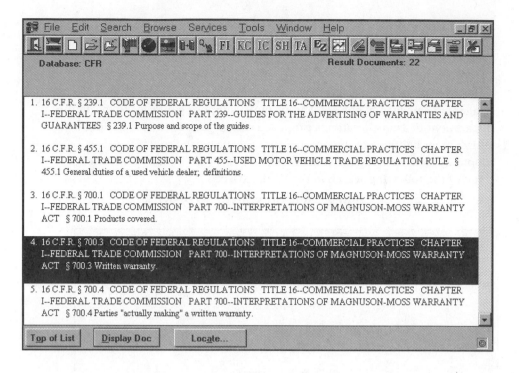

(b) Text of the Fourth-Ranked Document

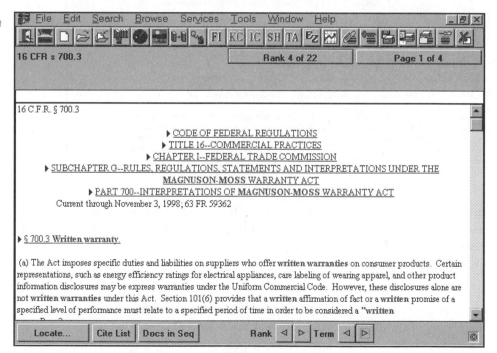

Occasionally, you may need regulations that were in effect during a certain year. The CFR databases are retrospective to 1984. If you want to find out how a regulation was stated in 1987, you would search the CFR87 database. For example, the rule requiring labels in wool products to carry certain information on the reverse side was revised in 1988. To see how the rule read in 1987, you would access the CFR87 database and type

reverse alternat! /s side /s label & wool

This search retrieves 16 C.F.R. § 300.10 (Figure 5.12).

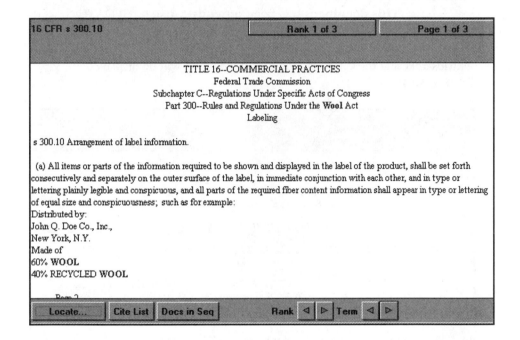

Figure 5.12
Searching for a Regulation
in a Particular Year

If you have a citation for the *Federal Register* or the C.F.R. document, you can retrieve it in a snap with Find. For example, to retrieve 62 Fed. Reg. 65850, click the **Find** button on the main button palette and type **62 fr 65850** in the *Citation* text box.

Updating the C.F.R. with the List of Sections Affected and the *Federal Register*

Since regulations are revised constantly, you must always update your regulation by checking for new revisions and deletions in the *Federal Register*. You cannot rely on a regulation as it is printed in the C.F.R. or in the CFR database on Westlaw without updating it.

On Westlaw, updating a C.F.R. section is easy. Just look for this Update message at the top of your screen:

This document has been amended. Use ▶ UPDATE.

See ▶ SCOPE for more information.

Click the **Update** button or the *UPDATE* Jump marker. Any *Federal Register* entries affecting the C.F.R. section you are viewing will be displayed (Figure 5.13).

Figure 5.13
Updating a Recently
Amended C.F.R. Provision

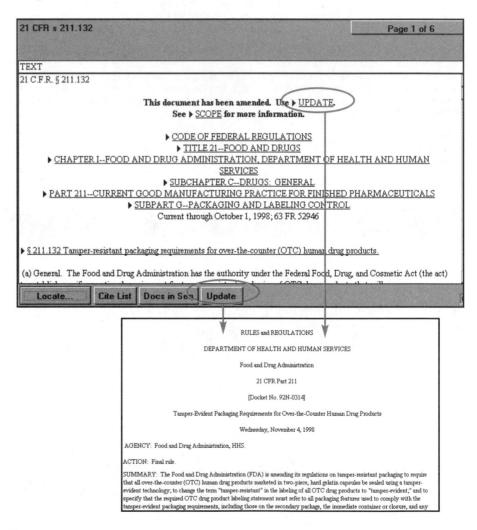

If you do not have access to Westlaw, you can still update your citation by using print sources (Figure 5.14). The following instructions may appear cumbersome, but the process is quite mechanical and will work if you follow the instructions carefully:

1. Look up your section in the most recent C.F.R. paperback volume. Note the date of revision on the front cover.

Figure 5.14
Updating a C.F.R.
Citation Using Print
Sources

20

LSA—LIST OF CFR SECTIONS AFFECTED

CHANGES JANUARY 2 THROUGH MARCH 30, 1990

TITLE 12 Chapter II—Con.

	Page
220.18 (a) and (b) amended	11160
221 OTC margin stock list	2631
224 OTC margin stock list	2631
225 Authority citation revised	6790
225.71—225.73 (Subpart H) Added; interim	6790
229 Appendix F amended	11358
264b.3 (a) revised	3576
(a) amended	11360

Chapter III—Federal Deposit Insurance Corporation

	Page
312 Technical correction	1912
312.1 (c) revised; (f) through added; interim	10412
312.4 Revised; interim	10413
312.5 Added; interim	10413
312.6 Revised; interim	10413
312.7 Revised; interim	10413
312.8 Added; interim	10414
312.9 Added; interim	10414
312.10 Added; interim	10414
357 Added; interim	11161

Chapter IV—Export-Import Bank of the United States

	Page
411 Added; interim	6737, 6747

Chapter V—Office of Thrift Supervision, Department of the Treasury

	Page
510.5 Added	7695
528 Revised	1388
545.75 (b)(3) revised; interim	11307
563.75 (i) removed	7300
563.80 (e)(2) revised	7300
563.93 Revised; interim	11307
563.132 (c) and (d) removed; (e) redesignated as new (c)	4602
563d.2 Revised	3041
567.13 Added	7478
571 Technical correction	696
571.19 (e) amended	126

Chapter VI—Farm Credit Administration

	Page
600.10 (Subpart B) Regulation at 54 FR 50735 eff. 3-6-90	7884
611.1162 Regulation at 54 FR 1148 corrected	10042
611.1167 Regulation at 54 FR 1148 corrected	10042
611.1172 Regulation at 54 FR 1148 corrected	10042
611.1174 Regulation at 54 FR 1148 corrected	10042
612.2150 Regulation at 54 FR 50736 eff. 3-6-90	7884
612.2160 Regulation at 54 FR 50736 eff. 3-6-90	7884
614.4280 Regulation at 54 FR 50736 eff. 3-6-90	7884
614.4320 Regulation at 54 FR 50736 eff. 3-6-90	7884
614.4321 Regulation at 54 FR 50736 eff. 3-6-90	7884
614.4340 Regulation at 54 FR 50736 eff. 3-6-90	7884
614.4345 Regulation at 54 FR 50736 eff. 3-6-90	7884
614.4460 Regulation at 54 FR 50736 eff. 3-6-90	7884
614.4511 Regulation at 54 FR 50736 eff. 3-6-90	7884
614.5040 Regulation at 54 FR 50736 eff. 3-6-90	7884
615.5104 Regulation at 54 FR 50736 eff. 3-6-90	7884
615.5135 Regulation at 54 FR 50736 eff. 3-6-90	7884
615.5143 Regulation at 54 FR 50736 eff. 3-6-90	7884
615.5190 Regulation at 54 FR 50736 eff. 3-6-90	7884
618.8060 Regulation at 54 FR 50736 eff. 3-6-90	7884

Chapter VII—National Credit Union Administration

	Page
700 Authority citation revised	1794
700.1 (h) and (i) removed; (j) through (m) redesignated as (h) through (k)	1794
701 Authority citation revised	1794
701.6 (d) added	1799
701.21 (c)(7) revised	1797
701.32 Heading revised; (d) added	1794
705 Authority citation revised	1794
705.3 Revised	1794
741 Authority citation revised	1794
741.5 Revised	1794
741.9 (k) added	1799

Step 2: Changes in 12 C.F.R. § 563 Listed in LSA

2. Consult the most recent monthly *List of CFR Sections Affected* (LSA) pamphlet to see if your C.F.R. section is listed (Figure 5.14 on page 111). The LSA directs you to changes in the C.F.R. that were published in the *Federal Register*. Entries for rules are arranged numerically by C.F.R. title, chapter, part, section, and paragraph. If there has been a change, the LSA will refer you to the pages in the *Federal Register* where the action appears. There will also be a descriptive word or phrase indicating whether the change was an addition, revision, or removal. Make certain the coverage of the LSA pamphlet begins the day after the date of revision on the paperback C.F.R. volume, and note the month printed prominently on the front of the LSA.

Figure 5.14
Updating a C.F.R. Citation Using Print Sources (continued)

Step 3: CFR Parts Affected Table

Federal Register / Vol. 55, No. 83 / Monday, April 30, 1990 / Reader Aids   ii

```
1011........................12369    Proposed Rules:                  15223, 15320–15900, 17421,   146........................14966
1012........................12369    2........................12370        17422, 17595, 17931      162........................17596
1013........................12369    30.............12374, 13542      73.................13761, 17931   171........................17596
1030........................12369    40.............12374, 13542      75........................17423   178.............12342, 17596
1032........................12369    50.............12374, 13542      91......13444, 15320–15900,      191........................17597
1033........................12369    55........................14288                           17736   Proposed Rules:
1036........................12369    60.............12374, 13542      95........................13762   101........................17633
1040........................12369    61.....12374, 13542, 13797      97.............15244, 17424       141........................12385
1044........................12369    70.............12374, 13542      121.............13326–13332
1046........................12369    72.............12374, 13542      125........................13332   20 CFR
1049........................12369    110............12374, 13542      129........................13332   404........................17530
1050........................12369    150............12374, 13542      135......13444, 15320–15900       416........................14916
1064........................12369    708............12668, 17453      382........................12336   626........................12992
1065........................12369    725........................15237  Proposed Rules:                  636........................12992
1068........................12369                                      Ch. I..........12383, 13798,      638........................12992
1075........................12369    11 CFR                                     15240, 17987          675........................12992
1076........................12369    110........................13507  13........................15134   676........................12992
1079........................12369    Proposed Rules:                  21........................12857   677........................12992
1093........................12369    106........................12499  23........................12857   678........................12992
1094........................12369    9003.......................12499  25.............12316, 13886       679........................12992
1096........................12369    9007.......................12499  29........................12316   680........................12992
1097........................12369    9033.......................12499  39.......12503, 12859–12863,      684........................12992
1098........................12369    9035.......................12499    13284, 13799, 13801, 14290,    685........................12992
1099........................12369    9038.......................12499    14292, 14426, 14428, 15243,    688........................12992
1106........................12369                                         17453, 17631, 17860, 17987–   689........................12992
1108........................12369    12 CFR                                                  17998     Proposed Rules:
1120........................12369    19.........................13010  71........12384, 13032, 13285–    416........................17999
1124........................12369    202...........12471, 14830         13287, 13802, 13803, 14293–
1126........................12369    205........................12635    14295, 17632                   21 CFR
1131........................12369    226...........13103, 17749        73........................13804   5.........................14916
1132........................12369    500........................13507  75........................13287   74........................12171
1134........................12369    543........................17584  91........................12316   101........................17431
1135........................12369    544........................13507  93........................17584   173........................12171
1137........................12369    545........................13507  119........................14404   176........................13518
1138........................12369    546........................13507  121.......12316, 13886, 14404     178.......12171, 12344, 13521
1139...............12369, 12848      550........................13507  125........12316, 14404           179........................14413
1485........................17618    552........................13507  127........................14404   300........................14968
1494........................17443    563........................13507  135.......12316, 13886, 14404,    430........................14239
1714...............12194, 12199      563b.......................13507                            17358   442........................14239
                                     563f.......................13507  241........................14296   444........................14968
8 CFR                                567........................13507  1266.......................13912   452........................14090
103........12627, 12628, 12815       574........................13507                                   455........................14378
210........................12629     584........................13507  15 CFR                           510.......13901, 13902, 14830,
235........................14234     614........................12472  776........................13121                            17951
242........................12627     615........................12473  779........................13121   514........................14831
287........................12627     620........................12472  799.......12635, 13121, 14089,    522...........13768, 13902
299........................12628     621........................12472                            17530   544........................13902
499........................12628     1609.......................14081  Proposed Rules:                  558........15099, 17598, 17951
Proposed Rules:                      Proposed Rules:                  295........................12504   610........................14037
103........................12666     21........................14424                                   640........................14037
                                     216........................12850  16 CFR                           801........................17599
9 CFR                                226........................13282  305........................13264   Proposed Rules:
1..........................12630     701........................12852  1700..........13123–13127         101........................14429
71........12631, 15320–15900         741........................12852  Proposed Rules:                  872........................17455
75........................13504      747........................12855  1027.......................13805
78........12163, 15320–15900         1611..........13543, 17715        1700.......................13157   23 CFR
82........................12631                                                                         658........................17952
91........................12632      13 CFR                           17 CFR                           Proposed Rules:
92........................12632      121........................17419  1..........................17932   655........................17634
Proposed Rules:                      122........................17267  30........................14238   1327.......................12509
3............12202, 12667            Proposed Rules:                  200........................17933
78........................12848      120........................17280  230........................17933   24 CFR
101........................15233                                      241........................17949   882........................14243
113........................15233     14 CFR                           Proposed Rules:                  885........................14243
156........................15236     13........................15110  155........................13288
201........................13796     14........................15110  156........................13545   26 CFR
318........................12203     21.....12328, 15214, 17589                                         1...........13521, 13769
381........................12203     23.....12328, 15214, 17589        18 CFR                           301........13289, 13521, 14244
                                     25........................13474  37........................14961   602........................14244
10 CFR                               39.........12332, 12473–12477,    270........................17425   Proposed Rules:
11........................14288        12815–12817, 13259–13261,      272........................17425   1...........13808, 14429, 14437,
25........................14288        13755–13760, 14411, 14412,     284........................12167                    17455, 17635, 17758
50........................12163        15217–15222, 17420, 17594,     381...........12169, 13899       31........................17758
72........................13883                         17927–17930                                    301........................12386
95........................14288      71........12336, 12482, 13263,    19 CFR                           602........14429, 14437, 17758
590........................14916       13264, 13761, 14234–14237,     141........................17596
                                                                      142........................12342
```

3. Consult the last issue of the month of the *Federal Register* for each complete month since the month on the cover of the LSA pamphlet. Check the CFR Parts Affected During [month] table near the back of the issue (Figure 5.14 on page 112). This table cumulates throughout the month so you only need to check the last issue for each month.
4. Consult the most recent issue of the *Federal Register* available and check the CFR Parts Affected During [month] table near the back. Note the date of the issue.
5. Finally, remember to check to see if the regulation is still valid. Check *Shepard's Code of Federal Regulations Citations* for cases that have interpreted the federal regulations.

i

Reader Aids

Federal Register

Vol. 55, No. 93

Monday, May 14, 1990

INFORMATION AND ASSISTANCE

Federal Register

Index, finding aids & general information	523-5227
Public inspection desk	523-5215
Corrections to published documents	523-5237
Document drafting information	523-5237
Machine readable documents	523-3447

Code of Federal Regulations

Index, finding aids & general information	523-5227
Printing schedules	523-3419

Laws

Public Laws Update Service (numbers, dates, etc.)	523-6641
Additional information	523-5230

Presidential Documents

Executive orders and proclamations	523-5230
Public Papers of the Presidents	523-5230
Weekly Compilation of Presidential Documents	523-5230

The United States Government Manual

General information	523-5230

Other Services

Data base and machine readable specifications	523-3408
Guide to Record Retention Requirements	523-3187
Legal staff	523-4534
Library	523-5240
Privacy Act Compilation	523-3187
Public Laws Update Service (PLUS)	523-6641
TDD for the deaf	523-5229

FEDERAL REGISTER PAGES AND DATES, MAY

18073–18302	1
18303–18584	2
18585–18716	3
18717–18850	4
18851–19046	7
19047–19232	8
19233–19616	9
19617–19716	10
19717–19870	11
19871–20110	14

CFR PARTS AFFECTED DURING MAY

At the end of each month, the Office of the Federal Register publishes separately a List of CFR Sections Affected (LSA), which lists parts and sections affected by documents published since the revision date of each title.

3 CFR

Proclamations:

6030 (See Proc. 6123)	18075
6122	18073
6123	18075
6124	18585
6125	18715
6126	18717
6127	19041
6128	19043
6129	19045
6130	19233
6131	19715
6132	20107
6133	20109

Executive Orders:

12675 (Amended by EO 12712)	18095
12712	18095
12713	18719
12714	19047
12715	19051

Administrative Orders:

Memorandums:

Apr. 26, 1990	18299

Presidential Determinations:

No. 90–17 of Apr. 25, 1990	18587
No. 90–18 of Apr. 25, 1990	18589

Order:

May 4, 1990	19235

5 CFR

1630	18851

7 CFR

2	18097
3	18591
13	18591
52	19001
210	18857
245	19237
301	19241
400	18097
704	19243
910	18858, 19717
920	19717
927	18097
979	19719, 19720
985	18859
993	19617
1012	18098
1139	18303
1478	19053
1980	19244

Proposed Rules:

220	18908, 20023
300	20023
301	18342
911	19740
929	19741
953	18909
1762	18606
1941	18607
1943	18607
1945	18607
948	19631
982	19632

8 CFR

286	18860

9 CFR

71	18099
78	19054
82	18099
85	19245
92	19245

Proposed Rules:

78	19200
94	18342
114	18346
308	19888
318	19888
320	19888
381	19888

10 CFR

590	18227

Proposed Rules:

Ch. I	19633
20	19890
30	19890
40	19890
50	18608
70	19890

12 CFR

207	18591
220	18591
221	18591
224	18591

Proposed Rules:

563g	18610
741	18613
1611	20023

13 CFR

302	18593
309	18594

Proposed Rules:

120	18614
124	18615
125	19633

14 CFR

13	18800
14	18800
15	18704
21	19050

Step 4: CFR Parts Affected Table in the Most Recent *Federal Register*

Figure 5.14 Updating a C.F.R. Citation Using Print Sources (continued)

Administrative Decisions

Agencies not only write rules but issue orders and opinions. Agencies report their opinions just as courts do. These reports are published by the U.S. Government Printing Office in either print format or microfiche.

An increasing number of agency decisions are available online on Westlaw. These decisions can be found in practice-area databases, such as the energy databases, which include decisions of the Federal Energy Regulatory Commission and the Nuclear Regulatory Commission, materials from two specialized publications, *Gower Federal Service* and *Public Utilities Reports,* and applicable regulations from the *Federal Register* and the *Code of Federal Regulations,* among other materials.

In addition to the official reports and Westlaw, administrative decisions can be located in various loose-leaf services. Loose-leaf services are so named because they are published in binders with removable pages. A loose-leaf service is constantly kept current with new pages. Loose-leaf services generally follow one of two formats. In the newsletter format, new pages are added at the end of each unit. *United States Law Week* (U.S.L.W.), which we discussed in Chapter 1, is an example of a newsletter format. The second type of loose-leaf service replaces pages that are out of date in addition to adding new information. The major publishers of loose-leaf services are The Bureau of National Affairs, Inc. (BNA), CCH Incorporated (CCH), and Prentice-Hall (P-H). Many loose-leaf reporters are now available online as well as in print format.

Presidential Documents

In discussing administrative materials, we cannot overlook the administrative actions of the president, who may direct agency action by issuing executive orders. The president may also issue proclamations that are either ceremonial in nature, such as the observance of National Library Week, or more substantive in nature, often concerning trade matters. Both types of actions have the effect of law.

The daily *Federal Register* prints presidential documents including proclamations and executive orders as well as other documents that the president orders to be published, such as determinations, letters, memoranda, and reorganization plans. All executive orders and proclamations published in the *Federal Register* are compiled annually in Title 3 of the *Code of Federal Regulations* and in West's *U.S. Code Congressional and Administrative News.* Proclamations and executive orders are available on Westlaw in the Presidential Documents database (PRES) (Figure 5.15).

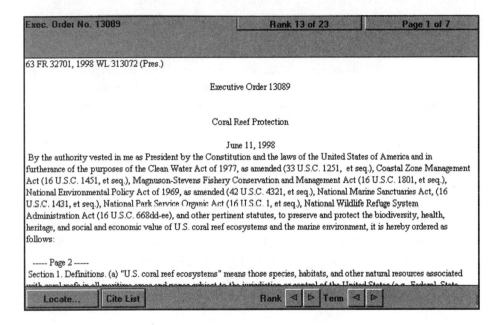

Figure 5.15
Presidential Documents
on Westlaw

State Administrative Law Materials

Administrative powers comparable to those of federal agencies are vested in state agencies, based upon the power of the states to regulate their internal commerce. Typical state agencies include state public service commissions and labor relations boards.

Many states have administrative codes similar in format to the *Code of Federal Regulations*. Many states also have registers similar to the *Federal Register*. But state administrative materials are frequently more difficult to find than federal materials and are less up-to-date if you do find them. Often an agency itself may be your best source for its own regulations and administrative decisions. Don't be afraid to make a phone call. You might well get things directly from an administrative agency that are not published in any organized manner.

State administrative law is voluminous; it is growing daily and prodigiously. More and more of it is now being added to Westlaw. Several administrative codes, especially for the largest states, are now on Westlaw. The Attorney General Opinions database (AG) contains the opinions of the attorneys general of all fifty states. Likewise, the Public Utility Reports database (PUR) has the decisions of public utilities regulatory commissions from all states. Additional administrative law materials are included in various practice areas, such as taxation, insurance, or workers' compensation. Online access to all of these materials makes life easier for everyone.

Conclusion

Administrative law has intimidated people for years. Since law school courses generally avoid it, many new associates are surprised by administrative regulations and decisions. Nevertheless, the *Federal Register* can be your pal—well, sort of—and the C.F.R., with its annual volumes and links to the *Federal Register* through the *List of CFR Sections Affected,* is quite a decent tool. This may be an area, though, where the Westlaw service is the best answer. It is updated for you, and you can search by unique terms. Try it for administrative law.

Secondary Legal Authority

Instead of beginning your research with one of the primary sources of the law, you may find it more productive—and less painful—to begin with various secondary sources of legal information. You can use secondary sources to become acquainted with a particular legal topic much as you used secondary sources to gather background information for your college research papers.

Secondary sources of legal information are known as *secondary authority*. Examples of secondary authority include annotations, legal periodicals, legal encyclopedias, treatises, restatements, dictionaries, and formbooks. Each of these sources may provide numerous citations to primary authority along with narrative discussions or summaries of legal principles and theories; thus, each can be a tool for finding the law as well as a source of legal analysis and background information. An added advantage is that secondary sources generally have good indexes. Consequently, the information they contain is easy to gather.

It is important to remember that secondary authority is not the law and is not binding on the courts. Therefore, you should never limit your research to secondary authority; you must always follow up by researching the primary sources of the law.

Figure 6.1
American Law Reports

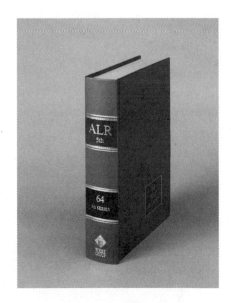

American Law Reports

We could have discussed the *American Law Reports* (ALR) in the chapter "Finding Cases" rather than in this chapter because the ALR is used both as a means of finding cases and as a source of analyses. The ALR is often an ideal starting place for your research (Figure 6.1).

The ALR, which is published by West Group, is known for its thoroughly researched annotations which leave no citation uncovered. An ALR annotation is a legal essay on a specific point of law. It traces the development of that point of law and presents its judicial treatment in all jurisdictions. As a law student, you will be surprised at how narrow the annotation topics tend to be. However, when you practice law you will be grateful for such well-defined topics, since your research will focus on narrow issues.

The ALR does not attempt to cover every legal topic, so it is possible that a topic will not appear. Generally speaking, the topics covered in the ALR are those the editorial staff believes to be of interest to attorneys in all jurisdictions, not solely to attorneys in a particular jurisdiction.

The ALR includes several series, as shown in Table 6.1. In general, if you are dealing with a federal problem, you will use ALRFed; if your issue is one arising primarily under state statutes or state case law, you will use the third, fourth, or fifth series.

Table 6.1
ALR Series

Series	Years	Coverage
ALR1st	1919–1948	State and federal issues
ALR2nd	1948–1965	State and federal issues
ALR3rd	1965–1980	State issues and federal issues until 1969
ALR4th	1980–1991	State issues only
ALR5th	1992–date	State issues only
ALRFed	1969–date	Federal issues only

You can access the ALR by using either the multivolume print *ALR Index* or Westlaw. The *ALR Index* provides subject access to all of the ALR series (except the first). Westlaw provides access to the index and to the full text of ALR annotations from the second, third, fourth, fifth, and federal series. You can also find references to ALR annotations by using the KeyCite citation research service on Westlaw.

To illustrate the features of the ALR, let's examine the following problem. Assume that your client is a hospital administrator who is concerned about her hospital's responsibility for administering blood transfusions. The *ALR Index* entry *Liability of hospital, physician, or other individual medical practitioner for injury or death resulting from blood transfusion* appears to be on target. Turning to the annotation in volume 20 of ALR4th, you find the text of one important representative case (*Fisher v. Sibley Memorial Hospital*) preceding the annotation. This case acts as the theme for the annotation. Following the case are an outline of topics covered in the annotation, a word index of topics for the annotation, and a table of jurisdictions represented so you can turn to cases from a particular state. The most useful part of the annotation is the case and statute analysis, where the weight of authority is noted along with the direction of emerging trends. Here the holdings of hundreds of cases are summarized (Figure 6.2).

Figure 6.2
Abstracts of Cases in an
Annotation

20 ALR4th   BLOOD TRANSFUSIONS   § 3[a]
20 ALR4th 136

Counsel for the patient may be in a position to claim that the transfusion itself was not necessary, in view of medical opinion that there are far too many unjustified transfusions. Nonvalid reasons for blood transfusions may include the use of transfusions as a tonic, to build body defenses, to combat infections, as a nutrient, to improve the patient's sense of well-being, to provide iron, to satisfy the desires of the patient, or to satisfy the wishes of the physician wanting to accomplish something with the patient.[15]

The fact that the consequences of improper transfusion techniques may not appear until a much later date raises obvious questions as to the time when the statute of limitations begins to run. Thus, counsel for the patient should be aware that in choosing among the various remedies available for recovery, he should consider whether questions of limitations would be avoided thereby.[16]

Counsel on either side may find the hospital's records a valuable source of evidence. In states adopting the Uniform Business Records as Evidence Act, or similar statutes, hospital records may be admitted into evidence if a proper foundation is laid. The courts, however, may still exercise considerable discretion over the admission of such records into evidence, and the qualification of a record generally may still leave specific parts of its subject to exclusion on grounds other than general hearsay rules. In states lacking such laws, the results may vary, but hospital records still are often admissible under one or another exception to the hearsay rule.[17]

II. Liability of hospitals or their employees

§ 3. Transfusing wrong or incompatible type of blood

[a] Application of view that transaction constitutes a service not giving rise to liability without fault

The courts have generally ruled that a supplier of a product may not be held liable without fault for injuries caused by the product, if the transaction involved the supplying of

---

15. The foregoing list of nonvalid reasons are utilized by some hospitals for the guidance of the staff. See 11 Am Jur Proof of Facts 331, Transfusions, Supplement.

16. See, for example, Smith v McComb Infirmary Asso. (1967, **Miss**) 196 So 2d 91, a statutory wrongful death action based upon negligence of a hospital in mistyping the blood of a mother, wherein the court held that the plaintiff's declaration was cast under the wrongful death statute and that the statute of limitations began to run from the date of the infant's death in December, 1964, and not from the time of the alleged negligent act in 1958, and that therefore the trial judge had erred in sustaining the plea of limitation, and the judgment was reversed and the cause remanded. The trial judge had based his opinion on the theory that the declaration of plaintiff was one charging malpractice and that the statute of limitations had run according to a rule that a cause of action for malpractice accrues and the statute begins to run on the date of the wrongful act or omission which constitutes the malpractice, and not from the time of the discovery thereof.

17. For example, the admissibility of hospital records tending to prove an incompatible blood transfusion was recognized in Joseph v W. H. Groves Latter Day Saints Hospital (1957) 7 **Utah** 2d 39, 318 P2d 330.
See, generally, 40 Am Jur 2d, Hospitals and Asylums § 43.
As to the admissibility of computerized hospital records, see § 8 of the annotation at 7 ALR4th 8.

Figure 6.3
An ALR Annotation

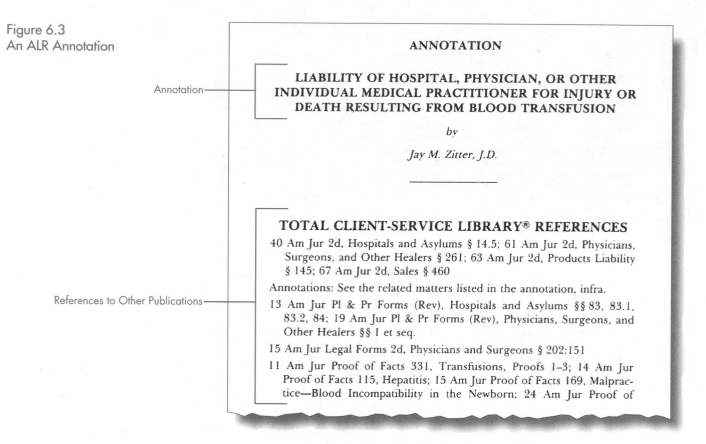

Annotation

References to Other Publications

ANNOTATION

LIABILITY OF HOSPITAL, PHYSICIAN, OR OTHER INDIVIDUAL MEDICAL PRACTITIONER FOR INJURY OR DEATH RESULTING FROM BLOOD TRANSFUSION

by

Jay M. Zitter, J.D.

TOTAL CLIENT-SERVICE LIBRARY® REFERENCES

40 Am Jur 2d, Hospitals and Asylums § 14.5; 61 Am Jur 2d, Physicians, Surgeons, and Other Healers § 261; 63 Am Jur 2d, Products Liability § 145; 67 Am Jur 2d, Sales § 460

Annotations: See the related matters listed in the annotation, infra.

13 Am Jur Pl & Pr Forms (Rev), Hospitals and Asylums §§ 83, 83.1, 83.2, 84; 19 Am Jur Pl & Pr Forms (Rev), Physicians, Surgeons, and Other Healers §§ 1 et seq.

15 Am Jur Legal Forms 2d, Physicians and Surgeons § 202:151

11 Am Jur Proof of Facts 331, Transfusions, Proofs 1–3; 14 Am Jur Proof of Facts 115, Hepatitis; 15 Am Jur Proof of Facts 169, Malpractice—Blood Incompatibility in the Newborn; 24 Am Jur Proof of

ALR annotations include helpful references to treatment of the issue in other publications (Figure 6.3). As a supplement to ALR4th and as part of the annotations of ALR5th, these references have been expanded to include citations to West digest topics and key numbers and sample electronic search queries (Figure 6.4).

Updating Your Research in the ALR

Since the annotations in the first and second series of the ALR were written before 1965, many of them have been subsequently rewritten and superseded. An important step in using ALR, then, is consulting the Annotation History Table, located in volume 6 of the *ALR Index* (Figure 6.5). This table will tell you whether or not an annotation has been supplemented or superseded. Always check the Annotation History Table before you read an annotation—you may not want to spend your time reading an outdated annotation.

Figure 6.4
Sample Electronic Search Queries and West Topics and Key Numbers in ALR5th

---

64 ALR5th   TRANSFUSION—AIDS
                            64 ALR5th 333

58 Am Jur Trials 1, Transfusion–Associated AIDS Litigation

Law Review Articles

Kelly, The Liability of Blood Banks and Manufacturers of Clotting Products to Recipients of HIV– Infected Blood: A Comparison of the Law and Reaction in the United States, Canada, Great Britain, Ireland, and Australia, 27 J. Marshall LR 465, 472 (1994)

Pieplow, AIDS, Blood Banks and the Courts: The Legal Response to Transfusion–Acquired Disease, 38 SD LR 609 (Fall 1993)

Electronic Search Query

WESTLAW® Search Query: (AIDS HIV HTLV "immune defic!") /10 transfusion

Natural Language Search Query: blood transfusion causing AIDS or HIV or Acquired immune deficiency syndrome

LEXIS® Search Query: (AIDS or HIV or HTLV or immune defic!) w/10 transfusion

West Digest Key Numbers

Consumer Protection 6, 30

Death 76

Hospitals 7, 810

Judgment 181(33), 185.3(21)

Physicians and Surgeons 15(8, 12, 15), 18.80(5)

Products Liability 46, 83

Figure 6.5
The Annotation History Table

ANNOTATION HISTORY TABLE

29 ALR3d 1021 Superseded 13 ALR4th 52	**36 ALR3d 735** Superseded 43 ALR4th 1062	**46 ALR3d 1383** Superseded 53 ALR4th 231
29 ALR3d 1407 Superseded 96 ALR3d 195 24 ALR Fed 808	**36 ALR3d 820** Superseded 74 ALR4th 277	**47 ALR3d 909** Superseded 47 ALR4th 134
29 ALR3d 1425 § 3[a], 3[b], 3[g], 3[i] Superseded 100 ALR3d 1205	**37 ALR3d 1338** Superseded 22 ALR4th 237	**47 ALR3d 971** Superseded 47 ALR4th 100
30 ALR3d 9 § 6 Superseded 76 ALR3d 11 § 14.1 Superseded 90 ALR4th 859 § 16, 19[d] Superseded 67 ALR3d 308 100 ALR3d 10 100 ALR3d 940 § 19[c] Superseded 99 ALR3d 807 99 ALR3d 1080 § 25 Superseded 7 ALR4th 308 § 26[c] Superseded 11 ALR4th 241 § 29 Superseded 69 ALR3d 1162	**38 ALR3d 363** Superseded 61 ALR4th 27 **39 ALR3d 222** Superseded 68 ALR4th 294 **39 ALR3d 1454** Superseded 1 ALR5th 132	**47 ALR3d 1286** Superseded 81 ALR3d 1119 **49 ALR3d 915** Superseded 97 ALR3d 294 **49 ALR3d 934** Superseded 49 ALR4th 1076
30 ALR3d 203 § 18 Superseded 46 ALR3d 900	**40 ALR3d 856** Superseded 85 ALR4th 365 **41 ALR3d 455** § 3[e, f] Superseded 91 ALR Fed 547	**50 ALR3d 549** § 4 Superseded 70 ALR3d 132 **51 ALR3d 8** § 2 [b] Superseded 65 ALR4th 346
30 ALR3d 1352 Superseded 110 ALR Fed 211	**41 ALR3d 904** Superseded 6 ALR4th 1066	**51 ALR3d 520** Superseded 65 ALR4th 1155

— A Superseded Annotation

— Most Recent Annotation

On Westlaw, an ALR annotation that has been superseded by a later one will contain a hypertext link to the later annotation so you can jump directly to it (Figure 6.6).

Figure 6.6
An ALR Annotation on Westlaw

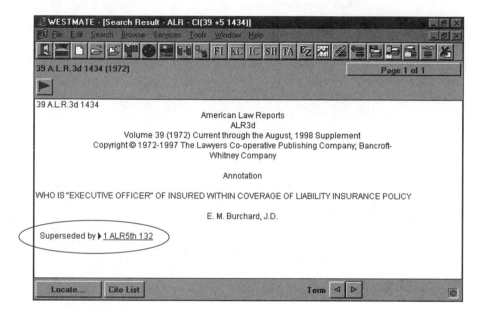

Obviously, the annotations in the ALR would lose their appeal if their citations to cases became outdated. Fortunately, you can update the cases that are cited in the text of the annotations by various means, depending on the series. For the third, fourth, fifth, and federal series, use the annual pocket parts inserted in the back of each volume (Figure 6.7). To update the cases in the second series, use the *ALR2d Later Case Service,* a separate supplemental set of books. For updates to the first series, check the set of books entitled *ALR1st Blue Book of Supplemental Decisions.*

On Westlaw, supplemental materials are integrated into the main text so you can view them in context. Also the ALR database on Westlaw is updated more frequently than the print publications.

Figure 6.7
A Pocket Part for the ALR

1 ALR5th 1-31   ALR5th

physical injury, regardless of whether plaintiff experienced physical impact as direct result of defendant's negligence. Plaintiff's observing worm in rice caused her to fear that she had eaten contaminated food, which was fear for her physical safety. Moreover, negligent infliction of emotional distress is type of negligence, and there is no distinction between law applicable to claims for negligence and breach of warranty where both are based on alleged injury caused by consumption of unwholesome food. Sowell v Hyatt Corp. (1993, **Dist Col App**) 623 A2d 1221, 20 UCCRS2d 1232.

---

1 ALR5th 132-162

Research References

16 Am Jur Proof of Facts 3d 583, Corporate director's breach of fiduciary duty to creditors.

§ 1. Introduction

[b] Related annotations

Validity, construction, and effect of "regulatory exclusion" in directors' and officers' liability insurance policy. 21 ALR5th 292.

Standard of liability applicable to action against directors or officers of failed depository institution pursuant to 12 USCS § 1821(k). 125 ALR Fed 435.

---

1 ALR5th 163-242

Research References

31 Am Jur Proof of Facts 3d 351, Establishing Liability of a State or Local Highway Administration, Where Injury Results from the Failure to Place or Maintain Adequate Highway Signs.

§ 1. Introduction

[b] Related annotations

Scope of provision in liability policy issued to municipal corporation or similar governmental body limiting coverage to injuries arising out of construction, maintenance, or repair work. 30 ALR5th 699.

§ 3. Barricade or barrier—dangerous or inadequate

[a] Liability established or supportable

Evidence supported jury verdict for plaintiff motorist in action against state transportation department for injuries resulting from penetration of windshield by portion of signpost incorporated into barrel marker delineating lane closure during highway project, where collisions with barrel markers were acknowl-

edged hazard of device's use, and department failed to build and place markers so as to minimize risk of windshield penetration during foreseeable collisions. Texas Dep't of Transp. v Henson (1992, **Tex App Houston (14th Dist)**) 843 SW2d 648, writ den (Jun 3, 1993) and rehg of writ of error overr (Jun 30, 1993).

[b] Liability not established or supportable

See Patti v State (1995, App Div, 3d Dept) 630 **NYS2d** 137, § 10(b).

State transportation department was not liable to estate of motorist whose automobile collided with construction equipment at highway-project site, where legally intoxicated driver drove past three separate barricades closing area off and warning motoring public to get to place at which loader was parked across roadway. Kennedy v Ohio Dep't of Transp. (1992, Ct Cl) 63 **Ohio Misc 2d** 328, 629 NE2d 1101.

State transportation department was not liable in action arising from multivehicle fatal injury accident on freeway detour at construction site, where department's use of asphalt median barrier to separate streams of traffic, rather than temporary concrete barrier, conformed to applicable highway design guidebooks and was reasonable choice that could not be considered negligent. Yinger v Ohio Dep't of Transp. (1992, Ct Cl) 66 **Ohio Misc 2d** 69, 643 NE2d 183.

§ 10. Guardrail

[b] Liability not established or supportable

Evidence supported judgment in favor of defendant state in action by passenger in vehicle that overturned after striking guardrail in gap of barricades directing traffic onto exit at terminus of highway, where barricade array conformed to safety standards, guardrail could be seen at sufficient distance to allow driver to interpret and avoid, and driver's inattention in face of clear physical directive provided by barricades was likely cause of accident. Patti v State (1995, App Div, 3d Dept) 630 **NYS2d** 137.

§ 15. Signal or sign—dangerous or inadequate

[a] Liability established or supportable

See Texas Dep't of Transp. v Henson (1992, **Tex App Houston (14th Dist)**) 843 SW2d 648, writ den (Jun 3, 1993) and rehg of writ of error overr (Jun 30, 1993), § 3[a].

---

1 ALR5th 243-268

Research References

19 Am Jur Proof of Facts 3d 107, Wrongful Death of Fetus.

6

For latest cases, call the toll free number appearing on the cover of this supplement.

An Update to the Annotation
in the Pocket Part

Figure 6.8
A Law Review Article Proposing
Legal Reforms

VOLUME 86   NOVEMBER 1972   NUMBER 1

HARVARD LAW REVIEW

CONTENTS

iii

Figure 6.9
Some Representative Law Reviews

Legal Periodicals

Many of the articles that appear in legal periodicals provide in-depth treatment of a topic and contain numerous references to primary and secondary authorities. Other articles, particularly those that appear in periodicals with a relatively short publication cycle—such as bar association publications, commercial journals, newsletters, and legal newspapers—cover the most current topics on the cutting edge of the law.

You may also find articles that propose legal reforms. One famous example of such an article is a piece by Gerald Gunther entitled "The Supreme Court, 1971 Term—Foreword: In Search of Evolving Doctrine on a Changing Court: A Model for a Newer Equal Protection," which appeared in the *Harvard Law Review* in 1972 (Figure 6.8). The information in articles proposing legal reforms can be very useful in supporting a point of view not currently held by the courts. Using a legal periodical article is often the best way to begin researching a new or rapidly developing area of the law.

Law school law reviews, a special type of legal periodical, include lengthy essays written by scholars or practitioners. Every law school has at least one law review (Figure 6.9). The authors discuss, in meticulous detail, aspects of the law that may not be covered in other sources. The extensive footnotes (there can literally be hundreds to thousands of footnotes in a single article) are a great aid in finding primary sources. In addition to the lengthy articles, law reviews generally include a "Notes and Comments" section, which contains short articles written by the law review staff.

You can locate periodical articles very easily on Westlaw or other online services, on laser disc, or in print format. In print, you can use the *Index to Legal Periodicals,* published by the H.W. Wilson Company, which dates back to 1908, or the *Current Law Index,* published by Information Access Company, which dates back to 1980.

Law schools have access through Westlaw to the Current Index to Legal Periodicals database (CILP), which is produced by the Marian Gould Gallagher Law Library at the University of Washington and indexes the most recent information from more than 300 legal periodicals; the Index to Legal Periodicals database* (ILP); and the Legal Resource Index database† (LRI), which includes all the material covered in the *Current Law Index* plus legal newspapers and law-related articles from the popular press. Each of these indexes is extremely convenient to use online.

Using the indexes online is preferable to searching through the print volumes since all of the indexes cumulate in one place and you can print or download your results. You can search periodical indexes on Westlaw using either the Terms and Connectors or the Natural Language search method. For example, to search the Legal Resource Index database (LRI) for articles published after 1997 whose titles refer to insider trading, access LRI and enter the following Terms and Connectors query:

ti("insider trading") & da(aft 1997)

Figure 6.10 shows the result of your search.

Figure 6.10
Legal Resource Index Online

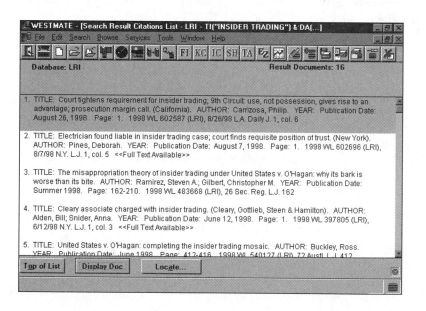

---

*Available to law school subscribers only if they subscribe to ILP on WILSONDISC or WILSONTAPE.
†Available to law school subscribers only if they subscribe separately to LegalTrac.

Using the indexes online is the most efficient way to research a current issue. If, however, you are dealing with an issue that is more retrospective in scope, such as the topic "dower," you should use the print *Index to Legal Periodicals* since that index dates back to the early 1900s, with its predecessors dating back to the early 1800s.

In addition to searching the indexes of legal periodicals online, you can also use Westlaw to locate the full text of articles. The Texts & Periodicals–All Law Reviews, Texts & Bar Journals database (TP-ALL) contains articles from law reviews, texts, and bar journals. You are able to access every word in the text and footnotes. TP-ALL may be searched using either the Natural Language or Terms and Connectors search method.

You can use Westlaw to search full-text articles for terms that may be associated with subtopics of the main topic. This is especially useful because subtopics are not normally found in the standard indexes. For example, if you are interested in articles on test anxiety, access the TP-ALL database and enter this Natural Language description:

test (exam) anxiety

Among the articles you retrieve is one entitled "The Bar Exam: Why Students Fail," 11–DEC NBA Nat'l B. Ass'n. Mag. 17 (1997); you might not retrieve this article in the standard indexes under the subject "test anxiety."

If you are looking for a specific article and you already know its citation, you can easily retrieve the article by using the Find service on Westlaw. For example, if the citation is 74 A.B.A. J. 55, click the **Find** button on the main button palette, type **74 abaj 55** in the *Citation* text box and click **OK**.

Legal Encyclopedias

The two national legal encyclopedias, *Corpus Juris Secundum* (C.J.S.) and *American Jurisprudence 2d* (Am Jur 2d), provide an elementary, objective statement of the law and cite hundreds of thousands of state and federal cases. These encyclopedias tend to concentrate on case law and ignore statutory materials. C.J.S. and Am Jur 2d are similar to general encyclopedias in that both sets contain alphabetically arranged summaries of legal topics and a multivolume index that provides easy access to the material.

In its introductory "Explanation," C.J.S., a West Group publication, defines its mission as "a complete restatement of the entire American law as developed by all reported cases." Due to this publishing philosophy, each page in C.J.S. contains a few lines of text and many lines of citations to cases and materials. The citations to cases are arranged alphabetically by state so that you can quickly find citations from the relevant jurisdiction.

The editors of C.J.S. are systematically replacing volumes in subject areas that have seen substantial changes and developments, such as the area of criminal law (Figure 6.11). The replacement volumes state the revised mission of C.J.S. to be "a contemporary statement of American law as derived from reported cases and legislation." As a result of the change in West Group's

Figure 6.11
Corpus Juris Secundum

concept of this encyclopedia, the number of cases cited has been reduced in the recompilation volumes.

Because it supplies West topics and key numbers for each entry, C.J.S. is perhaps most useful as a springboard into the West research system. Finding the topic and key numbers in C.J.S. circumvents the need to search through the Descriptive-Word Index when using West digests.

A five-volume *General Index* offers descriptive word entry into C.J.S. An alphabetical list of more than 430 subjects, called List of Titles, is located at the front of each volume. In using C.J.S., look up the most appropriate terms for your topic in the index. For example, if you were interested in an explanation of *nolo contendere*, after checking the C.J.S. index you would turn to Criminal Law § 398 (Figure 6.12).

Figure 6.12
An Entry in *Corpus Juris Secundum*

22 C. J. S.   CRIMINAL LAW § 398

ment or information is insufficient, from the standpoint of failing either to confer jurisdiction or to set forth facts sufficient to constitute a public offense, the plea of guilty confesses nothing,[62] and, accordingly, does not preclude accused from attacking the indictment or information on such grounds.[63] In fact, where the plea of guilty is to a void charge or one which fails to state facts sufficient to constitute a crime, the conviction is jurisdictionally defective and a nullity, and is not validated by the plea.[64]

A guilty plea does not waive a claim that the information or indictment, judged on its face, is constitutionally deficient in violation of the double jeopardy clause.[65]

Defects or irregularities in prior proceedings.

By pleading guilty to the charge contained in an indictment or information accused waives any technical defects or irregularities in prior proceedings[66] except such as go to jurisdiction.[67]

Involuntary plea.

Where a plea of guilty is so coerced that it is deprived of validity to support the conviction the coercion likewise deprives it of validity as a waiver of the right of accused to assail the conviction.[68]

Venue.

Since accused's plea of guilty is an admission of the material facts in the indictment or information, including the facts concerning the situs of the crime, the plea operates to waive any right to be tried in the county where the acts were actually committed, and the judgment cannot be collaterally attacked on that ground.[69]

Trial of accomplices.

Certainly, one who has pleaded guilty cannot question the procedure followed at the trial of his accomplices.[70]

2. **Plea of Nolo Contendere**

§ 398. In General

The so-called plea of "nolo contendere," also called "no contest," is not, strictly speaking, a plea, but a formal declaration by the accused that he will not contest the charge against him.

American Jurisprudence 2d (Am Jur 2d), also published by West Group, is more selective than C.J.S. and contains fewer footnote references, which cite only leading decisions. A *Desk Book* provides useful reference information such as the U.S. Constitution, the organization of the federal court system, and various tables. A ring-bound volume *New Topic Service* includes current topics such as alternative dispute resolution. Am Jur 2d is also available on Westlaw in the AMJUR database.

The complaint many law students have with legal encyclopedias is that some of the volumes are a bit musty. Encyclopedias do not always keep pace with the law as it rapidly grows and changes. Although both sets are kept up-to-date by pocket parts and replacement volumes, the encyclopedias are most useful for background information on traditional topics.

State Legal Encyclopedias

Many states have an encyclopedia that organizes and discusses the points of law applicable in that particular jurisdiction. State encyclopedias are extremely practical and timely and provide a great way to find state cases, statutes, and formbooks. West publishes several state encyclopedias. They provide references to West topics and key numbers, which makes it easy to access information in the state digests.

Legal Dictionaries

Undoubtedly you have already found it necessary to consult a legal dictionary. Since the legal field has its own jargon, the need for a law dictionary is constant. Probably several legal dictionaries are available in your library. The two most prominent are *Black's Law Dictionary* and *Ballentine's*.

Legal dictionaries may give case citations as well as define terms. A citation may direct you to a case that helps you fully understand the meaning of a term. Additionally, these dictionaries include a very handy table of abbreviations for just about any citation you need to interpret. You will also find that legal dictionaries are helpful in using the online services, since they may suggest synonyms or antonyms that you can add to your queries.

Black's Law Dictionary, 6th ed., is also available on Westlaw. Choose **Black's Law Dictionary** from the Services menu, type a term or phrase—such as **per stirpes**—in the *Term/Phrase* text box, and click **OK**. The definition is displayed (Figure 6.13).

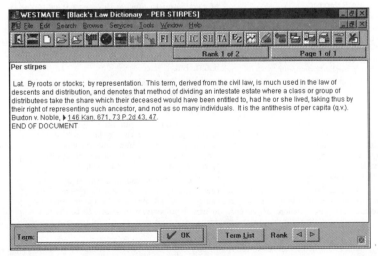

Figure 6.13
Checking Definitions on Westlaw in *Black's Law Dictionary*

West Group publishes *Words and Phrases,* an expanded multivolume dictionary. This set can be used to locate cases that have defined a particular term. Hundreds of thousands of definitions are alphabetically arranged, couched in the language of the court. For example, numerous courts have defined the term *enjoyment* (Figure 6.14). Although *Words and Phrases* is not available online, you can search the words–phrases field (wp) in case law databases on Westlaw to retrieve judicial definitions of terms or phrases.

Figure 6.14
Definitions in *Words and Phrases*

ENJOYMENT

ENJOYED WITHOUT LIMITATIONS

In a deed conveying a lot of land and "a free right of way for an alleyway 12 feet wide, extending from the rear end of said lot across another lot owned by said K. to the alley running to L. street," the word "free" qualifies and relates to "right of way" and is descriptive of the right of way, the thing granted, and not of the use to be made of the right of way. According to Webst.Dict., the word "free," when used in relation to a thing to be enjoyed or possessed, means "thrown open, or made accessible to all; to be enjoyed without limitations; unrestricted; not obstructed, engrossed, or appropriated; open." Applying that definition, the word "free," as used in the deed, indicates the condition and character of the right of way, which is the thing granted, and the thing to be enjoyed and possessed and, as thus interpreted, it means an unobstructed right of way as far as any future act of the owner of the servient lot is concerned. Flaherty v. Fleming, 52 S.E. 857, 859, 58 W.Va. 669, 3 L.R.A., N.S., 461.

ENJOYMENT

Cross References

Accumulate; Accumulation
Adverse Enjoyment
Exclusive Enjoyment
Full Benefit and Enjoyment
Natural Use and Enjoyment
Necessary to the Enjoyment
Personal Enjoyment
Possession, Enjoyment or Right to Income from

The words "enjoyment" and "enjoy", as used in statutes relating to estate and gift taxes, are not terms of art, but connote substantial present economic benefit rather than technical vesting of title or estates. C. I. R. v. Holmes' Estate, Tex., 66 S.Ct. 257, 260, 326 U.S. 480, 90 L.Ed. 228.

Where trustees, including settlor had power to accomplish a complete diversion of trust income and an invasion of corpus,

ENJOYMENT—Cont'd

settlor had power to alter the "enjoyment" of trust property, within Revenue Act. Jennings v. Smith, D.C.Conn., 63 F.Supp. 834. 838.

"Enjoyment", within statute levying tax on succession to property by deed, sale, assignment or gift without consideration substantially equivalent to full value of property, if intended to take effect in possession or enjoyment at or after grantor's, vendor's, assignor or donor's death, is synonymous with comfort, consolation, contentment, ease, happiness, pleasure and satisfaction. In re Heine's Estate, Ohio Pb., 100 N.E.2d 545, 554.

The rule that income is not taxable until "realized" is founded on administrative convenience, and is only a rule of postponement of the tax to the final event of "enjoyment" of the income, usually the receipt of it by the taxpayer, and not a rule of exemption from taxation where enjoyment is consummated by some event other than taxpayer's personal receipt of money or property. Helvering v. Horst, 61 S.Ct. 144, 147, 148, 311 U. S. 112, 85 L.Ed. 75, 131 A.L.R. 655.

The power to dispose of income is the equivalent of "ownership" and the exercise of that power to procure the payment of income to another is the "enjoyment", and hence the "realization" of the income by him who exercises it, so as to render the income subject to tax. Helvering v. Horst, 61 S.Ct. 144, 147, 148, 311 U.S. 112, 85 L.Ed. 75, 131 A.L.R. 655.

Under Internal Revenue Acts defining "gross income" in broad language, the power to dispose of income is tantamount to "ownership" of it, and exercise of that power in procuring payment to an assignee or nominee is the equivalent of the "enjoyment" of the income on part of him who exercises the right. Duran v. Commissioner of Internal Revenue, C.C.A.10, 123 F.2d 324, 326.

A use of economic gain, the right to receive income, to procure a satisfaction which can be obtained only by the expenditure of money or property, would seem to be the "en-

293

A Court's Definition

Treatises and Hornbooks

Simply put, treatises are books that describe an area of law. A treatise may consist of a single volume or multiple volumes. In your law school library, you will find thousands of treatises. In your course work, you probably are acquainted with hornbooks, a type of treatise (Figure 6.15).

Hornbooks explain the rudiments of a legal topic. The term *hornbook law* is often used to refer to points of law that are well settled by the courts. Hornbooks can be an excellent introduction to a topic in the traditional areas of law and can provide you with citations to key cases. Several publishers produce hornbooks. The two largest are West Group and Foundation Press. The West hornbooks often provide tips on search strategies and techniques for using Westlaw.

West Group also publishes a series of books called the Nutshell Series. These are paperback volumes, each of which is devoted to a single legal subject. Nutshells present the topic in a simplified format; hence, they are an excellent introduction to a subject.

You can locate a treatise by checking your library's catalog. In most law libraries, the hornbooks and most popular treatises, or those titles recommended for a course, will be on reserve—ask the librarian for help.

Figure 6.15
Hornbooks and Nutshells

Restatements

Your class work has probably introduced you to restatements. Restatements are written by scholars under the auspices of the American Law Institute. The purpose of the restatements is to state what the law is on a particular subject. Pertinent excerpts from restatements are usually included in casebooks or reprinted as supplements to your casebooks; for example, Section 402A from the *Restatement of Torts* will be included in your torts casebook. Restatements are also available on Westlaw.

Restatements cover twelve fields of law, several of which are typically encountered in first-year law school courses, such as Contracts, Torts, and Property. Each section begins with a boldface statement of principles, followed by comments intended to explain the statement. Since the series has a great deal of prestige among judges and scholars, you may want to present an issue using the restatement view.

Formbooks and Practice Manuals

At some point you may need materials that deal with legal procedure. Although many materials are written for the practicing attorney, they can be very useful to students tackling procedure and litigation courses. For federal law, you may look to Wright & Miller's *Federal Practice and Procedure* published by West Group—and available on Westlaw in the Federal Practice and Procedure database (FPP)—or West Group's *Federal Forms.*

Conclusion

This chapter has introduced secondary legal sources such as annotations, legal periodicals, legal encyclopedias, dictionaries, treatises, restatements, and formbooks. At this point in your law school career you may feel more comfortable with these sources than with primary sources because they are similar to the materials you used in your undergraduate or graduate days. But even as you gain experience in legal research, you will more than likely turn to these secondary sources first.

Nonlegal Background Sources

In previous chapters, we presented Westlaw as a fast, accurate way to find and update case law, statutes, and other legal materials. In this chapter, we will introduce you to some of the nonlegal materials Westlaw offers to help you round out your legal research. Because of the large amount of material in this category—literally thousands of individual databases—we cannot cover all nonlegal sources on Westlaw. We can, however, present an overview of some research tools that will come in handy during your first year of law school and beyond.

If you are like most students, you won't need a class assignment to begin exploring nonlegal materials on Westlaw. You'll quickly discover them on your own, particularly the full-text newspapers, magazines, and television and radio show transcripts.

Nonlegal materials, you will soon learn, contain some of the more entertaining items on Westlaw, such as movie commentary (in MAGILLS), notable quotes (in QUOTATIONS), celebrity news from *Entertainment Weekly* (in ENTWEEK), information from public opinion surveys (in POLL), the divergent world views of the *Village Voice* (in VILVC) and *National Review* (in NATREVIEW), and a breath of public radio's *Fresh Air* (in FRESHAIR). See Figure 7.1.

Most students have no problem finding the entertaining stuff. Our goal, on the other hand, is more practical: to help you incorporate nonlegal materials into your class work. We want to acquaint you with sources you can use to flesh out a journal article, seminar paper, or oral argument. For instance, we will show you how nonlegal materials can help you get a foothold when relevant case law is in short supply and how you can use nonlegal sources to develop a public policy argument. In short, this chapter is for those whose idea of entertainment is receiving an A or some other accolade for a well-supported legal argument.

Figure 7.1
A Document from the Quotations
Database

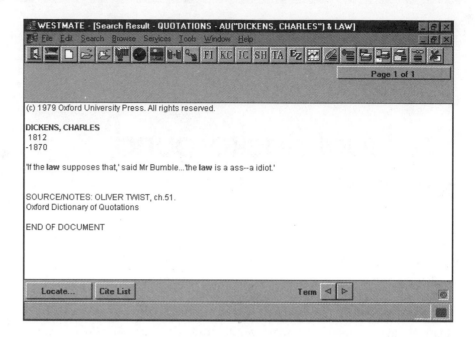

Unpublished Decisions and Out-of-Court Settlements

For all we hear about our litigious society and all we told you about how many judicial opinions have been published, you may be surprised by how often you are unable to find a case exactly on point. That's because a published opinion rarely accompanies the resolution of a legal dispute. Parties frequently settle out of court, submit to alternative dispute resolution, or simply drop their suit. Even if they go to court, a written opinion may be unnecessary, as when a jury resolves a factual dispute. If a written opinion is issued at the trial level, it is usually just filed in the courthouse.

So what fills all those handsome volumes in the law library? As we explained in Chapter 1, they are generally filled with appellate decisions that establish precedent within the jurisdiction or provide guidance on how courts will handle key issues. These decisions are published to make them easily accessible to legal practitioners. Trial-level opinions, by contrast, have no precedential value and are rarely published.

When there are no published decisions on point, it can be useful to find out how other parties have resolved similar issues. Unpublished decisions and out-of-court settlements, though not binding, may help you spot a trend that could persuade a court to decide in your favor. Westlaw contains a number of sources that make it easy to gather this kind of information.

Newspapers

The Newspapers database (NP) on Westlaw contains documents from more than 180 daily full coverage newspapers from the United States and other countries, including *The Wall Street Journal, USA Today, Los Angeles Times, The Washington Post*, and same-day coverage of the New York Times News Service (Figure 7.2). Newspapers are probably the best source for out-of-court settlement information because newspapers may at least mention the settlement and also provide useful background information.

Each individual paper in the Newspapers database can also be accessed in its own database. You can access the *Dallas Morning News*, for example, in the DALLASMN database. Individual newspaper databases are convenient for locating articles and features from a specific publication. For locating unpublished decisions and out-of-court settlements, however, we recommend that you begin with a broader database. You never know where the information you need may have been published originally.

Database Name	Identifier
Arizona Republic, The	ARIZREPUB
Boston Globe	BOSTONG
Chicago Sun Times	CHISUN
Chicago Tribune	CHICAGOTR
Dallas Morning News	DALLASMN
Detroit News	DETROITNWS
Houston Chronicle	HSTNCHRON
Los Angeles Times	LAT
Miami Herald*	MIA-HRLD
Newsday	NWSDAY
New York Daily News	NYDLYNWS
New York Times Abstracts*	NYT-ABS
New York Times News Service (same-day coverage only)	NYT
Plain Dealer (Cleveland)	PLDLCL
San Diego Union and Tribune	SDUT
San Francisco Chronicle	SFCHR
Star-Ledger (Newark, N.J.)	STLGRN
Star Tribune—Mpls & St. Paul	STTRMSP
St. Petersburg Times	STPTFTI
USA Today	USATD
Wall Street Journal, The	WSJ
Washington Post, The	WP

*Not included in the Newspapers database (NP)

Figure 7.2
Top-Circulation Newspapers
Available on Westlaw

This is illustrated by a case that made headlines some years back: Professor Cynthia Griffin Wolff sued the Massachusetts Institute of Technology claiming that her colleagues thwarted her career because they disagreed with her political views. If it were your task to find out how this litigation was resolved, you would think the *Boston Globe* or *Boston Herald* would be logical places to start. Yet neither of these local papers reported on the resolution of the dispute. Only by accessing a broader news and information database would you retrieve a *St. Louis Post-Dispatch* article that mentions a settlement. Why was the settlement reported in St. Louis but not in Boston? Who knows. But this story illustrates that you should start your research by casting your net broadly, even when logic suggests otherwise.

Narrowing Your Search Results

Broad databases have their drawbacks, however. Repetition of the same information in different newspapers can slow you down. To minimize this, rerun your search in a narrower database. You do not have to retype your search. For example, to narrow the result of a search in the Newspapers database (NP), rerun it in the Dow Jones Major Newspapers database (NPMJ). This database contains full-text articles from approximately forty of the most widely circulated newspapers in the United States. Choose **Change Database** from the Search menu, then select **Run query in different database**, type **npmj** in the *New Database Identifer* text box, and click **OK**. Your existing search will be run in the new database.

If you want to restrict your search to a specific geographic region, consider a regional database, such as the Western U.S. Newspaper Database (PAPERSWE), the North Eastern U.S. Newspaper Database (PAPERSNE), etc. Databases are also available for newspapers from individual states, such as California Papers (CANP), Massachusetts Papers (MANP), etc. Be aware, though, that these regional and state databases do not contain exactly the same papers as the Newspapers database. To check coverage for a database, use Scope.

Another easy way to narrow your result is by modifying your search. Say, for instance, you were researching verdicts or settlements involving psychotherapists accused of recklessly implanting false memories in the minds of their patients. Initially, you might type the following query:

"false memory" /s therapist psychotherapist psychiatrist /s jury verdict settl!

This search retrieves more than sixty documents in the Newspapers database. (Your search in the Newspapers database is automatically restricted to the past three calendar years unless you specify a different time period by adding a date restriction to your query.) Browse a few of the documents in your search result to see if you have retrieved repetitious information. You will notice several stories about a $10.6 million false memories award to a woman named Patricia Burgus. Do not waste time wading through every story. Once you know what you need to know about this particular case, exclude the redundant articles to make it easier to browse the others. For example, you can exclude all references to the name *Burgus* by editing your query as follows:

"false memory" /s therapist psychotherapist psychiatrist /s jury verdict settl! % burgus

As you continue browsing, keep modifying your search to exclude other repetitious material (Figure 7.3).

To exclude a term or concept, follow these steps:

Terms and Connectors

1. To recall your query for editing, choose **Edit Query** from the Services menu.
2. At the end of your query, type the BUT NOT connector (**%**) followed by terms you want to exclude. Westlaw excludes all documents containing terms that follow the %.

Natural Language

1. To recall your query for editing, choose **Edit Query** from the Services menu.
2. Click the **Control Concepts** button.
3. In the *Excluded Concepts* text box, type terms describing concepts you want to exclude and click **OK**.

Figure 7.3
Excluding Terms and Concepts
from a Westlaw Search

Public Policy Arguments

When you construct a legal argument in law school, you are expected to base it on the facts of the controversy and relevant legal precedent. For additional support, however, you may also include what are sometimes called *legislative facts*: evidence of a policy's overall impact. Named after the information-gathering a legislative body typically performs when considering legislation, the term also refers to information deemed to be within common knowledge. Such facts are frequently associated with court-made law.

For example, a party urging a court to adopt a strict liability standard may offer evidence that strict liability leads to efficient resource allocation. The opposing party may offer evidence that strict liability would render its industry uncompetitive. At other times a party may wish to debate whether custody modifications cause children psychological trauma, whether spraying aerial herbicides creates health risks, or whether the death penalty deters crime. None of these facts arises from the specific acts of the parties from which the dispute arose. Instead, they are generalizations designed to focus the court's attention on the broader context and impact of its ruling.

Perhaps the best-known purveyor of legislative facts was Louis Brandeis. In 1908 he filed a brief to the U.S. Supreme Court in *Muller v. Oregon.* This was the archetypal *Brandeis brief*—two pages of legal argument supported by 110 pages of economic and sociological data. Though this is not quite the balance—or length—you should strive for in your first-year writing assignments, it illustrates the long tradition of public policy argument in American law.

When you think legislative facts might help you bolster an argument, consider the fact-finding capabilities of Westlaw. The newspaper databases we have just discussed, for instance, are excellent sources for viewpoints on a wide variety of issues. Newspapers, after all, have long played an important role as a public forum and are a good source for gauging public opinion. In the next section we will introduce a few more sources you can use to measure the impact of a public policy: magazines, radio and television transcripts, and research studies.

Magazines

Searching magazines is a good way to find lengthy articles with extensive analyses. To search an assortment of the nation's top news and business magazines, access the Dow Jones Major Magazines database (MAGSMJ). It contains popular news weeklies such as *Time* and *U.S. News & World Report* plus respected business journals such as *Business Week, Barron's, Forbes,* and *Fortune.* Because it allows you to focus on just a few of the best-known publications, it is a good place to research issues that have been widely reported in the news media.

If your issue is more specialized, you may benefit by searching a broader range of publications. Consider the Magazines, Journals and Newsletters database (MAGSPLUS), which contains hundreds of news and business periodicals. Besides the familiar magazines we mentioned already, this database contains a wide variety of niche publications. Though you may not be familiar with the names of all these publications, they contain a gold mine of facts on an amazing range of topics. Here is a small sample of titles: *Air Conditioning, Heating & Refrigeration News*; *Biotech Equipment Update*; *Defined Contribution News*; *Flame Retardancy News*; *Industrial Health & Hazards Update*; *Internet Week*; *Monthly Labor Review*; *Securities Week*; and *Snack World.* When you are in practice, it is crucial to read what other attorneys who practice in the area read and what your clients read. These niche publications may be just the thing for keeping abreast of what is going on in an area. *Snack World* may be more important than you think.

Magazines that cover politics and current affairs are another excellent source of ammunition for a public policy debate. To find out what the pundits have written on your issue, consider targeting specific periodicals such as *Atlantic Monthly* (in ATLANTIC), *Commentary* (in COMMENTARY), *Harper's Magazine* (in HMAGAZINE), *The Nation* (in NATION), *The New Republic* (in NEWREPUB), and *The Progressive* (in PRGSVE). The Magazine Database* (MAGAZINE) provides extensive coverage of politics, current affairs, science and technology, social issues, business, consumer product evaluations, the performing arts, and much more. Besides containing selected full-text articles from more than one hundred magazines, the Magazine Database also tracks nearly four hundred additional titles to provide you with citations to and, in most cases, abstracts of relevant articles.

Television and Radio Transcripts

Once you learn how Jeffrey Rosen of *The New Republic* has analyzed your issue, do not stop there. Television and radio transcripts on Westlaw make it easier than ever to track the viewpoints of major governmental and political figures. Rather than making do with newspaper summaries of the Sunday morning news shows or fast-forwarding through a videotape, you can search every word of the discussion on Westlaw.

You may have to overcome an aversion to citing authority that is not in print. Keep in mind that in the context of a public policy argument, television can have far greater influence than print sources. World-renowned experts discussing policy in *The Wall Street Journal,* for example, may not generate the same level of scrutiny as a *Dateline NBC* story showcasing alleged police brutality videotaped by a hidden camera (Figure 7.4).

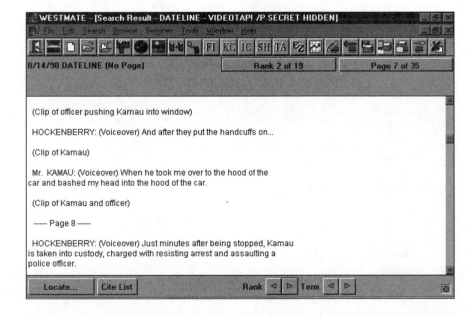

Figure 7.4
A Television Transcript
on Westlaw

*The Magazine Database is available to law school subscribers only if they subscribe separately to LegalTrac.

Television and radio transcripts often contain extensive discussion on matters that may be directly related to the legal issues you are deliberating. For example, if you are debating criminal justice and the rights of juveniles, you can access the Face the Nation database (FACENATION) to see how Senators Joseph Biden and Jeff Sessions discussed what should be done with juveniles who commit serious offenses. If you are debating tax reform, you can access the Meet the Press database (MTPRESS) to see how Representatives Bill Archer and Charles Rangel squared off over abolishing the federal income tax. And for coverage of the U.S. Supreme Court, you can retrieve Nina Totenberg's reports in the Morning Edition database (MORNED).

Research Studies

One of the most commonly repeated phrases in public policy debates is *studies show,* as in "studies show that housing discrimination is widespread" or "studies show that heavy ozone levels can trigger asthma attacks" or "studies show that 4 out of 5 dentists surveyed recommend ..."; well, you get the point. Citing a study in support of an argument is a time-honored practice. To help you locate scholarly studies, Westlaw offers a wide variety of databases that provide citations to and summaries of academic research.

Dissertation Abstracts Online (DAO), for example, contains citations for almost every doctoral dissertation accepted in the United States since 1861, along with thousands of Canadian, British, and other European dissertations (Figure 7.5). Business A.R.T.S. (BUS-ARTS) contains abstracts of articles from scholarly business publications that focus on the social, cultural, political, and psychological aspects of business. Selected full-text articles are also available. Coverage begins with 1976.

Figure 7.5
A Document from Dissertation Abstracts Online

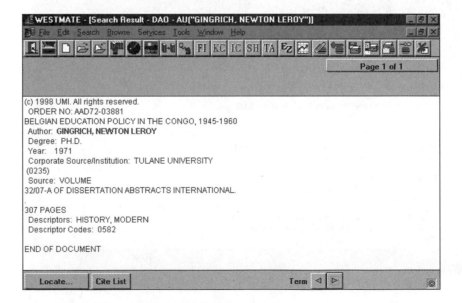

In addition, Westlaw offers a wide variety of databases that have a narrower focus. To locate environmental studies, for instance, your database choices include Environmental Bibliography (ENV-BIB), Oceanic Abstracts 1964 to Present (OCEAN-ABS), Pollution Abstracts (POLLUTION), and TOXLINE (TOXLINE).

Scholarly research databases are helpful not only for conducting your own research, but also for verifying uncited claims. For example, a few years ago when pundits were discussing Shannon Faulkner, a female student who sued for admittance to The Citadel, a publicly funded, all-male military academy, much of the debate centered on whether single-sex education was beneficial. (Note the classic appeal to legislative facts—the real legal issue was whether single-sex education at state-funded schools violated Equal Protection; however, many commentaries focused on the effects of a single-sex environment on learning.) Rather than accepting a commentator's assertions about the results of research in this field, you could sign on Westlaw and verify them yourself. In this case you might access a database such as Social SciSearch (SOCSCISRCH), an index of every significant item from the world's most important social science journals, plus social science articles from journals in the natural, physical, and biomedical sciences, with coverage beginning with 1972.

Because Westlaw provides so many specialized sources for scholarly research, tracking down the best database may seem daunting. Browsing the online Westlaw Directory, however, will help you get on the right track. All databases are arranged by subject, so you can quickly locate the database you need (Figure 7.6). You can also consult Westlaw practice-area brochures, which provide brief descriptions of Westlaw databases. Brochures are available for 23 areas of legal practice, such as bankruptcy, antitrust and trade regulation, and intellectual property law.

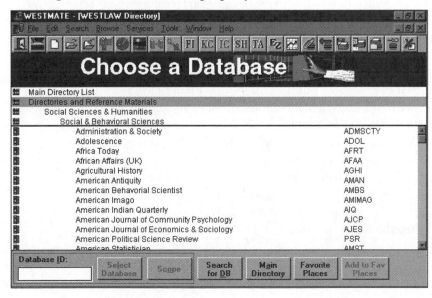

Figure 7.6
Browse the Westlaw Directory to Locate Scholarly Research Databases

Emerging Law

Believe it or not, there still exist spheres of human activity the government does not regulate. Unfortunately, this does not necessarily relieve legal professionals from having to advise clients on how to proceed within these areas. Keep in mind that, as an attorney, your role will generally involve more than simply finding the law and reporting back to your client. Clients will often rely on you for your expertise in predicting how a court or law-making body will react to a new enterprise they are contemplating.

For example, how would you advise a client who was about to devote substantial resources toward selling a product or service on the Internet? While no government entity currently taxes Internet commerce (at least as this book goes to press), what tax issues might arise in the future?

Broad Multibases

As we indicated earlier, the Newspapers database (NP) contains an abundance of information on legal trends. In this instance, though, the All News database (ALLNEWS) is probably better suited to our business-oriented hypothetical. All News contains hundreds of business-related trade journals, newsletters, and industry publications in addition to magazines, television and radio transcripts, and all the newspapers contained in the Newspapers database.

Because ALLNEWS contains so much material, Natural Language searching is a good way to keep your results manageable. For example, here is a description you might type to research our Internet hypothetical:

tax internet commerce

Figure 7.7 shows a partial list of articles this search may retrieve (new articles are added to Westlaw every day, so your results may differ).

Reviewing these articles can give you a sense of where law and policy is headed so you can alert your client. They may also remind you of existing laws or policies that can be relevant to your client's activities. For example, the fact that Internet commerce is not currently subject to taxation does not mean that clients doing business on the Net do not have to be concerned with wire fraud, copyright violations, or other acts that may lead to criminal or civil liability. Uncovering litigation in the news may lead you back to case law or statutes databases and help you locate relevant precedent.

Finally, you may have your own favorite source for staying current on legal trends. For instance, you may read the "Legal Beat" column in *The Wall Street Journal* every business day. You can retrieve this column on Westlaw by accessing The Wall Street Journal database (WSJ) and typing **pr,ti("legal beat")**.

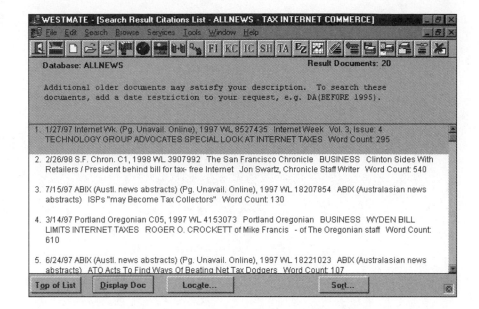

Figure 7.7
Natural Language Search Result
in ALLNEWS

Conclusion

If you rely only on traditional law-finding tools to prepare a legal argument, you are overlooking a wide range of persuasive authority. Beyond the periphery of official case reporters and legislative enactments lies a veritable El Dorado of influential data that can add power and eloquence to your side of the debate. Nonlegal databases on Westlaw can help you locate this information quickly and efficiently.

The Research Process

This book has tried to present you with an introduction to the full array of information that is available in the law library. We have discussed both traditional and computer-assisted legal research tools and techniques. Most of this material will become meaningful to you only when you actually work through it. The great Zen koan of legal research is that you can't understand the materials without using them, and you can't use them very well without understanding them.

In your first year of law school you will probably be assigned a series of research problems and you might participate in a moot court experience. This book has attempted to provide you with a series of ideas, explanations, and overviews that should make your first year significantly more successful.

In order to succeed, you must look at legal research materials functionally, understanding how they fit together and why they look the way they do. If you only understand one method of performing legal research, you will be lost when something goes awry. If you understand why the different sources of information work the way they do, however, you will be able to use them to better advantage.

This final chapter presents a few ideas on research methodology, i.e., how to go about attacking a research problem. We can't offer you a simple solution, but we would like to present you with a working model. Feel free to modify it as you wish; you may have to do so if you are to be successful. The point is that some model or plan is necessary. You have to have some overall concept of what you are doing, or you will simply drown in the mass of cases, statutes, administrative rules and regulations, and secondary sources that are available. Therefore, we propose the following four-step model.

Step 1: Deciding Where to Start

A large portion of your first year of law school will be devoted to sifting through facts and law, developing skills in how to glean what is important from what is not. This is a necessary first step in any research process as well. We urge you to carry this procedure one step further. Once you have identified the necessary issues, ask yourself what the ideal answer would be. In other words, what are you looking for?

You would be surprised how many people set out to research without really knowing what they want to find. This is dangerous because many lions, tigers, and bears lurk in the forest of the library. You have to know when you begin the journey what you expect or hope to find at its end. Are you looking for a statute? A case? An administrative rule or regulation? Updated citations? Analysis of a new or expanding area of law? Facts with which to bolster a policy argument? There are many different types of information that you can pursue and many different paths you might follow.

Only if you understand what your ideal answer is can you set out in search of it. It may turn out that your initial guess was incorrect and that once you get deeper into the problem your ideal answer turns out to be a dead end. But along the way you may also find a garden path.

Step 2: Thinking About How to Proceed

We hope this book has made you realize that a host of research systems is available. West Group has an intricate self-referencing system of materials. Based on the National Reporter System, it flows into the American Digest System and the Westlaw databases and filters into the family of annotated codes and other West products such as KeyCite. As we have pointed out, there is a coherent philosophy behind the West system. The same can also be said of other publishers. Indeed, many law firms have their own internal information systems, which consist of briefs and memoranda that have been written on various matters.

The successful researcher understands where to enter these research systems. Once you know what your ideal answer is, you must decide which research process and which research systems are the best means to that end. If what you really need is background information, for example, you are wise to use an encyclopedia like *Corpus Juris Secundum* or *American Jurisprudence 2d*. If you need to understand a landmark case, you should probably begin by reading the hornbook explanation or the headnotes written by West attorney-editors rather than the opinion itself.

The point is that you should follow one of our first rules of research—find someone who has done the work for you! Use the collective wisdom of legal publishers, legal scholars, and your own colleagues and professors as much as you possibly can. At the same time, do not lose sight of the distinction between a primary source (i.e., the law) and a secondary source (i.e., an interpretation of the law). If you understand where to enter the research systems, you can save yourself grief, time, and money.

Step 3: Legal Research and Economics

Once you are in practice, you will find that questions come with price tags attached. A partner may assign you a question for which you will be allowed to do only $500 worth of research. It is just as bad to do $5,000 worth of research on a $50 problem as it is to do $50 worth of research on a $5,000 problem.

Law students often have difficulty understanding this concept, partly because of their experience in law school. As a student, you have the luxury of time in which to rethink and revise your work again and again. And you're not wasting that time if you learn from your mistakes. Once you are in practice, however, you will learn that time-consuming mistakes can be very costly. You will be up against a hard edge of billable hours in a private firm, an overwhelming caseload in a public interest practice, or a stack of files from a government agency, and you will have to complete the assignment before the deadline. To do so, you will have to allocate and budget your research time appropriately. Start doing this now. Be a financial planner when it comes to your research. Consider how much time you have to invest in each part of the research process, and evaluate the potential risks and returns of your investments. Setting incremental goals for yourself will make the whole process easier.

If you have defined your question as we recommended in Step 1 and picked the quick entry places as we suggested in Step 2, then you can devise a time budget in Step 3. Doing so will allow you to be an efficient, effective researcher and will lead to far better results. There is no sadder sight than a student surrounded by piles of case reporters and statutory volumes working away late into the night in the law library. That student may have no concept of what to do with the problem or how much time should be spent on it.

The truly creative act is not locating materials, but reading and synthesizing them. That is why legal writing is such an important part of your first year. Remember, though, that you can't start on the truly creative part until you have assembled your materials. Factoring in time as a realistic constraint is part of that process.

Step 4: Knowing When to Stop

One of the steps law schools often fail to teach is how to judge when you should stop your research process. Once again, this is due to the idea that student time is infinitely elastic. In law school, you are asked to go back to the beginning and reinvent every wheel, to build each new research edifice from brick number one. In other words, you are expected to look at every case ever decided when writing your brief. In the real world, including the world in which you must live during your first year, you will have to make judgments about when you can successfully stop your research process. Devising stop rules is one of the current topics in legal research training. We suggest the following stop rules for your consideration:

1. *The loop rule.* This is the simplest rule for a first-year student to apply. When you start to see the same materials over and over again—the same cases, the same statutes, the same administrative agency rulings or regulations, the same types of citations—you should realize that you probably are done. This kind of loop can be deceptive, however, unless you are using the products of more than one publisher. Most publishers have an internal cross-referencing system. We have already urged you to use the dynamics of such systems in your research, but you should also use other research tools. However, once you understand the relevant cases, statutes, and rulings and have updated everything, you will know that you are in control of the problem. Remember there is almost never a perfect case. When you reach the point in your research where you are not seeing anything new, you are in a loop.

2. *The economic analysis or diminishing returns rule.* This rule suggests that when you are investing more in your research than you are getting in research returns, you should stop. The classic example of diminishing returns is the student in the library at 10:30 p.m. on Friday night who continues to read cases that seem to be less and less useful. Because of the built-in paranoia that goes with being a law student, students feel that if they stop, the very next case they would have read will turn out to be the perfect case. The experienced researcher can sense when less is coming back than is being put in. This is a difficult rule to follow, however. You must have confidence in your research abilities and understand the relationship between what the materials can tell you and the amount of time you can expend on them. This is a hard-body rule, one that is difficult for weak and puny first-year students. But if you want to be a mighty researcher, exercise your judgment.

3. *The Zen rule.* This is an aspirational rule, one for you to strive toward. When you are in practice and have been working in one area of the law for a long time, you will simply know when you are done. After a while you will become so familiar with the statutory and administrative architecture of your practice area—both the common law implications of what is going on and the rules of the lawmakers and law interpreters in your particular specialty—that you will be an expert resource. This is why we urge you to use a real live human being as a mentor for your research. Law school can sometimes be a very competitive experience, but it does not have to always be so. Instead of concentrating on competition, learn to ask for help. There is no shame in being a novice. So ask a master—a professor, a senior partner, a more experienced associate, or a colleague. In doing so you

can avoid many research roadblocks and may find a person who is a valuable long-term resource. Eventually you will become a master yourself, one who can pass along good karma and collegiality by helping a novice in turn.

When considering these rules, remember that the race went to the tortoise and that the result of consistent effort is success. No amount of methodology (or metaphor) can substitute for common sense. And common sense is what legal research is really all about. It is easy to get lost in the first-year experience, easy to be baffled by all the books on the shelves. But think back to the research skills that you mastered in high school and college and to all the intelligence and hard work that got you into law school, and you will find that legal research is not so bad. Carefully consider your problem, see clearly how the parts of the whole fit together, and you will ride the wave of legal research rather than be left to flounder in its wake.

Enjoy.

How to Search on Westlaw

Westlaw offers you a choice of search methods: WIN (Westlaw is Natural) and Terms and Connectors.

WIN allows you to use standard English—or Natural Language—to retrieve documents. Natural Language searching is available in most Westlaw databases.

Terms and Connectors searching allows you to enter a query consisting of key terms from your issue and connectors specifying the relationship between those terms. Terms and Connectors searching is available in all Westlaw databases.

The type of issue you are researching, your knowledge of the issue, and your expertise in performing research on Westlaw will determine which method is best suited to your needs.

This appendix will explain how to formulate a search request with WIN and with Terms and Connectors, how to perform a topic and key number search, and how to tailor search requests with field restrictions.

WIN Natural Language Search Method

The Natural Language search method (WIN) is easy to use and yields excellent results. Natural Language searching allows you to enter a description of your legal issue or fact pattern in standard English, e.g.,

do grandparents have visitation rights

or

admissibility of DNA evidence

When you enter your description, WIN completes the following steps:

1. WIN processes the description, removing common words such as *is* and *for.*
2. WIN identifies legal phrases, such as *summary judgment, child custody* and *res ipsa loquitor*, and puts them in quotation marks.
3. A stemming program generates variations of terms in your description, such as *defame, defamed,* and *defaming* for *defamation.*
4. The legal phrases and the remaining terms—which are considered the concepts in your description—are each given a weight:
   ▶ The more often a concept appears in the database, the less weight it is given.

▶ The more often a concept appears in the document, the greater weight it is given.

5. WIN retrieves the twenty documents that are most likely to match your description. These documents are ranked according to the probability that they match your description, from most likely to least likely.

Performing a Natural Language Search

Suppose your issue concerns whether a homeowner is liable for the actions of an intoxicated guest. To retrieve cases discussing this issue, first access an appropriate database such as the Multistate Tort Law Cases database (MTRT-CS). If the Terms and Connectors Query Editor is displayed, click the **Search Type** button and choose **Natural Language** from the drop-down list. Type a description of your issue (e.g., **is a host liable for an intoxicated guest**) in the *Natural Language Description* text box and click **Search**. You will retrieve the twenty documents that most closely match the concepts in your description, ranked according to their statistical relevance. The document that has the greatest likelihood of matching the concepts in your description is displayed first. (If you prefer to display the cases in chronological order, choose **Sort** from the Browse menu and select **Age** from the list of sort choices.)

If you've looked through all twenty documents and want to see more, choose **Next 10 Document** from the Browse menu to display the next ten documents. You can repeat this procedure to retrieve up to a total of one hundred documents for each Natural Language search. If you want to retrieve more than twenty documents each time you run a Natural Language search, access the Westlaw Options Directory by choosing **Westlaw Options** from the File menu. When the Options Directory is displayed, type the number corresponding to *Set the number of documents retrieved for Natural Language search* in the *Command* text box and click **OK**. Then type a number from 1 to 100 and click **OK**. The number you enter will become the default number of documents retrieved until you change it again.

Browsing Your WIN Search Results

Browsing your search result is essentially the same whether you use the Natural Language search method or the Terms and Connectors search method. You may choose to browse by search term or by page, move from one document to another, or locate particular terms in your search result by using the Locate feature. With Natural Language you have the advantage of an additional browsing mode: best. By clicking the **Best** arrows you can move directly to the portion of each document that most closely matches your description.

Adding Related Concepts to Your Description

You may add your own related concepts or access the Westlaw thesaurus for assistance in adding related concepts to your search.

To access the Westlaw thesaurus, enter a description in the *Natural Language Description* text box at the Natural Language Description Editor, then click the **Thesaurus** button. When the Westlaw Thesaurus dialog box is displayed, highlight a concept in the *Concepts in the Description* list box to view related concepts in the *Related Concepts* list box (Figure A.1).

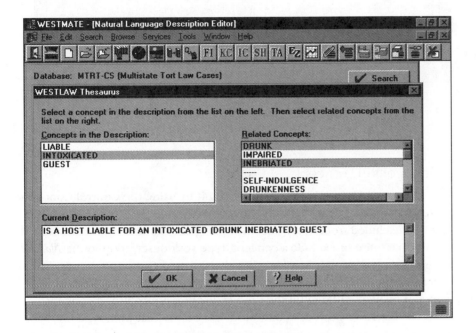

Figure A.1
Using the Westlaw Thesaurus to Add Related Concepts to a Natural Language Search

After reviewing the *Related Concepts* list, highlight a concept in the list to add it to your description. By viewing the *Current Description* text box, you can see how the related concept you select is placed in parentheses and added to your description following the concept to which it relates. When you finish using the thesaurus, click **OK**. Click the **Search** button to run your search.

You may want to add related concepts that do not appear in the thesaurus. For instance, antonyms do not appear in the thesaurus; if you want to add an antonym as a related concept, you must add it yourself. To add your own related concept, type it into your description immediately following the concept to which it relates, enclosing it in parentheses, e.g., **drunk (sober)**.

Figure A.2
Using Control Concepts in a
Natural Language Search

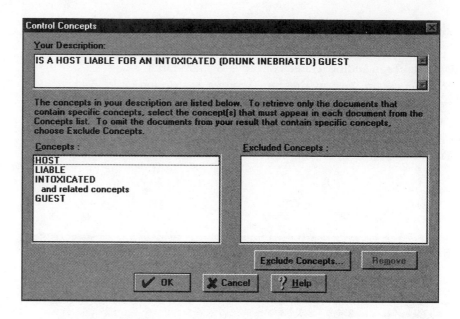

Using Control Concepts

You can further refine your search result by using the Control Concepts feature. Control Concepts allows you to specify concepts that must appear in or be excluded from every document in your Natural Language search result. To require or exclude a concept, type your description in the *Natural Language Description* text box and click the **Control Concepts** button. The Control Concepts dialog box is displayed (Figure A.2). You can require a concept by highlighting it in the *Concepts* list box. To exclude a concept, click the **Exclude Concepts** button. In the *Exclude* text box, type the concepts you want to exlude from the documents in your search result and click **OK**. When you finish using the Control Concepts dialog box, click **OK**. The Natural Language Description Editor is displayed. The *Restrictions Specified* box indicates the required or excluded concepts you have specified. Click **Search** to run your description.

Adding Restrictions to Your WIN Search

Adding restrictions allows you to limit your search. In a case law database, for example, you can limit your search by court, date, judge, attorney, or added date.

Double-click a restriction in the *Restrictions* list box to add it to your description. A dialog box is displayed to help you enter information related to the restriction you selected (Figure A.3). To remove a restriction, highlight it in the *Restrictions Specified* list and click **Remove Restriction**.

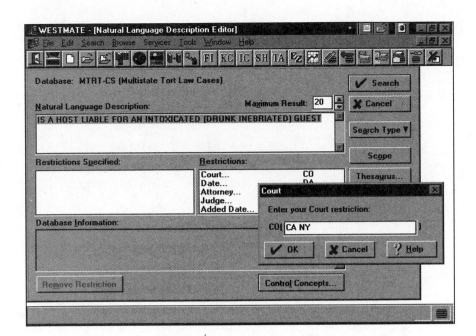

Figure A.3
Adding Restrictions
to a Natural Language Search

Terms and Connectors Search Method

The Terms and Connectors search method allows you to enter terms that you want to appear in retrieved documents and use connectors to specify the relationship between those terms. Terms and Connectors searching is especially useful when you know specific facts or details about a case or cases, such as the name of a party, judge, or product, or when you want to retrieve every document containing specific terms.

Formulating a Terms and Connectors Query

Follow these steps to translate your issue into a Westlaw query:

1. Choose search terms.
2. Decide which connectors to place between your terms.
3. Access a database, select the Terms and Connectors search method, if necessary, by clicking the **Search Type** button and choosing **Term Search** from the drop-down list, then enter your query.

▶ *Terms:* Choose search terms significant to your issue. Consider alternatives, such as synonyms and antonyms. You should also decide whether to retrieve variations of terms. Enter your terms in the singular, nonpossessive form—Westlaw automatically retrieves regular and irregular plurals and possessive forms. If you enter the plural form, only the plural is retrieved. If you enter the possessive form, only the possesive is retrieved.

If your term is an acronym, enter it with periods and without spaces to retrieve all variations of the acronym.

The Term	Retrieves
e.p.a.	*E.P.A.*
	E. P. A.
	E P A
	EPA

To retrieve various forms of a compound word, use its hyphenated form.

The Term	Retrieves
good-will	*good-will*
	good will
	goodwill

Consider synonyms or antonyms as alternative search terms. You may wish to consult the Westlaw thesaurus for assistance with synonyms.

The Term	Alternatives
attorney	**lawyer counsel**
constitutional	**unconstitutional**

Consider using a root expander (!) or universal character (*) to retrieve variations of word forms. The root expander is used to retrieve words with variant endings.

The Term	Retrieves
know!	*know*
	known
	knowing
	knowingly
	knowingful
	knowingfully
	knowable
	knows
	knowledge
	knowledgeable

The universal character (*) can be used to represent one variable character anywhere in a word, except at the beginning of the word. Think of the universal character as a blank Scrabble piece. When you place the asterisk within a term, it requires that a character appear in that position:

dr*ve retrieves *drive* and *drove*

When you place an asterisk or asterisks at the end of the term, you specify the maximum length of the term:

jur** retrieves *jury* and *juror* but not *jurisdiction*

▶ *Connectors:* After selecting terms for your query, choose connectors to specify the relationships that should exist between the terms. Double-click a connector in the *Connectors/Expanders* list to add it to your query.

1. Use the OR connector to search for alternative terms. Simply leave a space or enter **or** between a term and its alternatives. The query

attorney lawyer counsel

retrieves documents containing at least one of these terms.

2. Use the AND connector to retrieve documents containing both search terms anywhere in the document. Simply enter **and** or **&** between terms. The query

narcotic & warrant

requires both terms to appear somewhere in the document.

3. Grammatical connectors allow you to search for terms in the same sentence or paragraph. To retrieve documents with your terms in the same paragraph, use the paragraph connector (/p):

hearsay /p utterance

Documents with your terms in the same sentence can be retrieved with a sentence connector (/s):

design*** /s defect!

You can use a +s connector to specify the order in which the search terms should appear in a sentence. The +s requires that the first term precede the second term within the same sentence:

capital +s gain

4. Numerical connectors (/n or +n) require search terms to appear within a specified number of terms of each other, from one to 250:

attorney /5 fee

bill william +3 clinton

The +n connector is especially helpful when you are restricting your search to the citation field or searching for documents referring to a particular citation:

20 +5 1080

Function	WestMate 6.31 Command
Access the electronic citation research service (KeyCite)	Click the **Check a Citation** button at the Welcome to Westlaw window and choose **KeyCite** from the pop-up menu, click the **KeyCite** button on the main button palette, or choose **KeyCite** from the Services menu.
Access a list of cases cited by a case (Table of Authorities)	Click the **Table of Authorities** button on the main button palette or choose **Table of Authorities** from the Services menu.
Access the electronic clipping service (WestClip)	Click the **Clipping Service** button at the Welcome to Westlaw window or the **WestClip** button on the main button palette, or choose **WestClip Directory** from the Search menu.
Access *Black's Law Dictionary*	Choose **Black's Law Dictionary** from the Services menu.
Display the topic and key number outline (Key Number Service)	Click the **Key Number Service** button at the Welcome to Westlaw window or on the main button palette, or choose **Key Number Service** from the Services menu.
Display the table of contents for a statute, rule, or regulation (Table of Contents service)	Choose **Table of Contents Service** from the Services menu or double-click the Jump markers preceding a document's heading.
Update a statute, rule, or regulation (Update service)	From a search result, click the **Update** button or click the *UPDATE* Jump marker.

5. Westlaw also offers an exclusionary connector. With the BUT NOT connector (%), you can exclude documents that contain certain terms:

tax taxation % income /3 tax taxation

This search would not retrieve any documents containing the term *income* within three terms of *tax* or *taxation*.

6. To search for a phrase on Westlaw, place the phrase in quotation marks. For example, to search for *summary judgment,* type

"summary judgment"

Phrase searching should be used only when you are certain the phrase will not appear in other ways. For example, you might not want to use the phrase "**blood alcohol**" in your query because some cases could state "the amount of alcohol in the blood" instead. A more comprehensive query would be

blood /3 alcohol

Restricting Your Terms and Connectors Search by Field

Most Westlaw documents are composed of several parts, such as the citation and title, which reflect logical divisions of a document. These parts are called fields. As discussed in Chapter 2, you can restrict your Terms and Connectors search to a particular field or fields rather than search the entire document. Searching with field restrictions saves searching and browsing time and makes your search more efficient.

The available fields vary by database. Double-click a field restriction in the *Fields/Restrictions* list to add it to your query. For examples of case law fields, see Table A.1 on the next page.

▶ *Date restrictions:* A date restriction (da) allows you to limit your search to documents decided or issued on, before, or after a certain date, or between a range of dates. An added-date restriction (ad) allows you to update the result of a search you previously ran on Westlaw. "Added date" refers to the date a document was added to Westlaw. A dialog box is available to help you set up a date or added-date restriction. You cannot run a date restriction alone as your search. Use the & connector to add a date restriction to your search, as in the sample Terms and Connectors query below:

hypno! /s testi! & da(1993)

▶ *Court restrictions:* By using the court field (co) you can limit your search to cases from a specific court. After double-clicking **CO** in the *Fields/Restrictions* list, type the Westlaw abbreviation for the court within the parentheses. Attach this term to the rest of your query with the & connector. Following are examples of court field restrictions you can add to your search:

Field	Abbreviation	Contents	Sample Query
Attorney	at	Names, cities and firms of attorneys representing parties or participating in appeal, e.g., Ramsey Clark	**at(ramsey /3 clark)**
Digest	di	Combination of headnote and topic fields	**di(standing /p air /p quality pollut!)**
Headnote	he	West-prepared summary of a single point of law; also contains statute and rule citations, e.g., Texas Rule of Civil Procedure 308	**he(308)**
Judge	ju	Judge authoring lead opinion, e.g., Justice Breyer	**ju(breyer)**
Synopsis	sy	Brief description of the facts and holding of the case; includes court syllabus, where available	**sy(commerce /2 clause /p hodel)**
Topic	to	West digest topic name and number, hierarchy classification information, key number and key line text, and former key number, if any	**to(constitutional /2 law)** or **to(92)**

Table A.1
Case Law Fields

co(high)

restricts your search to a state's highest court, or to the highest courts of all states when entered in the ALLSTATES database.

co(low)

restricts your search to a state's lower courts, or to all lower courts in ALLSTATES.

co(tx fl)

restricts your search to Texas and Florida federal district court cases when entered in the DCT database.

▶ *Combining field searches:* To search for the same terms in more than one field, separate the field abbreviations with a comma but no space, e.g., **sy,di(coma! /p incompetent)**. Use the & connector to add a second field restriction or court or date restriction to your search:

sy,di(coma! /p incompetent) & da(aft 1970)

Topic and Key Number Searching

When you search using topic and key numbers you take advantage of West Group's editorial enhancements to case law documents. Every legal issue in a case published by West is identified and summarized, then assigned a topic and key number. West topic and key numbers allow you to focus your research and find relevant cases that might not include your exact search terms.

Finding West Topics and Key Numbers

Where can you find West topics and key numbers that may be relevant to your issue?

1. Headnotes in West case law reporters: When you read a headnote that you think is relevant to your issue, jot down the name of the corresponding topic and the key number.
2. West digests: As explained in Chapter 2, you can find relevant key numbers within topic categories in West's case law digests.
3. Headnotes on Westlaw: When you read a headnote on Westlaw that you think is relevant to your issue, select a Jump marker from the classification hierarchy above the text of the headnote (Figure A.4).
4. The Key Number Service on Westlaw: The Key Number Service contains the complete topic and key number outline used by West's editors to classify headnotes to specific topics and key numbers (Figure A.5).

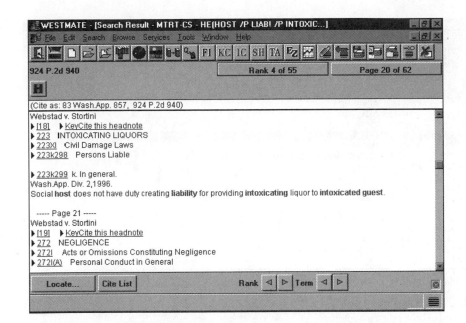

Figure A.4
A Topic and Key Number
Classification Hierarchy with
Corresponding Headnote on
Westlaw

To access the Key Number Service, click the **Key Number Service** button from the Welcome to Westlaw window or on the main button palette, or choose **Key Number Service** from the Services menu. You can also access the Key Number Service by selecting a Jump marker from the classification hierarchy of a case headnote.

After accessing the Key Number Service, you can browse the topic and key number outline by double-clicking a topic or key number. To run a search, highlight a topic or key number in the outline and click **Key Search**. The Key Search dialog box is displayed. Select a jurisdiction from the drop-down list and type optional descriptive terms in the *Additional Terms* text box. Then select a search method and click **OK** to run the search (Figure A.6).

Figure A.5
The Key Number Service
List of Topics

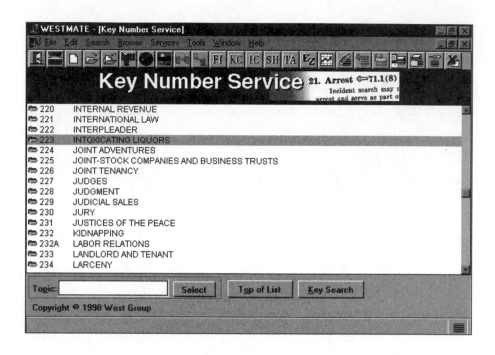

Figure A.6
The Key Search Dialog Box

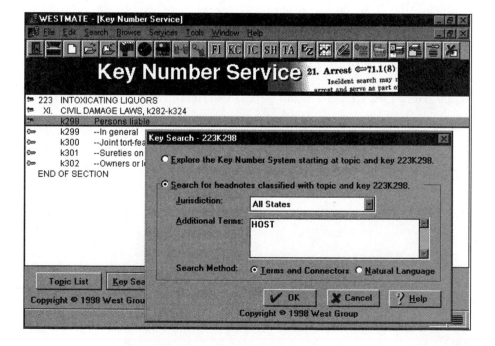

Common Westlaw Commands

Often, Westlaw commands can be entered in several ways: by clicking a button, choosing an item, or typing text.

General Commands

Function	WestMate 6.31 Command
Display explanatory messages	Choose the appropriate option from the Help menu.
Display database and service information	Click the **Scope** button or choose **Scope** from the Search menu.
Display the amount of chargeable time used or number of chargeable transactions	Choose **Project Log** from the Window menu and click the **Summary** button.
Change the client identifier	Choose **New Project** from the File menu.
Display the Westlaw Options Directory	Click the **Westlaw Options** button or choose **Westlaw Options** from the File menu.
Print or download documents or portions of documents	Click the **Print/Download** button on the main button palette or choose **Print/Download** from the File menu.
Display the Offline Print Directory	Click the **Offline Print Directory** button or choose **Offline Print Directory** from the File menu.
Display a list of publications and abbreviations that can be used in a service such as Find or KeyCite	Click the **Pubs List** button.
Return to the last database or service accessed	Choose the appropriate option from the Window menu.
View a list of the most recent databases and services accessed	Open the Window menu.
Sign off Westlaw	Click the **Sign Off Westlaw** button on the main button palette or choose **Sign Off Westlaw** from the File menu.

Search Commands

Function	WestMate 6.31 Command
Choose the Natural Language search method	Click the **Search Type** button at the Terms and Connectors Query Editor and choose **Natural Language** from the drop-down list.
Choose the Terms and Connectors search method	Click the **Search Type** button at the Natural Language Description Editor and choose **Term Search** from the drop-down list.
Return to the Westlaw Directory from a search result	Click the **Westlaw Directory** button on the main button palette or choose **Westlaw Directory** from the Search menu.
Access a new database	Type a database identifier in the *Database ID* text box at the Westlaw Directory window or the Welcome to Westlaw window.
Run a new search in the same database	Choose **New Search** from the Search menu.
Display the current query for editing	Click the **Edit Query** button on the main button palette or choose **Edit Query** from the Search menu.
Run the same search in a new database	Click the **Change Database** button on the main button palette, select **Run query in different database**, type the database identifier and click **OK**.
Edit a search in a new database	Click the **Change Database** button on the main button palette, select **Edit query in different database**, type the database identifier and click **OK**.
Require a concept in a Natural Language search result	At the Natural Language Description Editor, click the **Control Concepts** button.
Add restrictions to a Natural Language description	At the Natural Language Description Editor, select a restriction by double-clicking it, then type your terms and click **OK**.

Function	WestMate 6.31 Command
Display related concepts for terms in a query or description from the online thesaurus	Click the **Thesaurus** button at the Natural Language Description Editor or the Terms and Connectors Query Editor.
Display a list of all the queries and descriptions used in a current research session	Click the **Query List** button at the Natural Language Description Editor or the Terms and Connectors Query Editor.

Browse Commands

Function	WestMate 6.31 Command
Display the next search term in a result	From a search result, right-click to choose **Next Term** from the pop-up menu, or click **Term ▶**.
Display the next page	Right-click to choose **Next Page** from the pop-up menu, or choose **Next Page** from the Browse menu. To go to a particular page, right-click to choose **Go to Page** from the pop-up menu (or click the **Page** button in the document display header) to display the Go to Page dialog box, then type the desired page number.
Display the portion of each document retrieved by a Natural Language search that most closely matches the description	From a Natural Language search result, right-click to choose **Next Best** from the pop-up menu, or click **Best ▶**.
View additional documents retrieved by a Natural Language search	From a Natural Language search result, right-click and choose **Next 10 Documents** from the pop-up menu, or choose **Next 10 Documents** from the Browse menu.
Scan for terms within a document	Click the **Locate** button.
Display a list of documents containing a Locate term(s)	Click the **Locate List** button from the citations list.
Cancel a Locate request	Click the **Cancel Locate** button or choose **Cancel Locate** from the Browse menu.

Function	WestMate 6.31 Command
Display the next document in a search result	Right-click to choose **Next Document** from the pop-up menu, or click **Rank ▶**. To display a particular document, right-click to choose **Go to Document** from the pop-up menu (or click the **Rank** button in the document display header) to display the Go to Document dialog box, then type the desired document number.
Re-sort a Natural Language search result	From a Natural Language search result, choose **Sort** from the Browse menu.
Return the Natural Language search result order to statistical relevance ranking	At a Natural Language search result, choose **Sort** from the Browse menu. Select **Statistical Relevance** and click **OK**.
Display a citations list from a document	Click the **Cite List** button.
Display the status of a search	Choose **Search Summary** from the Browse menu.
Display the next statute, rule, or regulation even if it is not in the current search result (Documents in Sequence)	From a document display window, click the **Docs in Seq** button.
Cancel Documents in Sequence	Click the **Cancel Docs In Seq** button.
List available fields for the current database	Choose **Fields** from the Browse menu.
Cancel a field display restriction	Choose **Fields** from the Browse menu and click the **Display All** button.

Service Commands

Function	WestMate 6.31 Command
Retrieve documents by citation (Find)	Click the **Find a Document** button at the Welcome to Westlaw window or the **Find** button on the main button palette, or choose **Find** from the Services menu.